MW00425473

LIMITATIONS

OF

SCIENTIFIC

TRUTH

THE
LIMITATIONS
OF
SCIENTIFIC
TRUTH

*Why Science Can't Answer
Life's Ultimate Questions*

NIGEL BRUSH

Kregel
Academic & Professional

To my wife, Anne,
whose love and support made it
possible to complete this book, and
Dr. Reuben Bullard (1928-2004),
whose class at the Cincinnati Bible College
on science and Christianity first introduced me
to this subject.

*The Limitations of Scientific Truth: Why Science Can't Answer
Life's Ultimate Questions*

© 2005 by Nigel Brush

Published by Kregel Publications, a division of Kregel, Inc.,
P.O. Box 2607, Grand Rapids, MI 49501.

Library of Congress Cataloging-in-Publication Data
Brush, Nigel.
    The limitations of scientific truth: why science can't an-
swer lives ultimate questions / by Nigel Brush.
        p.   cm.
    Includes bibliographical references and index.
    1. Religion and science. 2. Science—History. 3. Science—
Methodology. 4. Apologetics. I. Title.
BL240.3.B78   2005   261.5'5—dc22   2005022166

ISBN 0-8254-2253-1

Printed in the United States of America

05 06 07 08 09 / 5 4 3 2 1

CONTENTS

INTRODUCTION

I AM A CHRISTIAN . . . and a scientist. To some this may seem a contradiction. Many people, in fact, want to know how I reconcile my faith with my scientific knowledge. Such a question can't be answered in a brief conversation, and that is my reason for writing this book.

This book is *not* an attack on science. As a *Christian*, I believe that God has given us conscious minds with which to think, and an entire universe to study, understand, and appreciate. As a *scientist*, I understand that science is a powerful tool for studying God's creation; those who reject science as a means of searching for truth will severely limit their mental horizons.

This book *is* about the limitations of the scientific technique as a means for obtaining absolute truth. A highly popular model of science that is often presented to the general public proclaims that scientific truth is superior to all other forms of truth. This model is built on the following four basic premises:

1. Scientists are completely objective in their interpretation of scientific facts.
2. Scientific methodology is totally rational.
3. Scientific truths are superior to religious or philosophical truths.
4. Scientific truths have generally disproved the existence of God.

As a scientist, I reject these four basic premises of this popular model of science, as do many of my Christian and non-Christian colleagues in

7

science. Nevertheless, the public debate between science and Christianity is often centered on this particular model of science. Further, some of the most vocal and well-known advocates of science—such as Carl Sagan, Richard Dawkins, or Lawrence Krauss—have attempted to further popularize this model.

Among the general public, many people who have only a limited knowledge of science have embraced this popular model of science. Indeed, some have come to the conclusion that scientific truth is the *only* form of truth. The usual justification for such belief is the many technological gifts that science has given to humanity. The modern world, it is true, has been shaped largely by the discoveries of science. In less than a hundred years, science has given us cars, airplanes, and spacecraft; radio, television, and computers; electric lights, microwave ovens, and atomic energy; antibiotics, artificial hearts, and genetic engineering. For these gifts, many people—scientists and non-scientists alike—have elevated scientific truth to a position of supreme honor.

Yet careful examination of this popular model of science will reveal that all four of these premises are false. Nonetheless, many people today—needing to be helped or healed, preserved or strengthened, inspired or enlightened—go first to science . . . rather than to God. Science, they say, will feed us, clothe us, entertain us, cure our diseases, heal our injuries, deliver us from natural catastrophes, and protect us from hostile nations. To many people, science has become the god of this age . . . but does science really deserve—or want—that honor?

Although the scientific method provides a powerful way of searching for truth, it has its limitations. Those of us who work in science on a daily basis are all too familiar with many of these limitations as we struggle to make sense of nature. Strong controversy often exists among scientists over many of the fundamental ideas at the very core of the scientific method. From the inside, science does not provide a great deal of confidence in the accuracy and completeness of scientific truth at any one point in time. Far from providing a finished product—the truth and nothing but the truth—science is a work in progress. Thus, the popular model of science discussed above is little more than wishful thinking on the part of some individuals.

This book, then, does not attempt to disprove science or reconcile the

Christian faith with current scientific truths. Rather, it suggests a replacement for the popular model of science, a more realistic model that is based on what natural scientists, social scientists, and philosophers of science have discovered about their own discipline and the limitations of its truths.

In doing so, part 1 addresses the human quest for truth, the ultimate questions of humanity, and alternate pathways for seeking truth.

Parts 2 through 6 present specific areas in which scientists have been forced to acknowledge the limitations of scientific truth.

Part 7 presents an alternative model of scientific truth, one in which both scientists and Christians acknowledge the limitations of their knowledge of the infinite.

Within part 7, chapter 18 discusses how the information in this book carries important implications for the Christian. A realistic understanding of the strengths and weaknesses of modern science can have a liberating impact on Christians who have lived in fear that science may negate or destroy their faith. Christ promised that "the truth shall set you free." A more accurate understanding of the limitations of scientific truth will allow Christians to enjoy the knowledge and insights that science provides, without the constant fear that every new scientific discovery or pronouncement will endanger their faith. Scientific truth is not absolute truth.

PART 1

THE HUMAN QUEST:
SEEKING TRUTH

*Then you will know the truth,
and the truth will set you free.*
—John 8:32

PATHWAYS TO TRUTH

AMONG ALL OF THE CREATURES of the earth, human beings are unique in our proclivity for asking questions. From the time we learn to talk until the day our mouths close in death, we continually ask questions.

Perhaps the most important questions we ask during the course of our lives are those that deal with our past, present, and future. Where did I come from? What is my purpose in life? What will happen to me when I die? Such questions cut to the very heart of human existence. Humanity generally longs to know how life originated, the meaning of life, and the ultimate fate of humanity.

Ultimate Questions

Because all peoples in all places and throughout all times ask the three questions of origin, purpose, and destiny, they are called "ultimate questions," and the attempt to answer these ultimate questions is both the beginning and the end of all human intellectual activity. It is the final objective of humanity's unrelenting quest for truth.

After thousands of years of study and searching, humanity's potential answers to the three ultimate questions are legion. In general, though, only two answers have come to dominate the modern world. One is that humans were purposefully created by God in the past, are meant to serve Him in the present, and have the opportunity to dwell with Him forever in the future. The alternate answer states that random processes created humans, that we have no particular purpose in the present, and that we will cease to exist when we die. Today, approximately 80 percent of the world's population espouses the belief that human existence involves both design and purpose, while some 20 percent believe that human existence is solely due to chance (Rubenstein 1994, 176).

People who eschew the various world religions usually find their answers to life's ultimate questions through philosophy or science. In the search for answers to our existence, science and philosophy, like religion, have been used to probe deeply into the past, present, and future. In the modern world, however, science has provided the most popular alternative to religion's answers.

Through such disciplines as archaeology, anthropology, biology, geology, and astronomy, scientists have attempted to answer the question of human origins, as well as the origins of life, the earth, the stars, and the universe.

Although scientists are by no means in agreement over their final answer to the question of human origins, some of the most vocal elements within the scientific community have popularized one answer: life evolved by random chance through natural processes.

Scientists who accept random chance as the answer to the first ultimate question, *Where did we come from?* deny themselves the opportunity of making a meaningful response to the second ultimate question, *What is our purpose in the present?* By rejecting a Creator, they must also reject purposeful design and, in doing so, any possibility of providing an ultimate meaning for humanity's existence in the present.

Those scientists following a strict random chance model have similar difficulty with the third ultimate question, *What is our destiny?* If life arose by random chance and natural processes, life can just as easily be extinguished in the same way. In the words of Macbeth,

> Life's but a walking shadow, a poor player
> That struts and frets his hour upon the stage,
> And then is heard no more: it is a tale
> Told by an idiot, full of sound and fury,
> Signifying nothing.
> —William Shakespeare, *Macbeth*, V, v, 17

Through statistical models, mathematical projections, and computer simulations, scientists have tried to see into the future, out to the very edge of space and time. But as to the continued existence of human life beyond death, the popular model of science offers little hope. Despite its inability to answer two of the three most important ultimate questions, however, the popular model of science has been elevated to the position of absolute authority in Western civilization.

Religion and the popular model of science have thus provided us with two alternative explanations to life's ultimate questions: (1) humans are created in the image of God and are meant to live in fellowship with Him throughout eternity; or (2) humans are advanced animals that were created by chance and have no ultimate purpose or destiny. It would be hard to imagine two answers to a single question that are more contradictory. Which answer, then, is true? Are the truths of popular science "truer" than the truths of religion?

Three Pathways to Truth

How can we know the truth? This is another age-old question with which humanity has struggled. What we often believe to be true, however, and what actually is true are often quite disparate. If we only knew the truth—in matters of our health, love, finance, eternal destiny—how different our lives would be! Both our happiness and our very survival are often tied to our ability to find the truth. Truth is the great liberator; truth, indeed, can make us free.

Throughout the ages, humans have sought truth by three primary ways: religion, philosophy, and science. Of the three disciplines, religion is the oldest and science is the youngest. Philosophers often trace the origin of their discipline to Thales (624–546 B.C.); scientists to Aristotle (384–322 B.C.). In contrast to philosophy and science, religion had been a daily part of human experience for thousands of years before the birth of Thales or Aristotle. Each of the disciplines of religion, philosophy, and science has its own unique methodology for discovering truth.

The search for truth begins with the realization that reality has deeper levels than the world we commonly perceive in our day-to-day activities. Truth is not a superficial phenomenon. Truth is not lying about on the ground waiting for anyone to pick it up. To find truth, writes Stumpf, we often must probe below the surface of external appearances to find the deeper reality:

> "What are things really like?" and "How can we explain the pro-
> cess of change in things?" What prompted these questions was
> the gradual recognition that things are not exactly what they seem
> to be, that "appearance" often differs from "reality." (1971, 3)

Religion seeks a knowledge of this "deeper reality" through supernatu-ral revelation. Thus, religion, by definition, is the belief that ultimate reality lies in a supernatural realm that exists outside the natural uni-verse. The visible events in the natural realm occur because of invisible events that are occurring in the supernatural realm. But because this lat-ter realm is "super" natural (above and outside the natural), it lies be-yond the reach of humans who live in the physical universe. We cannot use our senses to apprehend the supernatural, nor can we use our scien-tific tools to study it. The only way we can acquire accurate information about the supernatural realm is if beings in the supernatural realm choose to reveal themselves to us.

In this sense, humans are like a boatless people living on a small island in the middle of the Pacific Ocean. A whole world may exist beyond the coast of their tiny island, but these boatless people will never know about it unless someone from that broader world visits their is-land and tells them about it. Ultimately, therefore, religious truth is derived from supernatural revelation. The central core of Christianity is, in fact, the belief that ultimate truth has been obtained through su-pernatural revelation.

In contrast to religion, science attempts to apprehend truth through the natural realm, that is, the physical universe. Instead of seeking a revelation from the supernatural realm, scientists confine their search for truth to the visible universe. Because the supernatural realm is, by definition, beyond the natural realm, we cannot visit, map, measure, or quantify it. Many sci-entists, therefore, argue that the supernatural realm simply does not exist. The famous astronomer Carl Sagan (1934–1996), for instance, once said, "THE COSMOS IS ALL THAT IS OR EVER WAS OR EVER WILL BE" (1980, 4). If this belief is correct, all truth must indeed reside within the natural realm. Modern science itself, though, has found evidence that this belief may be incorrect—as will be discussed in chapter 13.

The scientific method of apprehending truth is built around the five human senses: seeing, hearing, smelling, touching, and tasting. Scientists attempt to learn about the universe by (1) using their senses to make empirical observations of the universe, (2) developing hypotheses to explain these observations, and (3) testing and refining these hypotheses by further empirical observations. Hypotheses that are repeatedly validated by physical observations assume the status of scientific law. Scientific laws, in turn, represent pieces of the ultimate, absolute truth. Many scientists believe that when scientific laws explain the physical universe in its entirety—including both its beginning and its end—absolute truth will have finally been achieved.

Both science and religion seek truth through sources that are external to the human mind, those sources being the natural realm or supernatural realm respectively. Philosophy, on the other hand, seeks truth within the human mind. Although philosophy borrows from science and religion, its focus and methodology are quite different. As Bertrand Russell (1872–1970) once explained, "Between theology and science there is a No Man's Land, exposed to attack from both sides; this No Man's Land is philosophy" (1945, xiii). Instead of revelation or empirical observations, philosophers seek truth through reason: "The history of philosophy exhibits man's search for Truth by the way of the discursive reason" (Copleston 1946, 1:6).

Most philosophers have not been overly concerned with the source of new ideas; revelation, empirical observation, or even daydreams may be equally fruitful sources of innovative insights. Rather, the philosopher's focus has always been to test these ideas to determine if they are logical or illogical, rational or irrational, true or false.

Philosophers have devised a variety of tools for critically examining their beliefs and hypotheses. These tools include the deductive and inductive methods (discussed in chapter 5), categorical propositions, syllogisms, a classification of formal and informal fallacies, quantification, and probability theory.

By using these techniques to test the clarity and rationality of human thought, philosophers hope to winnow the grain from the chaff, facts from fiction, and eventually arrive at absolute truth. "Philosophy," notes Popkin, "is the attempt to give an account of what is true and what is important, based on a rational assessment of evidence and arguments rather than myth, tradition, bald assertion, oracular utterances, local custom, or mere prejudice" (1999, 1).

Philosophers, because of their interest in logic and rational thought, are particularly helpful in ferreting out flaws in scientific methodology. Thus, although the focus of this present work is on the limitations of scientific truth, philosophical considerations must also be included. A subfield of philosophy that is particularly helpful in examining scientific method is epistemology. Epistemology studies the nature and grounds of knowledge, that is, how we know what we know. Many of the limitations of scientific truth that are discussed in this book were initially uncovered by philosophers and scientists working in the field of scientific epistemology. Some of the strongest charges, in fact, leveled against the superiority of scientific truth have been made by philosophers of science such as Hume, Kuhn, Popper, Lakatos, and Feyerabend (see chapters 5–7).

Therefore, although philosophy, science, and religion provide different pathways by which to search for truth, their paths often cross. Moreover, the methods and insights of one discipline may be used to critique, support, or attack theories or hypotheses in the other disciplines. Chapter 2 examines some of the disagreements that occur between these three disciplines.

DIVERGING PATHWAYS

RELIGION, SCIENCE, AND philosophy each have their own unique methodology for finding truth. Each discipline also has a unique source area in which the search for truth is conducted. Religion seeks truth in the supernatural realm through revelation. Science seeks truth in the natural realm through empirical observations. Philosophy seeks truth in the human mind through reason.

Most practitioners of these disciplines would agree, though, that the absolute truth they are all seeking is one and the same. Truth is truth wherever, whenever, or however one finds it. To believe otherwise is to deny that truth actually exists. Truth that is truth to only those who hold it is not truth at all but simply a manifestation of the human mind's ability to create false realities. It is also a demonstration of the human mind's proclivity for self-deception.

If only one absolute, ultimate truth exists, any contradictions and disagreements between so-called truths is a sure sign that absolute truth has not yet been achieved. If, for instance, a number of people desire to sail to Venice, they may start out in different oceans and with different types of boats, but when their boats finally achieve their destination, they will all be in Venice—not in Rome or Athens. Religion, science, and philosophy may have set out in their search for absolute truth by looking in different source areas and with different methodologies, but if they all eventually arrive at absolute truth, it will be the same truth.

The failure of humanity's attempts to find absolute truth is clearly demonstrated in that the truths of religion, science, and philosophy frequently contradict each other. In regard to science, conventional wisdom assures us that controversy is, in fact, natural—even proper—as scientists test one theory after another, rejecting the false and building upon the true. Science is a process of searching for the truth, and few things are more certain in science than that, as the process continues, current theories will be revised and eventually abandoned in favor of new theories. This process is the core of the scientific method.

Scientists, however, as well as theologians and philosophers, disagree not only with one another's disciplines about what is absolute truth; they also frequently disagree with their own colleagues in their chosen field of study. This disagreement clearly reveals that the various disciplines have not succeeded in finding the truth. Instead, this disagreement suggests that modern science, philosophy, and religion are composed of a mixture of truths, half-truths, misunderstandings, and absolute falsehoods. Harmony among such amalgamations of fact and fiction is, of course, impossible.

Such disunity, however, was not always the case. In earlier times, religion, philosophy, and science were not as clearly segregated as they are in the modern era. To many previous generations of scholars, all three of these disciplines were legitimate tools for seeking truth. Many early scientists were, in fact, also philosophers and theologians; they did not see these subjects as mutually exclusive.

Aristotle perfectly exemplifies the original unity between these disciplines, being at the same time one of the greatest philosophers, one of the earliest scientists, and also a theologian. Throughout the ages, many other famous scientists—such as Leonardo da Vinci (1452–1519), Francis Bacon (1561–1626), and Sir Isaac Newton (1642–1727)—have defied our modern stereotypes by their interests and writings in all three disciplines. Even modern scientists such as Carl Sagan reveal a similar proclivity for wandering beyond the boundaries of their chosen disciplines. Although Carl Sagan was an avowed atheist, in his science fiction novel *Contact* (1985) he was not above speculating about how God might have attempted to communicate with humanity—if there was a God. His Pulitzer Prize–winning book, *The Dragons of Eden: Speculations on the Evolution of Human Intelligence* (1977), also moved well beyond Sagan's chosen field of astronomy and discussed a number of issues that are more in the realm of religion or philosophy than of science.

That science, philosophy, and theology are usually considered as three totally separate fields is a relatively modern view, then, that is somewhat arbitrary and must occasionally be forced. All three disciplines seek, as stated above, the same ultimate truth. Thus, if science ever arrives at absolute truth, that truth cannot be different from the absolute truth at which religion or philosophy has also arrived. Two "truths" that contradict each other cannot both be part of the ultimate truth; one—or perhaps both—of these "truths" must be false.

Is There Absolute Truth?

Some people would argue that because religious truth, philosophical truth, and scientific truth often contradict each other, no such thing as absolute truth exists. Such people would argue that truth is relative and subjective. This argument has been around since the time of the sophists in ancient Greece and is no more valid today than it was thousands of years ago. It would be impossible, for example, to explain the technological advances that science has made over the past century if there were no physical absolutes such as (1) the laws governing the flow of electrons in an electrical current or (2) the laws governing the transmission of hereditary traits from one generation to the next through DNA. Universally recognized physical and moral absolutes exist—such as gravity, and the prohibition against murder—and we cannot defy these without wrecking our physical bodies or our moral character.

That a particular destination has not yet been attained has nothing to do with whether that destination actually exists. Just because one scientist contradicts another, or one discipline contradicts another, that in no way proves or disproves the existence of truth. What Copleston noted about religion and philosophy also applies to science: "As it is absurd to speak as if the existence of a variety of Religions *ipso facto* disproved the claim of any one religion to be the true Religion, so it is absurd to speak as though the succession of philosophies *ipso facto* demonstrated that there is no true philosophy and can be no true philosophy" (1946, 1:4). Thus, the disagreement between the truths of religion, science, and philosophy only provides evidence that these disciplines have not yet arrived at their chosen destination—absolute truth.

Who Has the Truth?

Given the lack of agreement between the truths found in religion, science, and philosophy, one is naturally led to speculate about which discipline's truths might at least be closer to absolute truth. Religion argues that it has already been given absolute truth while science argues that it is advancing steadily toward ultimate truth. Philosophy, in the modern world, has largely been relegated to the sidelines as science and religion vie for supremacy.

Philosophy, although it has continued its search for absolute truth, has never arrived at a set of truths that have been mutually agreed upon by the majority of philosophers. Instead, philosophy has fragmented into a mosaic of conflicting theories and schools of thought. Although some of the followers of these various theories and schools may believe that they have arrived at absolute truth, most people outside philosophy, as well as many within philosophy, are not convinced: "The ambition of philosophy is to achieve truth of a kind which transcends what is merely local and temporal; but not even the greatest of philosophers have come near to achieving that goal in any comprehensive manner" (Kenny 1994, 368).

Most religions agree with the argument that absolute truth is external to both nature and humanity. Because most religions believe that God or gods created both nature and the human mind, ultimate truth can reside only with the Creator or creators of those entities. Therefore, absolute truth must come from the supernatural realm, from God Himself—or from the gods.

Some people would argue that religion is every bit as fragmented as philosophy. Jews believe there is only one God. Christians believe that God has three manifestations: Father, Son, and Holy Spirit. Muslims believe that Allah is God and that Muhammad is his prophet. Hindus believe that as many as 330 million gods may exist. Nevertheless, despite the obvious differences among the world's religions, equally obvious similarities exist. There is remarkable agreement among the world's religions regarding, for instance, moral absolutes. Many of the statutes contained in the Ten Commandments are legislated repeatedly among the world's great religions. Moreover, most of the world's great religions agree on the existence of a divine being (or beings) to which humans owe their existence and obedience. The Devil, as some people might say, is in the details.

Science, unlike philosophy and religion, has been able to maintain a semblance of unity—at least within its various disciplines. Scientists in general often point with pride to the great strides that have been made over the past centuries in their understanding of the physical universe. Most astronomers believe in the big bang theory, most geologists believe in the theory of plate tectonics, and most biologists believe in the theory of evolution. Moreover, most scientists across the various disciplines share a common belief in the effectiveness of the scientific method for studying the physical universe.

Nevertheless, forces and trends are at work that threaten to shatter science's appearance of cohesion. To some scientists, the rapid pace of scientific advancement in the twenty-first century constitute more a source of concern than a reason for pride. Absolute truth does not change, but scientific truth continues to change with each new discovery. Consequently, some scientists are beginning to express doubt as to the absolute character of scientific truth. Others have even begun to question the ability of the scientific method to apprehend absolute truth.

The following chapters examine some of the limitations of scientific truth that scientists themselves have identified. Such critical self-examination of science *by scientists* can provide the Christian a unique window into the workings of science.

PART 2

SHIFTING SANDS:
THE TEMPORAL LIMITATIONS OF SCIENTIFIC TRUTH

All your words are true;
all your righteous laws are eternal.
—Psalm 119:160

CHAPTER 3

REVOLUTIONS IN SCIENTIFIC
UNDERSTANDING

THE FIRST AND PERHAPS greatest limitation of scientific knowledge is that it is constantly changing. Few things are more certain than this: that which is current scientific knowledge today will be outdated scientific knowledge tomorrow. Old scientific textbooks are relatively useless, their only value being as historical curiosities or collector's items. Even used bookstores try to avoid buying or selling used science textbooks. Many publishers of college textbooks now try to release a new, updated edition of each science text every three years. Such is the accelerated pace of scientific discovery that our understanding and explanations of the natural world can literally change over the course of a few days, months, or years.

While the rapid pace of scientific advancement is certainly exciting—you never know what's going to turn up tomorrow—it is not the kind of environment that provides much intellectual or emotional security for the scientist. If you are not on the cutting edge, your work likely will be plowed under and forgotten. Moreover, such a rapidly changing field does not provide one with a great deal of confidence about the current pronouncements of science. As they say about the weather in southern England, if you don't like it, wait a little while; it will change. If what is scientific truth today turns out to be scientific falsehood tomorrow, then what will happen to the scientific truths of tomorrow?

The truths of science are constantly being revised because they are neither perfect nor complete. This is why, as will be more thoroughly discussed in chapter 18, adapting Christianity to fit science is highly un-desirable. As John Casti notes in his book *Paradigms Lost: Images of Man in the Mirror of Science*, trying to harmonize science and religion "is self-defeating since scientific views are always changing. As a result, a theol-ogy that attaches itself to one scientific family today will surely be an orphan tomorrow" (1989, 65).

Introductory textbooks in science often discuss the birth of modern science and its conflict with the beliefs of Christianity. In these text-books—such as those concerning astronomy (Seeds 1993, 61–62); geol-ogy (Tarbuck and Lutgens 1994, 576–577); or physical anthropology (Nelson and Jurmain 1991, 28)—one of the most commonly cited con-flicts dates back to the 1500s. At that time, the Polish cleric and astrono-mer Nicolaus Copernicus (1473–1543) advanced an idea that was to revolutionize our understanding of the heavens. He postulated that the sun, not the earth, was the center of the universe. This idea ran counter to fourteen hundred years of scientific (and religious) belief. To under-stand this debate in its historical setting, it is necessary to do a little sleuth-ing into the past.

Revolutions in Astronomy

Perhaps the oldest of all of the sciences is astronomy. And little won-der, considering that the sun governs our days upon the earth; the moon rules our nights. The heavens are filled with a starry multitude that dances across the night sky from hour to hour and season to season. Thus, an-cient humanity could hardly have escaped pondering the objects in the sky that so dominated life on the earth.

One of the greatest puzzles that early astronomers sought to explain was the movement of the heavenly host across the sky. The early Greeks believed that the sun, moon, and planets were gods. The god of the sun was Helios, who had a chariot with wheels of shining gold that was pulled by four fiery horses. Each day, the god Eos opened the gates of dawn, and Helios drove his fiery chariot across the sky, bringing light and warmth to the world. At night, Selene, goddess of the moon, drove a silvery chariot pulled by two white horses.

By the fifth century B.C., however, ideas advanced by the Greeks to ex-

plain the heavens were more scientifically oriented. Anaxagoras of
Clazomenae (ca. 500–428 B.C.), for instance, argued that the moon shines
by reflected sunlight, explaining the phases of the moon in terms of the
earth passing between the moon and the sun. Plato (ca. 427–347 B.C.) believed that the heavenly bodies were perfect spheres that moved in perfect
circles around the earth. Eudoxus (ca. 408–355 B.C.), a student of Plato,
realized that the movement of the planets could not be explained in terms
of perfectly circular orbits, so he created a model of nested spheres to explain the erratic movements of some of the planets across the night sky.

Claudius Ptolemy's Universe

In A.D. 141, the Greek astronomer Claudius Ptolemy (ca. A.D. 75) wrote
a book titled the *Almagest*. In *Almagest* Ptolemy summarized the previous seven hundred years of Greek scientific and philosophical speculation about the heavens. Living in Alexandria, Egypt, Ptolemy had access
to the greatest library of the ancient world—containing more than half a
million scrolls. This great library was eventually destroyed and many of
the ancient sources for the *Almagest* lost forever. Ptolemy's work sur-
vived, however, and for the next fourteen hundred years came to dominate Western civilization's understanding of the heavens.

Ptolemy, following Plato and Eudoxus, argued that the earth lay at the
center of the universe, and the sun, moon, and stars orbited around the
earth in a series of invisible spheres. Ptolemy created a model of these
spheres that allowed astronomers to explain the movement of the planets across the sky and even predict their future pathways. One of the
greatest difficulties in explaining the motion of the planets is that they
periodically exhibit retrograde motion, that is, although the planets usually travel from west to east across the night sky, they occasionally seem
to move backward, traveling from east to west. Today we know that this
retrograde motion is due to the planets' having different orbital velocities around the sun. Ptolemy, however, used epicycles (circles within
circles) to explain this apparent retrograde motion.

In addition to fulfilling humanity's need to explain the movement of
the sun, moon, planets, and stars across the sky, Ptolemy's model of the
universe also seemed to fit in very well with the teaching of the Bible.

Although the book of Genesis tells us that God created both the heavens and the earth, the focus of the Bible is clearly upon the earth. Since Ptolemy was developing his model of the universe at the same time that Christianity was beginning to spread across the Roman Empire, it is not surprising that early Christians merged Ptolemy's teachings with their understanding of the Bible. The Jewish and Christian doctrine that, "In the beginning God created the heavens and the earth" (Gen. 1:1), was easily merged with the Ptolemaic belief that the earth was the center of this creation. This successful merger of scientific and religious thought lasted for some fourteen hundred years, probably due in large part to the onset of the Dark Ages, the era that followed the collapse of the Roman Empire, during which little scientific research was conducted.

Thus, modern science traces its origin to the Renaissance, which began in Italy in the 1500s. During this great awakening, many of the modern scientific disciplines—including astronomy, geology, and biology—came into existence.

Nicolaus Copernicus's Universe

Nicolaus Copernicus is often called the founder of modern astronomy. In 1543, he published his most famous work, *De Revolutionibus Orbium Celestium (On the Revolutions of Heavenly Spheres)*, in which he abandoned Ptolemy's model of the universe and argued that the planets revolved around the sun, not the earth. His model could account for many observations that Ptolemy's model had failed to explain.

To the Roman Catholic Church, however, the idea that the earth was a planet orbiting the sun was nothing less than heresy. Copernicus's theory clearly contradicted more than fourteen hundred years of church teaching and removed the earth from the center of creation. Since *De Revolutionibus Orbium Celestium* was not actually published until the year in which he died, Copernicus was not personally caught up in this controversy. Giordano Bruno (1548–1600) was, however, burned at the stake in 1600 for promoting this idea. Galileo (1564–1642) spent the last ten years of his life under house arrest for using his telescope to help confirm Copernicus's heliocentric (sun-centered) model. Thus, many scientists argue that the church attempted to halt the development of modern science.

Nothing in the Bible, of course, states that the earth is at the center of the universe. Christians in the twenty-first century have no problem believing in a heliocentric model of the solar system because the Bible simply does not address this issue. Today, we understand at a much deeper level than Copernicus could have ever comprehended that the earth is not even remotely close to the center of the universe. As Carl Sagan pointed out, "We have examined the universe in space and seen that we live on a mote of dust circling a humdrum star in the remotest corner of an obscure galaxy" (1980, 20). Nonetheless, the Bible is undeniably earth centered and human oriented. Thus, to Christians, the growing scientific knowledge of the universe—far from destroying our faith—makes us ever more likeminded with David, who said, "When I consider your heavens, the work of your fingers, the moon and the stars, which you have set in place, what is man that you are mindful of him, the son of man that you care for him?" (Ps. 8:3–4).

Science is the search for truth, and most people, far from desiring to halt science, would agree that for science to exist, it must have the freedom to grow and develop. Science must be able to replace older, faulty theories with better, more advanced models. Scientific knowledge of the universe did not, in fact, reach perfection with the heliocentric model of Copernicus. In just a little more than one hundred years, the heretical ideas of Copernicus were swept away by an even more advanced theory of the heavens. Although Copernicus had abandoned the earth-centered model of Ptolemy, he had retained Ptolemy's circular orbits. This forced Copernicus to also retain Ptolemy's epicycles to explain the retrograde motion of the planets.

As more and more precise measurements were made of planetary motions, however, it gradually became apparent that the planets did not travel in circular orbits around the sun. Johannes Kepler (1571–1630), a German astronomer, is credited with first recognizing that planets travel in elliptical orbits. The question remained, though, *Why do they do so?*

Isaac Newton's Universe

Sir Isaac Newton, an English mathematician, discovered the forces that make elliptical orbits possible. In 1687, Newton published his famous

Philosophiae Naturalis Principia Mathematica (Mathematical Principles of Natural Philosophy), in which he not only described the three laws of motion that became the basis for developing classical mechanics, but also identified one of the fundamental forces in nature—gravity. Whereas Ptolemy had explained the movement of stars and planets by imagining that they were attached to invisible celestial spheres that spin slowly around the earth, Newton was able to explain how moons, planets, and stars move through space under the force of gravity. Moreover, according to his first law of motion (the conservation of momentum), the natural tendency of a body in motion (such as a planet) is to travel in a straight line. The force of gravity, however, bends this straight line of motion into an elliptical orbit.

Although Copernicus had correctly placed the sun at the center of the solar system, Newton identified the forces governing the movement of the planets around the sun. Therefore, Newton's model of the universe explained a number of things that Copernicus's model couldn't. In fact, Newton's model was so precise that some scientists began to think of the universe as a clock whose parts could be individually studied and explained. Yet, as scientifically sophisticated as it was, Newton's model was also flawed and after two hundred years, it also was replaced.

Albert Einstein's Universe

The German physicist Albert Einstein (1879–1955) showed that parts of Newton's model of the universe are based on illusion. Einstein revolutionized our understanding of space-time itself. In contrast to the mechanistic model of the universe that had been developed on the foundation of Newtonian physics, Einstein showed that some of the physical characteristics—that is, mass, length, and time—that scientists had used to quantify this mechanistic universe were themselves not absolute but relative.

In 1905, Einstein published a series of papers dealing with his special theory of relativity, which focused on the effects of high-speed motion. Newton had identified the basic laws of motion, but Einstein went on to explain what effect motion has on the physical properties of an object. He argued that because no fixed or immovable objects exist in space, all motion is relative. In other words, you can say that something is in motion only as it relates to another object—which is also in motion.

Moreover, Einstein went on to make the astonishing statement that some of the basic physical properties of an object are not fixed but are relative to the velocity at which the object is moving. Einstein was able to prove mathematically that the mass of an accelerating object (be it a spaceship or a planet) increases while its length decreases. Perhaps even more shocking was his statement that time runs more slowly for an object that is accelerating; if an object could be accelerated to the speed of light (186,200 miles per second), time would come to a standstill. The reverse of these events happens to an object that is decelerating: mass decreases, length expands, and time speeds up.

Although these relativistic effects do not become apparent until an object is approaching the speed of light (and then, only to an observer outside the accelerating object), the process can be explained as similar to our experiences in cars and jets. In a rapidly accelerating car, our bodies are thrust back into the seat for a few seconds before the body catches up with the speed of the car. The effect is even more pronounced during the acceleration of a fast jet plane. Fighter pilots talk about experiencing several "Gs" (multiples of earth's gravity) during takeoffs, steep dives, or sharp turns. Of course the speeds achieved in even our fastest jets are— relative to the speed of light—so small that any real increase in a body's mass would be negligible. Nevertheless, we "feel" for a short time like our mass has significantly increased.

Einstein also showed that the two principal entities in the physical universe, energy and matter, are not distinct from each other but are, in fact, equivalent. In his famous equation $E = mc^2$, Einstein showed that matter can be transformed into energy and energy can be transformed into matter. This idea is demonstrated in our nuclear power plants, where uranium is partially transformed into energy. Such transformations in the very structure of matter and time make it difficult to reduce the universe to a set of equations, because some of the very qualities we use to quantify the universe are themselves subject to change. With the introduction of Einstein's *special* theory of relativity, then, the tame, predictable, machinelike character of Newton's universe was thus transformed into a much wilder and more unpredictable universe.

In 1915, Einstein published his *general* theory of relativity, which dealt specifically with the effects of gravity. Again, Newton had first identified the law of gravity, but Einstein went on to explain how gravity worked. He showed that the mass of an object warps the space that surrounds it, as the surface of a trampoline is warped when one stands upon it. Planets orbit the sun because the great mass of the sun warps space to such a degree that planets are caught in the depressed space that surrounds the sun. Calculations based on Einstein's equations predict that, if an object is massive enough, the warping of space is so strong that even light cannot escape—a black hole develops. In Einstein's universe, the movement of planets around the sun, the nuclear fires that burn at the hearts of stars, the spiral shapes of galaxies, and even the passage of time can all be explained in terms of the effects of relativity. Einstein's model of the universe explained a number of things that Newton's model could not explain.

Probing the Depths of Truth

In the end, who was right—Ptolemy, Copernicus, or Newton—or did Einstein give us the final and absolute truth? Each man was partially right; each found jewels of truth that for a time sparkled with brilliance. But in the end, each theory was shown to be inadequate. Each model of the universe was created with only partial truths that were later replaced by better, more comprehensive truths—or simply different truths. Scientists, in fact, are already beginning to speculate about who will be Einstein's successor (Calder 1979, 237–245). Problems exist in some of Einstein's theories that even he was unable to resolve. Who will break the path to even deeper truth that will resolve these problems?

Every generation thinks that its scientific truth is the definitive, ultimate truth. This belief includes a certain amount of not only pride but also self-deception. As with astronomy, a brief look at the history of any scientific discipline demonstrates how far each field has come, but we can only guess about the distance that still remains to be traveled. How long will it be before science reaches the whole and complete truth? Is the end in sight, or are we dealing with an infinite regression of knowledge? Does each answer pose even more questions? We simply don't know. On the scale of the very small, it was once thought that atoms were the ultimate building blocks from which the universe had been constructed. The atom, by definition, was indivisible. But then it was discovered that the atom itself is built out of subatomic particles: electrons, protons, and neutrons. Later, scientists were able to subdivide protons and neutrons into quarks. Now it is known that six types of quarks exist, each with its own spin, charge, color, and flavor. The question has naturally arisen, *Of what are quarks made?* One theory is that they are made of "strings" (see chapter 13).

On the scale of the very large, a pattern of infinite regression has also been found. The ancient Greeks and the peoples of medieval Europe believed that the earth was the center of the universe. Then Copernicus showed us that the earth is just one of several planets that orbit the sun. It was subsequently discovered that our sun is just one of some 100–200 billion stars that make up the Milky Way Galaxy. In the 1920s, Edwin Hubble (1889–1953) found that other galaxies existed beyond the Milky Way. Astronomers now estimate that at least one hundred billion galaxies exist, stretching to the very edge of space and time. The galaxies themselves are clumped together into clusters and even superclusters. Although the local cluster to which the Milky Way Galaxy belongs is composed of only some thirty galaxies, the Virgo supercluster may contain tens of thousands of galaxies (Sagan 1980, 247). In the mid 1980s, astronomers found that galactic superclusters are only filaments of even larger structures. Groups of superclusters are strung together into lacy chains of galaxies that stretch across (at least) a quarter of the observable universe (Lerner 1991, 15–25). This latticework of superclusters is composed of millions upon millions of individual galaxies. Thus, every star and galaxy seems to be but a subset of a larger structure.

Whether speaking of the very small or the very large, nature becomes more and more complex the deeper we probe. Like an onion, each layer of skin we remove reveals only another, deeper layer. Such complexity presents difficulties for the scientist in search of truth, but such complexity is not unexpected in a universe that was created by an omnipotent (all-powerful) and omniscient (all-knowing) God: "He performs wonders that cannot be fathomed, miracles that cannot be counted" (Job 9:10).

CHAPTER 4

WHY SCIENTIFIC
REVOLUTIONS OCCUR

MODERN SCIENTISTS ARE NOT unaware of the transitory nature of scientific knowledge. In the past, however, centuries or even millennia might elapse before a new scientific theory would revolutionize humanity's understanding of the world. Thus, the temporal nature of scientific knowledge was not readily apparent. In more recent times, the pace of scientific research has accelerated, and so has the rate of change in scientific knowledge. Today, each new space probe, accelerator, or genetic experiment seems to revolutionize our understanding of the universe. Information is often outdated before it can even be published. This growing flux in scientific truth is beginning to have an impact on science that is shaking it to its very foundations. Scientists are growing more introspective, and the history of science has become an important field of study. Epistemology has become an important auxiliary to scientific research.

One of the best known historians of science in the latter half of the twentieth century was Thomas Kuhn. In 1962, Kuhn published a book titled *The Structure of Scientific Revolutions*, in which he explained how scientific truth changes through time. This book was to have its own revolutionary impact on the minds of many scientists. Older models of scientific development were generally pyramidal in character—the acquisition of scientific knowledge was thought to be a gradual, accumulative process in which layer upon layer of facts were built up until the pinnacle of modern scientific truth was achieved. Kuhn argued, however, that the actual practice of science is a much more erratic process than the standard models suggested. Based on his historical studies of scientific development, Kuhn concluded, "Perhaps science does not develop by the accumulation of individual discoveries and inventions" (1970, 2).

The Ruling Paradigm

Kuhn's observation is grounded in the reality that scientific facts have no significance in and of themselves. Facts must be incorporated into an interpretive framework before they have any meaning. In the old *Dragnet* series from the 1950s, gruff police detective Sergeant Friday always attempted to cut through the emotionally charged atmosphere of a crime scene by demanding that the witnesses give him "just the facts." Facts by themselves, however, have no meaning. Facts are given significance only by our hypotheses and theories. In the hands of a good detective (like Sergeant Friday), the facts can be woven together into a recreation of what actually happened at the crime scene. The observational statement *I saw a flash of light at 10 p.m.* is a factual statement that has no significance unless we attempt to explain it. The flash of light that I saw at 10 P.M. could, for example, have been lightning, an explosion, car headlights cresting a hill, a plane wreck. Facts of any kind become interesting only when we try to explain what they mean.

A good scientist can collect scientific observations of the natural world and piece them together into an explanation of how the world works. Any given body of facts, though, can be arranged and interpreted in a great many ways. Kuhn has argued that periodically science goes through a revolution in the way it looks at and interprets scientific facts. Therefore, scientific knowledge does not necessarily grow in a linear fashion by the simple accumulation of more and more scientific facts. Instead, the history of science is periodically marked by "revolutions," during which time scientific facts are given completely new and often radically different interpretations. As Kuhn noted, "It is rather as if the professional community had been suddenly transported to another planet where familiar objects are seen in a different light and are joined by unfamiliar ones as well" (1970, 111).

In his book, Kuhn argued that during periods of "normal science," the majority of scientists will share a similar understanding and interpretation of scientific facts; they will see and interpret the world in a similar manner. He called this shared worldview a "paradigm":

> The term "paradigm" is used in two different senses. On the one hand, it stands for the entire constellation of beliefs, values, techniques, and so on shared by the members of a given community. On the other, it denotes one sort of element in that constellation, the concrete puzzle-solutions which, employed as models or examples, can replace explicit rules as a basis for the solution of the remaining puzzles of normal science. (1970, 175)

A paradigm is composed of not one but a number of theories that, taken together, explain the world. The unique perspective that a paradigm provides gives rise to certain types of problems that need to be solved; it also specifies the types of techniques that can be used to solve those problems. The paradigm provides direction as to (1) which scientific questions should be asked, (2) which scientific facts are relevant to answering those questions, (3) which techniques can be used to study those facts, and (4) how those facts should be interpreted. Therefore, every paradigm is a self-directed model for seeking and identifying truth (Kuhn 1970, 103).

According to Kuhn, every mature science operates within a well-defined paradigm. For instance, the current paradigm in modern geology is plate tectonics. The plate tectonic paradigm is based on the idea that the earth's crust is composed of a series of rigid plates that are in motion. Based on the composition of these plates and their motion relative to each other, geologists have developed a number of secondary theories. These secondary theories attempt to answer a variety of geologic questions, including: (a) What was the position of the continents in the past? (b) Why do some areas have frequent earthquakes? (c) Why do volcanoes often occur in linear belts? (d) How were metal rich ore bodies formed? (e) Why do mountain ranges commonly occur at the edge of continents? and (f) How are deep ocean trenches created? Although each of these secondary theories will have its own unique set of assumptions, hypotheses, analytical techniques, and data bases, they all attempt to answer questions about the earth in terms of the composition and movement of rigid plates that form the earth's crust. A modern geologist who does not believe in plate tectonics is a scientist who is badly out of sync with his or her discipline. Such geologists are probably seeking answers to questions that no one else is asking (or even interested in).

Although the use of the plate tectonics paradigm to study the earth is providing geologists with solutions to many previously unanswered questions, it is also raising new problems that require further research. Therefore, over time, a paradigm and its secondary theories continues to evolve. The paradigm is a sort of game plan for seeking truth; it not only delineates what questions are relevant but also provides guidelines as to how to solve those questions. According to Kuhn, if you want to participate in the scientific endeavor, you must attempt to answer the questions that are posed by the current scientific paradigm.

Paradigm Evolution

Most scientists spend their lives conducting what Kuhn has called "normal science." Initially, the fit between a new paradigm and the scientific facts that it attempts to explain is far from complete. Many implications must be followed up; many problem areas must be resolved; many applications wait to be made. A new paradigm offers an exciting and potentially more fruitful approach to understanding the world, but most of the details need to be worked out. This is where normal science comes in:

> The success of a paradigm . . . is at the start largely a promise of success discoverable in selected and still incomplete examples. Normal science consists in the actualization of that promise, an actualization achieved by extending the knowledge of those facts that the paradigm displays as particularly revealing, by increasing the extent of the match between those facts and the paradigm's predictions, and by further articulation of the paradigm itself. (Kuhn 1970, 23–24)

As an example of the actualization of promise, during the past 200 years, most geologists have believed that the earth was shaped by slow, gradual processes, not rapid, catastrophic events. This paradigm is called uniformitarianism. In the early 1980s, however, a new paradigm (catastrophism) was introduced into geology. This paradigm was based on the idea that, occasionally, catastrophic events can generate rapid changes that significantly alter the earth. Initially, the primary data supporting the catastrophism paradigm was a correlation between the disappearance of the dinosaurs at the end of the Cretaceous Period and rocks of the same age that contained an excessive amount of a metal (iridium) that is commonly found in meteorites. Since the early 1980s, scientists have actually found the crater that was produced by this asteroid impact at the end of the Cretaceous Period. They have also identified a couple dozen other lines of evidence supporting this catastrophic event. In addition, geologists have now identified over 200 additional impact craters of various sizes and ages across the earth. Some of these larger craters are associated with other mass extinctions—some of greater magnitude than that which led to the disappearance of the dinosaurs. Thus, catastrophism provides a classic example of a paradigm actualizing its potential by (1) starting out with a limited amount of supporting evidence, (2) subsequently expanding its data base, and then (3) finding new areas of application.

Despite the dominant influence a paradigm exerts over a scientific community, it will not be able to answer every question that arises during the course of normal scientific research. Initially, the paradigm can be stretched to cover new observations or modified to better fit the data. Thus, the paradigm continues to grow and develop—the model becomes more refined. But inevitably, anomalies will be discovered that simply cannot be explained by the theories in the current paradigm. As these anomalies continue to build, the inadequacy of the paradigm slowly becomes apparent.

An everyday example of this process might be a young couple who have just purchased their first home. Initially the house meets all of their needs. As they buy new furniture and have their first child, they expand into rooms that they had previously used for storage. With the acquisition of more furniture and the birth of additional children, they modify the existing rooms or perhaps add on an addition. If their family continues to grow, however, it will eventually become apparent that the house is

simply too small, and further modifications will not solve the problem—
a new and bigger house is needed.

In the same manner, a paradigm may function for a considerable period of time as a viable explanation for various natural phenomena. Eventually, however, its premises can be expanded no further and its defects
can be excused no longer. It will have to be replaced with a new paradigm that better addresses the current needs and problems.

Ptolemy's earth-centered model of the universe, for example, was viable for more than fourteen hundred years, but it was eventually swept
away by the heliocentric model of Copernicus. Today, as the pace of scientific research accelerates, anomalies build faster, and paradigms must
be replaced after a much shorter time. This is exactly the reason scientists such as Kuhn have begun to recognize the transitory nature of scientific knowledge. If a paradigm were able to answer every question that
arose, then absolute truth would finally be achieved, and work in the
discipline would slowly come to an end as all of the questions were answered. In the real world, no scientific paradigm has yet proven itself
infallible.

Paradigm Extinction

The transition from an old paradigm to a new paradigm is not an easy
one. Scientists like to portray themselves as impassioned seekers of truth,
but the all-inclusive nature of a paradigm ensures that the scientific community will exhibit a great deal of resistance at the prospect of old theories being swept away.

Older scientists who have spent their careers developing a paradigm
in their field are not anxious to discard their life's work in favor of a new
set of theories. Eminent European archaeologist Vere Gordon Childe
(1892–1957), for instance, spent much of his career developing a chro-
nology for prehistoric Europe that was based on stylistic changes in arti-
fact typologies. When in the 1950s the radiocarbon dating technique
began to revolutionize our understanding of European prehistory, Childe
chose to commit suicide rather than stand in the way of scientific
progress—or see his life's work invalidated. Many other scientists have
gone to their graves embittered because their theories and research were

eventually made obsolete by newer theories and paradigms. Even the preeminent scholars in a field may eventually find themselves becoming the rear guard and finally the old fogies of their discipline.

Science is not a very good rewarder of those who diligently serve it. Therefore, according to Kuhn, every paradigm has a great deal of built-in inertia in the form of scientific careers and personal egos that must first be overcome before a scientific revolution can occur. Often, nothing less than death or retirement finally silences the advocates of the old paradigm (1970, 151–52).

The New Paradigm

Thomas Kuhn argued that the anomalies that build during the course of normal scientific research eventually result in a "scientific revolution." In other words, the long, stable periods of normal science are periodically disrupted by chaotic episodes in which the old paradigm ceases to provide an adequate explanation for many of the known scientific facts. A period of intellectual confusion follows, during which a number of competing paradigms may be introduced into the field. Eventually one of the competitors wins out, and the other paradigms are rejected. The winning paradigm is usually the one that best explains the anomalies that the old paradigm failed to explain (Kuhn 1970, 153). The new paradigm, however, is directed at solving those particular anomalies, and it may provide a very different view of the world than did the old paradigm. The new paradigm is directed at solving a different set of problems and consequently generates a different set of theories to achieve this end. The scientific view of the world is remade, and science once more settles into another stable period of problem solving, during which the implications of the new paradigm are thoroughly examined, tested, and applied.

Paradigms and Absolute Truth

It should be obvious by this point that the transitory nature of scientific truth, which was documented in the preceding chapter, has been explained thoroughly in Thomas Kuhn's book *The Structure of Scientific*

Revolutions. The transformations in our understanding of the universe that followed the work of Ptolemy, Copernicus, Newton, and Einstein can be modeled in terms of paradigm change, but it can be suggested that each new paradigm was more powerful than its predecessor. This view implies that, although none of these paradigms represented absolute truth, science was at least advancing in the right direction—each new paradigm was a little closer to the truth. Kuhn, however, has argued otherwise: "We may, to be more precise, have to relinquish the notion, explicit or implicit, that changes of paradigm carry scientists and those who learn from them closer and closer to the truth" (1970, 170). Kuhn seems to have taken this position for at least three reasons:

1. Scientific revolutions are the end result of *paradigm failures*, not successes;
2. Scientific revolutions often result in radically *different scientific agendas*;
3. *Teleological arguments* (i.e., nature was designed for a specific purpose) are inconsistent with modern scientific thought.

In regard to *paradigm failures*, most scholars traditionally believed that scientific advances are made by the gradual accumulation of knowledge and facts. Kuhn recognized that such growth does occur "within" a paradigm. Indeed, he has described normal science as a period of "mopping-up" or "puzzle-solving" (1970, 24, 36). Researchers, during the course of normal science, gradually solve many of the problems that a new paradigm poses at its inception. Kuhn, however, has also shown that the most important episodes in the history of science—the scientific revolutions—are generated not by the accumulation of facts but by the inevitable failure of the paradigm to explain the anomalies that have also accumulated during the course of normal scientific research. Thus, in the final analysis, scientific revolutions and the new paradigms they generate are not the result of advancements in our understanding of truth. When the previous paradigm collapses, scientists must rebuild from the ground up. According to Kuhn, the new paradigm may be no closer to the truth than the old paradigm; it may be even farther away.

The only reason for choosing a particular new paradigm is that it seems capable of explaining the anomalies.

Concerning *different scientific agendas,* once the explanatory power of a paradigm has largely been exhausted, science simply abandons it. A new paradigm is then chosen primarily on the basis of its ability to offer possible explanations for anomalies that the old paradigm could not explain. Consequently, a new paradigm often bears little resemblance to the old one. Many of the problems and solutions that were of central importance to the old paradigm may be irrelevant to the new one. The epicycles of the Ptolemaic universe, for instance, were retained by Copernicus but were completely abandoned by Newton. Therefore, when a new paradigm is built upon the structure of the preceding paradigm, it is often difficult to show continuity; instead of representing quantitative increases in knowledge, new paradigms are often little more than shifts in perspective. The process could be compared to the old baseball parks that had wooden fences around their outfields. People unable to afford a ticket into the park could still watch the game by looking through the knotholes in the fence. Each knothole, though, gave a different view of the playing field. A hole in the left field fence gave a good view of the left fielder and third base, but the center fielder might be completely out of sight. Each knothole in the fence provided the viewer with a different perspective of the game. Paradigms are somewhat akin to knotholes in that each gives only a limited view of the universe, never the whole picture. The primary value of a new paradigm is that it offers radically new insights into problems that have become the center of scientific attention.

Finally, in addition to the two preceding problems, Kuhn also rejected the belief that paradigm change carries us closer to the truth. He did so because of the *teleological implications* of such a belief. Teleology is based on the idea of purpose or design in nature. According to this doctrine, everything that exists has a cause. In other words, the universe has meaning because it was brought into existence not by chance but by design. As Kuhn has noted, even the pre-Darwinian evolutionary theorists believed that evolution was a directed process, ultimately culminating in the appearance of humanity. Charles Darwin (1809–1882), however, rejected any teleological arguments for evolution; he believed that evolution was governed solely by chance. Kuhn suggested that Darwinian evolution provides a good model for the evolution of human knowledge: we do not have to worry about whether science is drawing nearer to the truth because there is no absolute truth:

> Does it really help to imagine that there is some one full, objective, true account of nature and that the proper measure of scientific achievement is the extent to which it brings us closer to that ultimate goal? If we can learn to substitute evolution-from-what-we-do-know for evolution-toward-what-we-wish-to-know, a number of vexing problems may vanish in the process. (1970, 171)

Kuhn's idea that new paradigms do not necessarily reflect actual advances from what-we-do-know is quite disturbing to many scientists. The rapid changes taking place in scientific knowledge have forced most scientists to recognize that current scientific theory is transitory, and they have taken solace in the belief that science is at least advancing toward the truth. Yet, according to Kuhn, even this belief may be illusionary. Therefore, whereas some scientists hold Kuhn in high esteem and regard him almost as a prophet, others see his work as little more than blasphemy and condemn him as a "betrayer of the truth" (Theocharis and Psimopoulos 1987, 597).

Because of the rapid pace of scientific research in the latter half of the twentieth century, scientific knowledge is in an accelerating state of flux. This situation has led many scientists to realize that scientific truth cannot be equated with absolute truth. At best, scientific truth is only partial truth—and sometimes, not even that. Science is, after all, a way of searching for truth by using the scientific method of theory formation and hypothesis testing. Thus, careers in science are made by being creative, not necessarily by being right. The entire purpose of testing theories is to eliminate those that are wrong or inadequate. The process has yet to produce, however, a theory that has withstood the test of time. Eventually, all scientific theories are replaced by better or different theories. To stop learning in science is, in fact, to stagnate. In one sense, scientists are very much like the Athenians of Greece, whom Luke said "spent their time doing nothing but talking about and listening to the latest ideas" (Acts 17:21).

The recognition that scientific truth is constantly changing has led historians of science such as Thomas Kuhn to document how science moves from paradigm to paradigm by periodic scientific revolutions. Each new scientific paradigm, however, and the theories it contains, does not represent absolute truth but only an internally consistent set of theories that attempt to explain specific aspects of the physical universe. Scientific knowledge thus cannot be equated with absolute truth. At best, scientific truth is only partial truth. Science moves from paradigm to paradigm, "but the word of the Lord stands forever" (1 Peter 1:25).

PART 3

FAULTY FOUNDATIONS:
THE LOGICAL LIMITATIONS OF SCIENTIFIC TRUTH

. . . always learning but never able to acknowledge the truth.
—2 Timothy 3:7

CHAPTER 5

FOUNDATION BUILT
AND UNDERMINED

THE PRIMARY OBSTACLE TO harmonizing religious truth with scientific truth is that scientific truth is constantly changing. Thomas Kuhn, in his book *The Structure of Scientific Revolutions,* explained *how* scientific truth changes. The question remains, however, *Why does scientific truth change?* An answer can be found by examining the logical limitations of the modern scientific method.

Why have scientists, using the scientific method, been unable to arrive at absolute truth? Why must we continue to update our textbooks on all of the sciences from astronomy to zoology? Why does every science have a history that is littered with brilliant hypotheses and theories that have had to be discarded?

The answer lies at the heart of scientific methodology. As early as the first half of the 1700s, philosophers realized that the logical foundations of modern science were faulty. In other words, the methods being employed in science were not powerful enough to achieve the ends that scientists wanted to achieve—absolute truth. These problems were never resolved, and they have resurfaced in the twenty-first century with a vengeance.

Francis Bacon: The Inductive Method

To understand the logical limitations of modern science, we must first understand its foundation. Francis Bacon is usually credited with being the creator of the inductive method of scientific research (B. Russell 1945, 541). Bacon, like many other early scientists, was also a Christian. He believed that science and reason held a role that was separate from theology in God's dealings with humanity. This belief is called the doctrine of double truth. Bacon thought that theology is primarily directed at restoring humanity's spiritual relationship to God, which was lost when Adam and Eve disobeyed God in the Garden of Eden. Science, on the other hand, can help restore humanity's physical dominion over nature, which was also lost because of Adam and Eve's disobedience (Bacon 1901, 290). Through the publication of two major books, *Advancement of Learning* in 1605 and *Novum Organum* in 1620, Bacon attempted to establish science upon a solid foundation so that it could be used to recover humanity's power over the natural world. Indeed, Bacon is often credited as being the originator of the statement "Knowledge is power" (B. Russell 1945, 542).

The most important contribution that Francis Bacon made to modern experimental science was his insistence that the *inductive* method—that is, arguing from specific instances to general/universal statements—was the only proper way to conduct scientific research. Before Bacon, Aristotle had dominated scientific thinking for nearly two thousand years. In his famous work *The Organon* (Aristotle 1955), Aristotle stated that *deduction* (arguing from general principles to specific instances) was the only proper method of logic. The scientist needed to find specific instances in nature that would confirm his or her hypotheses about nature. The deductive method proceeds as follows:

- Deduction: We start with a hypothesis without necessarily making any specific observations.
- Hypothesis: Dogs are smarter than cats.
- Confirming the Hypothesis

1. My dog can retrieve a ball; my cat can't.
2. My dog can pull a wagon; my cat can't.
3. My dog can protect me; my cat can't.
4. Dogs chase cats; cats don't chase dogs.

• Negating the Hypothesis

Although there may be as many (or more) instances that negate the hypothesis as confirm it, because the researcher has started out with a hypothesis that is often based on personal opinion or bias (rather than observation), it is usually far easier to confirm the hypothesis than to negate it.

Because of this asymmetry between confirmation and negation, the deductive method often tells us far more about how the scientist wants to see the world, than how the world actually is.

Despite its flaw, scientists and philosophers over the next two millennia continued to follow Aristotle's deductive methodology. Francis Bacon achieved fame in the 1600s by strongly opposing Aristotle's "philosophical approach" to knowledge. Instead, Bacon championed the "experimental approach." Although he recognized deduction as a valid methodology for logic or mathematics, he argued in *Novum [New] Organum* that the only proper method of reasoning for a scientist was by *induction* (arguing from specific instances to general/universal statements) (Asimov 1972, 89):

There are and can exist but two ways of investigating and discovering truth. The one [deduction] hurries on rapidly from the senses and particulars to the most general axioms, and from them, as principles and their supposed indisputable truth, derives and discovers the intermediate axioms. This is the way now in use. The other [induction] constructs its axioms from the senses and particulars, by ascending continually and gradually, till it finally arrives at the most general axioms, which is the true but unattempted way. (Bacon 1901, 15)

Bacon believed that if a scientist really wanted to understand nature, he or she should begin by observing nature. On the basis of these observations (specific instances), scientists could then formulate hypotheses (generalizations) in an attempt to explain what had been observed. A professional detective, for example, always begins his murder investigations with no assumptions (hypothesis). In a new murder case, the detective found several pieces of evidence: (1) the wife lacked an alibi on the night of the murder; (2) there was no evidence that a window or door had been forced open; (3) the smell of perfume lingered on the murder weapon; (4) a large insurance policy had recently been taken out on the husband. These lines of evidence suggested a hypothesis—the wife did it. This methodology stands in sharp contrast to Aristotle's deductive approach to science whereby the scientist begins with a series of preconceived generalizations about how nature works and then attempts to identify specific instances that would validate these beliefs (Casti 1989, 19). An *amateur* detective, for example, begins his murder investigations with the assumption (hypothesis) that the butler did it. In a new murder case, the detective is soon able to find evidence to justify his belief: (1) the butler lacked an alibi on the night of the murder; (2) the butler had shifty eyes; (3) the butler talked with a foreign accent; (4) the butler didn't like cats, dogs, or children. These lines of evidence validated his hypothesis—the butler did it.

Based on Bacon's scholarly expositions on the role that induction should play in science, the inductive method was eventually incorporated into the very warp and woof of experimental science. Today, it forms the foundation of the scientific method. A modern scientist begins his search for truth by making a number of specific observations on selected phenomena in the physical world, such as the movement of the stars, the chemical properties of different types of rocks, or the behavior of various types of animals. On the basis of these specific observations, the scientist then begins to formulate a hypothesis (generalization) that will explain these observations. Based on his or her observations, a scientist might hypothesize, for example, that the stars in our galaxy are in orbit around a central galactic nucleus, hard rocks have iron in them, or Canada geese mate for life. This is the process of induction—reasoning from specific facts to general principles, moving from individual occurrences to broad patterns.

Despite Bacon's dislike for deduction as a means for generating scientific hypotheses, he nevertheless retained deduction as a means for testing a hypothesis. In Bacon's scientific method, once a hypothesis has been formulated by means of induction, it must be tested. Deduction (reasoning from the general to the specific) allows the scientist to make predictions about the physical world that should be true . . . if the hypothesis is correct. If, for instance, the hypothesis that bright colors in sedimentary rocks are derived from trace amounts of iron oxide (generalization) is true, then a brightly colored rock, such as red sandstone (specific instance), should contain measurable amounts of iron oxide. Thus, a hypothesis is based on a finite number of specific instances. The hypothesis is tested by specifying a number of additional instances in which a similar pattern should also be found. The scientific method proceeds as follows:

- **Induction:** We create a hypothesis after making a number of specific observations:
  1. Rock A is brightly colored and contains iron oxide.
  2. Rock B is brightly colored and contains iron oxide.
  3. Rock F is brightly colored and contains iron oxide.
  4. Rock I is brightly colored and contains iron oxide.
  5. Rock K is brightly colored and contains iron oxide.

- **Hypothesis:** Based on the preceding specific observations, we might arrive at the following inductive conclusion (general/universal statement): *All* brightly colored rocks contain iron oxide.
- **Deduction** (testing the hypothesis): If "*all* brightly colored rocks contain iron oxide," then the following brightly colored rocks (which have not previously been studied) should also contain iron oxide:
  1. Rock M is brightly colored; it *should* contain iron oxide.
  2. Rock O is brightly colored; it *should* contain iron oxide.
  3. Rock R is brightly colored; it *should* contain iron oxide.

- **Confirming the Hypothesis:** If rocks M, O, and R do indeed contain iron oxide, then our hypothesis that "all brightly colored rocks contain iron oxide" is confirmed, or,
- **Negating the Hypothesis:** If one or more of the rocks M, O, and R do *not* contain iron oxide, then our hypothesis that "all brightly colored rocks contain iron oxide" is negated.

The larger the number of times a hypothesis has been tested and confirmed thus, the greater is our confidence that the hypothesis is true.

For the past three hundred fifty years, the experimental approach to
truth has been the hallmark of modern science. Although this approach
uses both induction and deduction, induction is, by far, the more important of the two reasoning techniques. Each scientist begins his search for
truth with the inductive method; it is the first step that each scientist
must take to practice the scientific method. Therefore, Francis Bacon
was quite successful in his attempt to firmly establish modern science on
a foundation of induction.

David Hume: The Problem of Induction

Having shown that modern science is built on the foundation of induction, we now return to our initial question: Why is scientific truth
not absolute; why has it continued to shift upon its foundation? The
Scottish philosopher David Hume (1711–1776) believed that the problem lay in the foundation itself.

Within one hundred years of the publication of *Novum Organum,*
Bacon's inductive method involving observation and experimentation
had assumed such an important role in humanity's search for truth that
some scientists and philosophers concluded that this methodology was
the only way to find truth. These advocates of experimental science either ignored or attacked the earlier ways of seeking truth (logical deduction and supernatural revelation). The philosopher John Locke
(1632–1704), in his influential 1690 publication *An Essay Concerning
Human Understanding,* argued that all knowledge comes from experience (observation and experimentation):

> Whence has it [the mind] all the materials of reason and knowl-
> edge? To this I answer, in one word, from *experience;* in that all
> our knowledge is founded, and from that it ultimately derives
> itself. Our observation, employed either about *external sensible
> objects, or about the internal operations of our minds perceived
> and reflected on by ourselves, is that which supplies our under-
> standings with all the materials of thinking.* These two are the

fountains of knowledge, from whence all the *ideas* we have, or can naturally have, do spring. (1961, 77)

This philosophy came to be known as empiricism. David Hume was a self-proclaimed empiricist. He was interested in those things that could be apprehended only through the senses, things that could be experienced. Could you see it, smell it, hear it, touch it, taste it? Could you weigh it, measure it, dissect it? If so, Hume and other empiricists were interested. Hume, however, saw religion (knowledge through divine revelation) and metaphysics (the study of ontology or epistemology) as being essentially meaningless because they did not have these properties. In his major 1748 philosophical work, *Enquiries Concerning Human Understanding and Concerning the Principles of Morals,* he wrote,

> When we run over libraries, persuaded of these principles, what havoc must we make? If we take in our hand any volume; of divinity or school metaphysics, for instance; let us ask, *Does it contain any abstract reasoning concerning quantity or number?* No. *Does it contain any experimental reasoning concerning matter of fact and existence?* No. Commit it then to the flames: for it can contain nothing but sophistry and illusion. (1975, 165)

From Hume's point of view, since the supernatural or metaphysical realms cannot be studied empirically, any books written on those subjects will just be wasting space on library shelves.

While Hume became an empiricist by choice, he was forced to become a skeptic out of necessity. Because of his love for empiricism, Hume decided to accept no knowledge that could not be proven through experience. This decision had disastrous consequences: at the heart of the inductive method is the assumption that an association of events implies causation. In other words, if, in our experience, A and B are always found together, then one must cause the other. If every time we eat strawberries, for example, we break out in hives, we assume that (A) eating strawberries (B) causes us to have hives. On a more general level, if every brightly colored rock that we examine contains iron oxide, we come to the inductive conclusion that "all brightly colored rocks contain iron oxide"; we assume that (A) iron oxide causes (B) rocks to have bright colors.

When, however, Hume attempted to prove the truth of empiricism on the basis of the inductive method, he found that it could not be done: past and current experiences (specific instances) could not be used as a bridge to future expectations (general instances or universal statements). Merely because we have experienced certain associations in the past or present does not ensure that we will continue to experience such associations in the future (Hume 1978, 139): Perhaps it was not the strawberries that caused our hives, but the milk that we had with the strawberries; perhaps other minerals than iron oxide will also cause rocks to be brightly colored.

Hume thus came to realize that inductive generalizations have no logical basis. Therefore, no inductive generalization (A causes B) can ever be proven by experience—unless one makes an infinite number of observations or experiments. According to Hume, only when one has examined every rock in the universe can one justifiably make the universal statement that "all brightly colored rocks contain iron oxide." Because it is obviously impossible to make an infinite number of observations in one or many human lifetimes, inductive statements can never be absolutely proven. As a result of this line of thought, Hume, in his 1739–1740 book *A Treatise of Human Nature*, concluded that "all our reasoning concerning causes and effects are deriv'd from nothing but custom; and that belief is more properly an act of the sensitive, than of the cogitative part of our natures" (1978, 183).

Hume's empiricism eventually led him to the realization that *scientific truth cannot be equated with absolute truth*. Because, ideally, all scientific hypotheses are derived from induction, they can never be proven on the basis of empirical observations. In the past, for example, you may have observed the wind blowing from the west to the east on ten thousand consecutive days, but no way exists to prove empirically that it will continue to blow from west to east in the future. Only by making a nonlogical, inductive leap of faith can you derive universal statements/laws from a finite number of specific observations. This fatal flaw in the inductive method became known as "Hume's Problem."

Hume's Problem was so called not only because he was the first person to call attention to this weakness in the scientific method but also, perhaps, because many other scientists and philosophers simply ignored the problem; it was Hume's problem, not theirs. These scientists pointed out that, whatever the inherent flaws in the scientific method might be, it was still a very powerful tool for accomplishing great and marvelous things—and, indeed, it is. Similarly, although your car might not run with the precision of a Swiss watch, as long as you can drive it, it's better than walking. Nonetheless, those more philosophically minded scientists who took the time to consider Hume's arguments and to probe deeply into the foundations of modern science were disquieted by what they found. As Bryan Magee (1985, 17) observed, "That the whole of science, of all things, should rest on foundations whose validity it is impossible to demonstrate has been found uniquely embarrassing." Indeed, the eminent philosopher and scientist Bertrand Russell has stated,

> It is therefore important to discover whether there is any answer to Hume within the framework of a philosophy that is wholly or mainly empirical. If not, there is no intellectual difference between sanity and insanity. The lunatic who believes that he is a poached egg is to be condemned solely on the ground that he is in a minority, or rather—since we must not assume democracy— on the ground that the government does not agree with him. This is a desperate point of view, and it must be hoped that there is some way of escaping from it. (1945, 673)

If, then, according to Russell, universal statements in science that are based on empirical observations can not be absolutely verified, then these statements, indeed, have no stronger claim to truth than the statements of a lunatic, which are based on subjective feelings. Perhaps the lunatic really is a poached egg and the rest of society is deluding itself by thinking otherwise?

Despite David Hume's eighteenth-century critique on the fatal weakness of the scientific method, scientific truth continued to exert an ever more powerful influence on the collective mind of humanity throughout the eighteenth, nineteenth, and twentieth centuries. Yet

Hume's Problem remained unanswered, and many of the brightest minds of the next three centuries continued to wrestle with the inevitable question that arose from it: "If all scientific theories are equally unprovable, what distinguishes scientific knowledge from ignorance, science from pseudoscience?" (Lakatos 1978, 1:3). Indeed, if all scientific theories are equally unprovable, what distinguishes scientific truth from metaphysical truth . . . or even religious truth?

CHAPTER 6

FOUNDATION REPAIRED

AND UNDERMINED

THAT HUME'S PROBLEM remained unanswered was a state of affairs that, for many scientists, was intolerable.

It was obvious to these scientists that scientific truth was clearly superior to religious and metaphysical truth. Yet scientific truth was derived from induction and the problem of induction—that inductively derived scientific truths could not be conclusively proven—would not go away. Consequently, a major attempt was mounted in the early twentieth century to resolve this problem through a philosophical movement known as "logical positivism." This movement attempted to merge the ideas of many eighteenth-, nineteenth-, and twentieth-century scholars to provide the ultimate answer as to what distinguishes science from metaphysics and religion.

The Vienna Circle: Logical Positivism

The roots of logical positivism can be traced back to the early 1920s, when a group of Austrian philosophers, scientists, and mathematicians in Vienna, under the leadership of Moritz Schlick, attempted to place science on a more solid foundation. This group became known as the "Vienna Circle." Members of the Circle had one primary goal in mind: to create a unified approach that would be equally applicable to the various disciplines in the natural (hard) sciences (astronomy, biology, chemistry, geology, physics, etc.) and the social (soft) sciences (anthropology, economics, psychology, sociology, etc.). To accomplish this goal, they drew on the works of a number of philosophers and scientists (Ayer 1959, 4), but three of the most important pillars of logical positivism were derived from (1) the empiricism of David Hume, (2) the positivism of Auguste Comte (1798–1857), and (3) the linguistic logic of Ludwig Wittgenstein (1889–1951).

In regard to the first pillar—the empiricism of David Hume—the members of the Vienna Circle, and most other modern scientists, were interested only in things that could be studied empirically. They believed that they could sidestep Hume's Problem by using inductive logic to speak in terms of *probabilities* rather than absolutes: [1st pillar]

> Inductive logic set out to define the probabilities of different theories according to the available total evidence. If the mathematical probability of a theory is high, it qualifies as scientific; if it is low or even zero, it is not scientific. Thus the hallmark of scientific honesty would be never to say anything that is not at least highly probable. Probabilism has an attractive feature: instead of simply providing a black-and-white distinction between science and pseudoscience, it provides a continuous scale from poor theories with low probability to good theories with high probability. (Lakatos 1978, 1:3)

While no scientific theory based on induction could ever hope to be proven absolutely true—barring an infinite number of observations—empirically based theories could be shown to be highly probable—which was the next best thing.

[Unity of Method] The second major pillar of the Vienna Circle's logical positivism was the positivism of Auguste Comte. Born in Montpelier, France, Comte set out to emulate his hero, Benjamin Franklin, by becoming "perfectly wise" (Durant 1953, 265). In his quest for wisdom, Comte came to believe that human knowledge in any area or discipline always exhibits three stages of development. In the first or "theological stage," natural phenomena are explained in terms of the actions and will of God or other supernatural beings. In the second, more advanced "metaphysical stage," these same natural phenomena are described according to abstract entities and forces such as the "nature" or the "vital force." In the third and final stage of human knowledge the world is understood through the application of scientific or "positive" laws of cause and effect that are derived through reason and observation (Comte 1853, 1:2). According to Comte, this final, positive stage of knowledge is the one toward which all of the natural sciences and social sciences are moving, and he proposed "to consolidate the whole of our acquired knowledge into one body of homogeneous doctrine . . ." (1:16). In other words, all "real" truth would be derived from positive (scientific) knowledge, regardless of the particular scientific discipline within which that truth was discovered.

Although the various social and natural sciences often study radically different aspects of the physical world, Comte believed that unity among the sciences could be achieved through a unity of method, which would be centered on mathematics. Comte taught that the basis of all positive knowledge was mathematics, and that a natural phenomenon that could not be quantified could not be studied scientifically.

Today, more than two hundred years after Comte's birth, we still feel his influence. If, for instance, a social science such as anthropology or psychology wants to become more like a hard science (such as chemistry or physics), what must it do? It must, Comte asserted, quantify its data and look for statistically significant patterns:

> Geometrical and Mechanical phenomena are the most general, the most simple, the most abstract of all—the most irreducible to others, the most independent of them; serving, in fact, as a basis to all others. It follows that the study of them is an indispensable preliminary to that of all others. Therefore must Mathematics hold the first place in the hierarchy of the sciences, and be the point of departure of all Education, whether general or special. (1853, 1:33)

Based on Comte's argument, the Vienna Circle used the methodology of mathematics to provide a clear demarcation between the truths of science and the truths of religion and metaphysics. Scientific truth would be based on mathematical probability. Therefore, although the Vienna

Circle derived its empiricism from David Hume, they gained both their desire for a unified science and their emphasis on the importance of mathematics from the positivism of Auguste Comte.

The third, and perhaps most important pillar of thought contributing to the development of logical positivism in the twentieth century was the work of the Austrian philosopher Ludwig Wittgenstein (1889–1951). At about the same time that the founders of logical positivism were beginning to hold their meetings in Vienna, Wittgenstein was preparing to publish one of his two major philosophical works, *Tractatus Logico-Philosophicus* (1922). Although Wittgenstein never became a member of the Vienna Circle, the Circle frequently discussed his work during their meetings, and he maintained close personal contacts with several members of the Circle, including Moritz Schlick.

Wittgenstein was particularly interested in the logical structure of language. He argued that for language to work, some type of logical correlation must exist between a statement and the thing about which the statement is made. Wittgenstein initially believed, in fact, that "the structure of reality determines the structure of language" (Pears 1971, 13). For this to be true, however, one must infer that the reality about which one is speaking is empirically knowable through the five senses. In other words, we cannot speak about that which we cannot apprehend through our senses or, as Wittgenstein himself put it at the very end of *Tractatus Logico-Philosophicus,* "Whereof one cannot speak, thereof one must be silent" (1922, 189). To the empirically and positivistically minded members of the Vienna Circle, this obviously meant that statements about abstract entities and forces (metaphysics) or God and the supernatural (religion) that cannot be empirically verified or mathematically quantified cannot be known. Anything spoken about those things that we cannot apprehend through our senses is simply meaningless nonsense. As A. J. Ayer (1959, 11) once noted, "The originality of the logical positivists lay in their making the impossibility of metaphysics depend not upon the nature of what could be known but upon the nature of what could be said." In other words, since God or abstract forces (such as the "vital force") can't be apprehended with our senses, we can say nothing about them because we know nothing about them. This belief fit in very well with Comte's positivism, which held that theology and metaphysics were nothing more than inferior modes of thought that should be replaced by the "positive" knowledge of science.

Based on Wittgenstein's work on the logical structure of language, members of the Vienna Circle attempted to develop a common language for science. If the sciences were to be welded into a unified whole, as Comte had once dreamed, then a shared, common language would be essential. This language would set scientists apart from all other disciplines. Moreover, such a scientific language would provide another clear demarcation between scientific truth and the pronouncements of religion or metaphysics. The hallmark of this new language of logical positivism was the "verification principle." If one is going to make statements about a thing, one must include information that will verify the existence of the thing. If one cannot verify and quantify empirically the thing about which one is talking, then one is speaking nonsense because one has no knowledge of that thing. This is just reaffirming, of course, what the founder of empiricism, John Locke, said in 1690: all knowledge comes from experience (1961, 77).

The philosophy of logical positivism that grew out of the Vienna Circle in the 1920s and 1930s contained, then, five primary elements that would distinguish scientific truth from religious or metaphysical truth:

1. A strong belief that all knowledge is derived through the senses (empiricism);
2. An attempt to circumvent Hume's Problem by using mathematical probabilities (inductive logic);
3. A strong desire to merge the natural and social sciences into a unified whole (positivism);
4. An attempt to develop a common methodology of science based on mathematics (positivism);
5. An attempt to develop a common language of science based on the verification principle (linguistic logic).

In 1929, members of the Vienna Circle held an international congress at Prague to introduce scholars from other countries to their new synthesizing approach to science. As a result of this congress, particularly strong ties were developed between members of the Vienna Circle and other scientists and philosophers working in Germany, Britain, and Scandinavia. During the 1930s, subsequent congresses were held at Konigesberg, Copenhagen, Paris, and Cambridge. In 1930, members of the Vienna Circle also began to publish their own journal, *Erkenntnis,* to further the spread of their ideas, but it was through the publication of A. J. Ayer's book *Language, Truth and Logic* (1936) that logical positivism was to have its greatest impact on the general public—particularly in the English-speaking world (Hanfling 1981, 2–3).

Logical Positivism Crumbles

It is ironic—as well as illustrative of the temporal nature of scientific truth—that while the influence of logical positivism was spreading around the world in the 1930s, the Vienna Circle itself was beginning to fall apart. Disagreements among some of the leading members of the movement were becoming more pronounced as the group attempted to refine the methodology of logical positivism. Moritz Schlick, the individual most responsible for the cohesion of the group, was murdered by a student in 1936. Moreover, the Nazis, who were gaining power in Germany and among other German-speaking populations, came to believe that certain aspects of logical positivism—such as relying on empirical evidence rather than on Nazi propaganda—were detrimental to the Nazi political agenda. With the annexation of Austria by Germany in 1938 and the eventual outbreak of World War II, members of the Vienna Circle were dispersed across the face of the earth, many of them eventually ending up in colleges and universities in Scandinavia, Britain, and America (Hanfling 1981, 3–4; Ayer 1959, 6–9).

Although logical positivism was to have a considerable influence on the thinking of both scientists and the general public throughout the rest of the twentieth century, the movement itself eventually died out. "'Logical positivism,' we are told in the *Encyclopedia of Philosophy*, 'is dead, or as dead as a philosophical movement ever becomes.' It is safe to say that few philosophers nowadays would be willing to describe themselves as Logical Positivists or Logical Empiricists" (Hanfling 1981, 1). Even A. J. Ayer, one of the leading advocates of logical positivism in the 1930s, ultimately became disillusioned with this philosophy. In the 1970s, after the collapse of logical positivism, Ayers was asked what he thought were its main defects. He answered, "Well, I suppose the most important of the defects was that nearly all of it was false" (Ayer 1978, 131). That is, indeed, a rather grave flaw. Yet, in retrospect, the collapse of logical positivism's structure was inevitable, considering the weakness of its three main pillars: empiricism, positivism, and linguistic logic.

The first of the pillars to crumble was empiricism. Although the latter part of logical positivism's name comes from the positivism of Comte, the former part of its name is derived from the Vienna Circle's heavy reliance on inductive logic and linguistic logic. Mathematics (in the form of inductive logic) was supposed to become the methodology of science; Wittgenstein's linguistic logic was supposed to become the language of science. Inductive logic would allow scientists to circumvent Hume's Problem of Induction by couching inductive statements in terms of probabilities rather than absolutes. Linguistic logic would separate scientific statements from theological or metaphysical statements by the rigorous application of the "verification principle."

Soon, however, logical positivists tripped over the same stumbling block that had been David Hume's empirical downfall—the problem of induction. Inductive logic failed because it was found that most inductive statements could not be assigned high probabilities. As was noted earlier, it would take an infinite number of observations to prove an inductive statement. The number of observations that a scientist can make over the entire course of a lifetime, is, of course, very small when compared to infinity. Linguistic logic failed for the same reason. When the verification principle was applied to statements derived through induction, it was found that few statements of real substance were empirically verifiable. Unless scientists wished to confine themselves to making probabilistic statements about common occurrences (e.g., the sun will rise in the morning), or empirically verifiable statements about the obvious (e.g., water is wet), Hume's Problem was still very much their problem. Thus, as Casti notes, perhaps the greatest weakness of logical positivism was its inability to resolve the problem of induction (1989, 32). Empirical observations cannot be used to generate universal statements that can be (1) empirically verified (linguistic logic), or (2) shown to be highly probable (inductive logic).

The second pillar to crumble was Comte's positivism. The logical positivists had hoped that mathematics would be able to save them from the skepticism of David Hume, as well as provide science with a common methodology. The failure of mathematics to achieve the former has been discussed above. In regard to its providing a common methodology, it is true that mathematics holds a unique and preeminent position among the sciences. Invariably, the more scientific a discipline is considered to be, the more it is able to reduce its theories and discoveries to mathematical formulae.

The scholar who would venture into the hardest of the hard sciences—physics and chemistry—without a strong background in mathematics will not travel far. Chemistry and physics, in turn, are stepping-stones for those who would study such sciences as geology, astronomy, and biology. Therefore, for a scientist working in the hard sciences, a solid knowledge of mathematics is of fundamental importance. Mathematics is often, in fact, considered to be the queen of the sciences. Above the door of Plato's Academy were written these words: "Let no one ignorant of mathematics enter here" (Asimov 1972, 15).

It was unfortunate for the members of the Vienna Circle that, as they attempted to elevate mathematics to the primary methodology of science, the absolute character of mathematical knowledge began to unravel. All mathematical systems were subsequently found to be seriously flawed.

The weak links in the mathematical chain were first discovered by the Austrian mathematician Kurt Gödel (1906–1977). Although Gödel was initially involved in the deliberations of the Vienna Circle, he subsequently sought to distance himself (Dawson 1988, 5). He was particularly interested in the relationship between mathematics and logic. If mathematics was to be the final arbiter of scientific truth, Gödel and other scientists wanted to prove that mathematical systems are themselves "complete"—that is, every true statement of number theory can be derived from within the system itself—and "consistent"—that is, mathematical statements contain no contradictions (Hofstadter 1979, 23–24).

To test the logical unity of mathematics, Gödel devised a coding system that could convert the symbols of mathematical logic into numbers (Gödel-numbering). This numbering system allowed mathematics to make logical statements about itself. Using this self-referential system of mathematics, Gödel made the startling discovery that *all* formal mathematical systems are both incomplete—in that mathematics would not be able to prove all possible truths—and inconsistent—in that mathematical theories could not even prove themselves (Hofstadter 1979, 18–19).

In 1931, Gödel published his findings in a seminal paper on the consistency and completeness of mathematics titled "On Formally Undecidable Propositions of *Principia Mathematica* and Related Systems I." His famous "First Incompleteness Theorem" is found in Theorem VI of this paper: *"For every w-consistent recursive class k of* FORMULAS *there are recursive* CLASS SIGNS *r such that neither v Gen r nor Neg (v Gen r) belongs to Flg (k) (where v is the* FREE VARIABLE *of r)"* (Gödel 1986,173). Scholars who can understand Gödel's First Incompleteness Theorem have attempted to translate it into less formidable language (apparently, with only limited success): "All consistent axiomatic formulations of number theory include undecidable propositions" (Hofstadter 1979, 17), or "For every consistent formalization of arithmetic, there exists arithmetic truths that are not provable within that formal system" (Casti 1996, 163). Basically, what Gödel's First Incompleteness Theorem did was to show that *all* mathematical systems are incomplete because they are unable to encompass every possible truth. In other words, some things exist that we absolutely know to be true but cannot prove through the use of any mathematical system. (Given the complexity of Gödel's arguments, readers must simply take his conclusions to be correct.) "Put more prosaically, there is an eternally unbridgeable gap between what can be *proved* and what's *true*" (Casti 1996, 153). Therefore, Gödel's First Incompleteness Theorem proved mathematically that mathematics would never allow us to apprehend all possible truths. All mathematical systems are thus incomplete.

Gödel was also able to show that all mathematical systems are inconsistent in that they contain contradictions. By substituting the idea of "proof" for "truth," Gödel was able to introduce into mathematics the famous Epimenides Paradox. Epimenides was a sixth-century B.C. poet from Crete who made the paradoxical statement, "All Cretans are liars." This statement is an example of what Hofstadter calls a "strange loop":

"The 'Strange Loop' phenomenon occurs whenever we, by moving upward (or downward) through the levels of some hierarchical system, unexpectedly find ourselves right back where we started" (1979, 10). The Epimenides Paradox forever trapped philosophers in just such a strange loop because they could never determine whether Epimenides' statement, "All Cretans are liars," was true or false. Epimenides was a Cretan, so in saying, "All Cretans are liars," he must be lying. If he was lying, however, then the statement, "All Cretans are liars," must be true. But if the statement is true, then he must be lying, because he is a Cretan, and so forth. Gödel took the core out of the Epimenides Paradox—"This statement is false"—and transformed it into a mathematical concept: "This statement of number theory does not have any proof" (Hofstadter 1979, 17–18). By doing so, Gödel was able to show that mathematical systems can contain contradictions and are therefore inconsistent. (This contradiction is true only of theories or systems, not of mathematical givens such as $2 + 2 = 4$.)

In addition to proving that mathematical systems can be inconsistent, Gödel also showed that mathematical systems are incapable of validating their own consistency. In his 1931 paper, Theorem XI (Gödel 1986, 1:193), known as the "Second Incompleteness Theorem," specifically addresses the consistency of mathematical systems and demonstrates that all formal mathematical systems are too weak even to prove their own consistency (Casti 1994, 141–43; 1989, 279–82). Therefore, how can mathematics be used to validate the empirical observations of scientists if it cannot be used even to validate its own consistency? In plain language, it cannot.

Here, then, was indeed a dilemma; according to logical positivism, mathematics was to provide the absolute base on which all scientific methodology was to be built. Alfred North Whitehead (1861–1947) and Bertrand Russell, in their massive three-volume work *Principia Mathematica* (1910, 1912, 1927), had attempted to provide such a base. Gödel, however, was able to prove that no mathematical system—be it Whitehead and Russell's or any other—could logically contain all of the truth that the world holds. Therefore, although Gödel's early interest in the problem of completeness and consistency in mathematical systems may have been stimulated by his discussions with members of the Vienna Circle, his subsequent work on these problems led him to philosophical views "which were, in large part, almost diametrically opposed to the views of the logical positivists" (Feferman 1986, 1:4). Much to the detriment of Comte's positivism and the Vienna Circle's logical positivism, Gödel ended up proving that mathematical systems are neither complete (able to encompass all true statements) nor consistent (contradiction-free).

Based, then, on the work of both Hume and Gödel, the conclusion is inescapable that absolute truth cannot be confined within the bounds of logical (inductive) or mathematical (probabilistic) systems. At best, all that can be done with induction or mathematics is to apprehend a part of the larger truth that is out there; the systems being used are simply not robust enough to capture the entirety of this truth. Gödel's work clearly shows that, although mathematics might be the queen of the sciences, she nonetheless has feet that are made of clay:

> The ultimate foundations and the ultimate meaning of mathematics remain an open problem; we do not know in what direction it will find its solution, nor even whether a final objective answer can be expected at all. "Mathe-matizing" may well be a creative activity of man, like music, the products of which not only in form but also in substance are conditioned by the decisions of history and therefore defy complete objective rationalization. (Weyl 1949, 219)

The third pillar to crumble beneath the edifice of logical positivism was the linguistic logic of Ludwig Wittgenstein. Building largely upon Wittgenstein's ideas about the relationship between language and reality, the Vienna Circle attempted to develop a universal language of science that would be based on the principle of verification: only statements that could be verified empirically or mathematically would be considered scientific.

It is ironic that, while the members of the Vienna Circle were building logical positivism around the ideas found in Wittgenstein's *Tractatus Logico-Philosophicus*, Wittgenstein himself was laying the foundation for a new philosophy that would contradict the verification principle (Casti 1989, 29). In his second great work, *Philosophical Investigations* (1953), published two years after his death, Wittgenstein had "abandoned the idea that the structure of reality determines the structure of language and suggested that it is really the other way around; our language determines our view of reality because we see things through it" (Pears 1971, 13). As an example, some languages have only two words for color—such as red or blue—and those colors are the only ones that the users of this language can distinguish. What we see as different colors, they see as different shades of the two colors.

Therefore, while the logical positivists were attempting to create an objective scientific language that could be verified by empirical observation of the physical world, Wittgenstein had concluded that language is actually subjective and has meaning only within the cultural context in which it occurs. Reality does not give rise to the structure of language; instead, language provides the structure for how we see reality. Thus, although Wittgenstein's early work had inspired the members of the Vienna Circle, his later work significantly undermined one of the central tenants of logical positivism—the verification principle. If language itself governs how we see reality, how could logical positivists trust their empirical observations of reality to create a common scientific language that only made statements about things which had been verified empirically? Logical positivists were once again caught in the circular logic of a strange loop that had no final end or answer.

The three main pillars on which the edifice of logical positivism had been erected—empiricism, positivism, linguistic logic—were found, then, to be incapable of bearing the weight of absolute truth. The mathematical work of Kurt Gödel and the philosophical work of Ludwig Wittgenstein were instrumental in pointing out some of the most glaring deficiencies in this system. Eventually, the entire structure of logical positivism began to teeter and ultimately came crashing to the ground. The dust of this collapse filled the latter half of the twentieth century and clouded the minds of many scientists and philosophers with the murky particulates of skepticism and relativism.

Karl Popper: The Principle of Falsification

Even before the final collapse of logical positivism, certain philosophers were beginning to doubt its underpinnings. One of the first individuals to see clearly the inadequacies of logical positivism was another Austrian scholar, Karl Popper (1902–1994). Born in Vienna at the turn of the century, Popper became involved in the discussions of the Vienna Circle during the early 1920s. It soon became evident, however, that his philosophical views were incompatible with those of logical positivism (Casti 1989, 32). Indeed, in his later career, he, of all twentieth-century philosophers, would produce the most sustained attack against this philosophy, leading one of the members of the Vienna Circle to nickname him "the Official Opposition" (Magee 1985, 5).

Like many members of the Vienna Circle, Popper left Austria in 1937 because of the impending occupation of his homeland by Nazi Germany. Popper first moved to New Zealand where he obtained a teaching position at Canterbury University College. Later, he moved to England and found a permanent home teaching philosophy at the London School of Economics.

In his early philosophical work, Popper focused directly on the Problem of Induction that Hume had introduced some two hundred years earlier. By 1934, Popper had concluded that the mathematical probability of all scientific theories was zero (Lakatos 1978, 1:3; Popper 1976, 146–47). In his 1934 groundbreaking work, *The Logic of Scientific Discovery*, Popper stated, "My own view is that the various difficulties of inductive logic here sketched are insurmountable. So also, I fear, are those inherent in the doctrine, so widely current today, that inductive inference, although not 'strictly valid,' *can attain some degree of 'reliability' or of 'probability'*" (Popper 1968, 29). Popper saw that the attempt by the logical positivists to use mathematical probabilities to circumvent Hume's Problem was doomed to failure. He argued that it was simply impossible to *prove* any inductive hypothesis on the basis of empirical observations or mathematical probabilities. Therefore, rather than continue to labor over a technique that was clearly inadequate for discovering truth, Popper decided to lay out a different path.

Popper's solution to Hume's Problem was somewhat similar to Alexander the Great's approach to the Gordian knot. Alexander visited Gordium—home of the famous Gordian knot, which according to local legend King Midas had tied. King Midas also predicted that the man who could untie the knot was destined to rule the world. Legend states that Alexander, after thoroughly examining the intricately tied knot, simply took his sword and sliced the knot in half. Similarly, Popper was able to dispense with Hume's Problem of Induction simply by dismissing induction as a necessary component of the scientific method. This was, of course, a rather drastic departure from the scientific orthodoxy that had been in force since the time of Francis Bacon but, from Popper's viewpoint, continued adherence to an inductive methodology was little more than an exercise in futility—it simply didn't work.

Popper argued that it makes little difference from where a hypothesis comes: induction, deduction, poetic inspiration, or the tea leaves at the bottom of your cup (1968, 31–32). What really matters is whether a hypothesis is true or false. Popper therefore shifted the attention of science away from the question of origins—from where a hypothesis comes—and focused it squarely on content—what the hypothesis actually *says*. It was impossible, though, to prove the truth of any hypothesis that contained a universal statement (*all* stars, *every* rock, etc.), as centuries of labor on the problem of induction had demonstrated; logic dictated that it would take an infinite number of observations to prove that a universal statement is true. To solve Hume's Problem, Popper had not only to break science's addiction to the inductive method but also to find a workable methodology for testing the truth of a hypothesis.

Popper's second major breakthrough was his recognition of the "*asymmetry* between verifiability and falsifiability" (1968, 41). Two ways, he pointed out, can be used for testing a hypothesis: (1) by proving it true (verification); (2) by proving it false (falsification). Based on a casual observation of swans, for example, one might easily formulate the hypothesis, "All swans are white." The only way, of course, to verify this statement would be to examine every swan in the universe to be absolutely certain that all swans are, indeed, white. Popper, however, pointed out that an infinite number of observations would not be necessary to prove that this statement is false. A single observation of a black swan would be sufficient to falsify the statement, "All swans are white" (Magee 1985, 18–19). Popper showed, therefore, that while it is forever beyond our ability to prove absolutely (verify) a universal statement, it is well within our means to disprove (falsify) such a statement.

The logical positivists had attempted to use the verification principle to establish a clear demarcation between scientific statements and statements derived from religion or metaphysics. Karl Popper took the exact opposite approach. He said that all truly scientific statements must be written such that they can be falsified—not verified. This became known as the "principle of falsification" and was the hallmark of Popper's approach to science. As Popper stated, "the criterion of the scientific status of a theory is its falsifiability, or refutability, or testability" (Popper 1965, 37). He said that instead of presenting a hypothesis in rather vague terms (e.g., geese come in various colors) in the hope of protecting it from attack, a hypothesis should be stated such that its weak points are immediately obvious and testable (e.g., geese are always white—never black, brown, or any other color). As one of Popper's students would later note, "A theory is 'scientific' if one is prepared to specify in advance a crucial experiment (or observation) which can falsify it, and it is pseudoscientific if one refuses to specify such a 'potential falsifier'" (Lakatos 1978, 1:3). Thus, false hypotheses can more readily be identified and abandoned and new, more powerful hypotheses developed.

Popper's principle of falsification is somewhat similar to General George Patton's approach to warfare. As Patton prepared his Third Army for the campaign in France during World War II, he gave his troops these marching orders: "I don't want to get any messages saying that, 'We are holding our position.' We're not holding anything! Let the Hun [German] do that. We are advancing constantly and we're not interested in holding on to anything except the enemy. . . . We have one motto, '*L'audace, l'audace, toujours l'audace*'" (Boldness, boldness, always boldness!) (D'Este 1995, 623).

Patton knew that his army would soon encounter towns and villages that were heavily fortified by the Germans. His solution to this problem was to act with daring and *l'audace*. His army would simply sweep around these pockets of resistance, thereby leaving the enemy isolated from their supply lines, as his Third Army raced on across France toward Germany. Similarly, Popper argued that scientists have spent too much time trying to defend indefensible positions and outdated hypotheses. The path of progress for science is to make every hypothesis easily testable (falsifiable) so that the weak and erroneous ones can be identified quickly and swept aside, and new, better theories developed. The successful scientist must act with daring and boldness by continually testing the frontiers of knowledge and looking for weak spots in current theories that will allow the scientist to gain footholds in previously unoccupied territory— *l'audace, l'audace, toujours l'audace!*

Many scholars found Popper's approach to science liberating. Over the past centuries, a great deal of scientific theory had crystallized into dogma: This is the way the world is; this is absolute truth—case closed. Those who questioned the dominant theories of science (such as Darwinian evolution) did so at their professional peril. Such dissenters were often viewed by their colleagues as little more than heretics and were soon relegated to the lunatic fringe of their discipline, their careers in shambles. But, from Popper's perspective, no aspect of scientific knowledge was sacred. He believed that

> The old scientific idea of *episteme*—of absolute certain, demonstrable knowledge—has proven to be an idol. The demand for scientific objectivity makes it inevitable that every scientific statement must remain *tentative for ever.* It may indeed be corroborated, but every corroboration is relative to other statements which, again, are tentative. Only in our subjective experiences of conviction, in our subjective faith, can we be "absolutely certain." (Popper 1968, 280)

To many scientists, knocking over the idol of scientific certainty opened the door to creativity. Released from the straitjacket of conventional knowledge, they could test and probe into every corner of science, looking for flaws, examining weak areas, hoping (even expecting) to make dramatic breakthroughs that might revolutionize our understanding of the world. It is not surprising, then, that a number of Nobel Prize winners attribute their success, at least in part, to Popper's influence. These Nobel Prize winners—all in Medicine—include Sir Peter Medawar (1960), Sir John Eccles (1963), and Jacques Monod (1965). Other eminent scientists and scholars who have been strongly influenced by Popper's work include astronomers (Sir Herman Bondi), art historians (Sir Ernst Gombrich), and politicians (Sir Edward Boyle) (Magee 1985, 3–4).

It is unfortunate, however, that in addition to the positive results that

Popper's work has generated there has also been a downside. In rejecting induction as a necessary prerequisite of the scientific method and abandoning the false hope of ever being able to prove or verify scientific hypotheses absolutely, Popper had inadvertently opened the doorway to relativism and skepticism. Gone was the old straitjacket of scientific orthodoxy, but so too was the security that had accompanied the scientist's belief in the absoluteness of scientific truth. Popper himself was aware of these consequences. In another of his books, *The Open Society and Its Enemies* (1966), Popper discusses how any increase in freedom also leads to an apparent decrease in security. In this book, he noted that the apparent trade-off of security for freedom is one of the primary reasons for the appeal of totalitarian government down through the ages. People frequently do not like the increased responsibilities that come with freedom, even though their actual (versus perceived) security under a totalitarian system is often minimal (1966, 1:1–5; Magee 1975, 87–90).

Scientists, of course, were never really secure in their scientific knowledge because the foundation on which that knowledge was built was flawed. Nonetheless, many scientists *believed* themselves to be secure, and perceptions (even false ones) are very important to one's sense of security. In the brave new world of modern science that followed the collapse of logical positivism and the introduction of Popper's philosophy, scientists may *believe* in the existence of absolute truth (as did Popper), but they are also aware that the scientific truths with which they daily work can never be *proven* absolutely.

One might conclude that such a recognition would cause many scientists to temper their total devotion to scientific truth and reexamine the claims of Christ, who said that He is the source of all truth. Some have, but many others have sunk ever deeper into skepticism and the belief that all truth is relative. As we noted earlier, this is exactly the position in which Thomas Kuhn found himself. He brilliantly identified how scientific knowledge evolves through a series of paradigm shifts, then he found himself in a dilemma: Did such shifts bring scientists closer to the truth ... or merely give them a different set of questions? (Kuhn 1970, 170).

CHAPTER 7

FOUNDATION REPAIRED, UNDERMINED, AND ABANDONED

ALTHOUGH KARL POPPER HAD a powerful impact on science in the twentieth century, his principle of falsification was by no means accepted universally. Other philosophers of science pointed out that Popper was "prescribing" rather than "describing" how science actually worked. In a perfect world, scientists might be willing to open up their work to criticism by pointing out the weak parts of their theories; under ideal conditions, scientists might willingly abandon pet theories as soon as they found them to be false. But in the real world things are quite different.

Imre Lakatos: Scientific Research Programs (SRPs)

One of Popper's students at the London School of Economics, Imre Lakatos, was very much aware of this deficiency in his mentor's philosophy:

> Is, then, Popper's falsifiability criterion the solution to the problem of demarcating science from pseudoscience? No. For Popper's criterion ignores the remarkable tenacity of scientific theories. Scientists have thick skins. They do not abandon a theory merely because facts contradict it. They normally either invent some rescue hypothesis to explain what they then call a mere anomaly or, if they cannot explain the anomaly, they ignore it, and direct their attention to other problems. Note that scientists talk about

anomalies, recalcitrant instances, not refutations. History of science, of course, is full of accounts of how crucial experiments allegedly killed theories. But such accounts are fabricated long after the theory had been abandoned. (Lakatos 1978, 1:3–4)

Popper's principle of falsification fails, then, to set science apart from pseudoscience. Scientists, naturally having a vested interest in the outcome of their work, are far more prone to justify than to falsify their theories.

Imre Lakatos (1922–1974) was born in Debrecen, Hungary, but later fled from his homeland during the 1956 Hungarian uprising. He subsequently moved to England and attended college at Cambridge University, where he began to achieve fame as a philosopher of mathematics and science. He spent the later part of his life teaching at the London School of Economics. Lakatos's most famous work, *Proofs and Refutations*, was published posthumously in 1976 by his students. In this book, Lakatos follows in Gödel's footsteps, that is, continuing the attack on the formalist philosophy of mathematics that had been the methodological centerpiece of logical positivism. In the introduction to that book, Lakatos stated his antipathy to the Vienna Circle's pillars: "The dogmas of logical positivism have been detrimental to the history and philosophy of mathematics" (1976, 3). Perhaps his most important contribution, however, was outlined in another posthumously published book, *The Methodology of Scientific Research Programmes* (1978).

That book presented Lakatos's view of science as a series of "scientific research programmes," or SRPs (1:4). Lakatos argued that science is not just a number of isolated hypotheses that must be verified or falsified. Instead, science is actually an entire research program that is composed of many hypotheses and assumptions. These hypotheses and assumptions form several distinct layers, which might be compared to the skin, flesh, and core of an apple. At the heart of any SRP are seeds of truth or the "hard core"—a collection of hypotheses that are considered noncontestable because they have been so thoroughly substantiated. Surrounding this core is a "protective belt" of auxiliary hypotheses that arise out of the hard core and are presumed to be true—if the hard-core hypotheses are true. Like the flesh of an apple, these auxiliary hypotheses protect the seeds of truth in the hard core from direct attack or falsification. Whenever experimental data are collected that seem to contradict (falsify) the core hypothesis, some of the auxiliary hypotheses in the protective belt can be modified to explain these apparent anomalies. Finally, the entire SRP is covered with a "heuristic skin"—a powerful problem-solving methodology that suggests how data are to be gathered, interpreted, and used to support or modify the auxiliary hypotheses in the research program (1:4; Casti 1989, 35–36).

Imre Lakatos presented a much more complicated picture of how science works than the one that Karl Popper offered. Lakatos showed that science is more than simply falsifying weak hypotheses and creating stronger ones. As he noted, each SRP "at any stage of its development, has unsolved problems and undigested anomalies. All theories, in this sense, are born refuted and die refuted" (1978, 1:5). Therefore, according to Lakatos, Popper's principle of falsification cannot serve as the demarcation between science and pseudoscience, "since all programmes grow in a permanent ocean of anomalies" (1:6). This brings us right back to the same thorny question that unfortunately continues to resurface century after century: If neither induction, empiricism, verification, mathematical probability, nor falsification can be used to separate scientific truth from religious or metaphysical truth, what can?

Lakatos also attempted to answer the recurring question, *What makes scientific truth superior to other types of truth?* He suggested that a scientific or progressive program of research "leads to the discovery of hitherto unknown novel facts." In pseudoscientific or degenerating programs, on the other hand, "theories are fabricated only in order to accommodate known facts" (1978, 1:5).

Lakatos has thus given a very utilitarian definition of what is scientific: if it works—if it gives us hitherto unknown novel facts—it is scientific; if it doesn't work or has stopped working, it is not scientific. As Lakatos himself noted, however, all SRPs have a heuristic skin that helps explain away anomalies and thereby preserves the integrity of the core hypothesis. Therefore, any SRP may simultaneously be generating unknown, novel facts and fabricating theories to accommodate known facts. Moreover, Lakatos argued that "it is not dishonest to stick to a degenerating programme and try to turn it into a progressive one" (1978, 1:6). Consequently, the border between progressive research programs—those that provide new facts and insights—and degenerative ones—those that fail to provide new facts and insights—is a very thin one indeed, a border that can be and frequently is crossed. Many scientists have thus found Lakatos's demarcation between science and other disciplines to be unsatisfactory.

Popper cracked the floodgates of relativism by embracing fully Hume's argument that it is impossible to prove (verify) a scientific hypothesis. Lakatos inadvertently opened the gates still wider by demonstrating that entire SRPs are not absolute; they can degenerate into nonproductive, pseudoscientific approaches, or they can be revived once more, to start producing novel facts. Therefore, it is difficult to judge which SRPs are nearest to absolute truth because the programs themselves are constantly changing.

Lakatos's vision of the scientific enterprise is far richer than Popper's in that his notion of heuristics [the skin of the apple] directs attention to important aspects of scientific practice not stressed by Popper at all. Nevertheless, the difficulties with [Lakatos's] SRPs cast aspersions on the kinds of views of scientific "reality" that can be expected from any such program (Casti 1989, 37).

In terms of how scientists try to preserve their hypotheses from falsification, Lakatos's SRPs are more realistic than Popper's model. His criteria, however for judging the usefulness of any particular SRP is very relativistic.

As discussed in the introduction to this book, one of the reasons scientists have been so concerned with delineating the differences between scientific truth and religious or metaphysical truth is their belief that scientific truth is superior to all other forms of truth. Yet Francis Bacon's induction, John Locke's empiricism, Auguste Comte's positivism, the Vienna Circle's logical positivism, Karl Popper's principle of falsification, and Imre Lakatos's SRPs all have failed to provide an adequate demarcation between scientific truth and religious or metaphysical truth.

Paul Feyerabend: Scientific Skepticism

After nearly four hundred years of failed attempts, it is not surprising that at least one philosopher of science—Paul Feyerabend (1924–1994)—

came to the long-overdue conclusion that, in reality, there is no difference between scientific, religious, and metaphysical truth. Truth is truth no matter where you find it; it is the one immutable object in the universe. As Albert Einstein concluded, "All religions, arts and sciences are branches of the same tree" (Bradley, Daniels, and Jones 1969, 615). Science itself, concluded Feyerabend, is a religion:

> Thus science is much closer to myth than a scientific philosophy is prepared to admit. It is one of the many forms of thought that have been developed by man, and not necessarily the best. It is conspicuous, noisy, and impudent, but it is inherently superior only for those who have already decided in favor of a certain ideology, or who have accepted it without ever having examined its advantages and its limits. And as the accepting and rejecting of ideologies should be left to the individual it follows that the separation of state and church must be complemented by the separation of state and science, that most recent, most aggressive, and most dogmatic religious institution. (Feyerabend 1978, 295)

Feyerabend appears to follow the old proverb: If it looks like a dog, acts like a dog, and smells like a dog—it must be a dog. If science is going to become the voice of authority that religion once was, if science is going to provide explanations for the ultimate questions that religion once provided, if science is going to castigate doubters and nonbelievers as religion once did, then science must be a religion.

Such scientifically heretical ideas as those of Feyerabend did not go over well in many scientific circles. In a 1987 article in *Nature* titled "Where Science Has Gone Wrong," two English physicists discuss recent cutbacks in government funding of scientific projects and the likely correlation of those cutbacks with growing public skepticism about the value of scientific research. They blamed much of this recent skepticism on several philosophers of science whose work they believed was undercutting public confidence in the pronouncements of science. They included in their article photos of four philosophers whom they thought were particularly good candidates for the title "betrayers of the truth": Karl Popper,

Imre Lakatos, Thomas Kuhn, and Paul Feyerabend. Feyerabend, however, they singled out as "currently the worst enemy of science" (Theocharis and Psimopoulos 1987, 596).

It is not surprising that Feyerabend's name would be linked with Popper, Lakatos, and Kuhn. Paul Feyerabend, yet another Austrian-born philosopher of the early twentieth century, was too young to become involved in the early deliberations of the Vienna Circle, but he subsequently studied under Karl Popper at the London School of Economics and became best friends with Imre Lakatos. Despite his notoriety in the eyes of some scientists, he was always in great demand as a professor and once simultaneously held tenured positions at four separate universities. During the latter part of his career, he alternated his yearly teaching schedule between the University of California at Berkeley and the Federal Institute of Technology in Zurich, Switzerland.

Feyerabend's most famous book, *Against Method* (1978), is a collage of essays and arguments that he had presented during the previous twenty years (Feyerabend 1995, 139). In this book, Feyerabend argued, "Science is an essentially anarchistic enterprise . . ." (1978, 17), which should not "be run according to fixed and universal rules . . ." (295). Feyerabend noted that such attempts to create a rigid definition of the scientific method had ultimately failed. He believed that this failure was inevitable, given the complexity of the universe in which we live—no single approach could ever hope to encompass all the multifaceted aspects of nature.

Feyerabend argued that scientific progress (i.e., new theories and paradigms) occurs only when individual scientists are willing to step outside the bounds of conventional scientific knowledge and attempt to explain the natural world in new and unique ways:

> We find then, that there is not a single rule, however plausible, and however firmly grounded in epistemology, that is not violated at some time or other. It becomes evident that such violations are not accidental events, they are not results of insufficient knowledge or of inattention which might have been avoided. On the contrary, we see that they are necessary for progress. (1978, 23)

Many great scientific discoveries, in fact, are owed to such violations "occur[ring] only because some thinkers either *decided* not to be bound by certain 'obvious' methodological rules, or because they *unwittingly broke* them" (Feyerabend 1978, 23).

Feyerabend taught that strict adherence to any particular methodology of science (be it induction, empiricism, falsification, etc.) was only a waste of time that ultimately inhibited the creativity of the human spirit. "All methodologies have their limitations and the only 'rule' that survives is 'anything goes'" (1978, 296). Moreover, in the search for truth, Feyerabend said that, because no preferred or superior methodology exists, the human mind should simply make use of every pathway that it finds available. He believed, consequently, that many areas of study that the scientific community had shunned might prove rich repositories of knowledge: "It is, therefore, necessary to re-examine our attitude towards myth, religion, magic, witchcraft and towards all those ideas which rationalists would like to see forever removed from the surface of the earth (without having so much as looked at them—a typical taboo reaction)" (298–299).

Given the preceding excerpts, it is evident that both the scientific skepticism that beset Hume and his fellow empiricists and the relativism that surfaced with the work of Kuhn and Popper came to full force in the writings of Paul Feyerabend. Although some of Feyerabend's ideas are like a breath of fresh air in the desert of scientific rationalism, his philosophy is not without its own unique set of problems. It is an unfortunate reality, for instance, that the same mind that initially won't believe anything, will eventually end up believing everything. If all truth is relative, the very idea of truth loses its significance. Consequently, the relativist loses the ability to distinguish between truth and falsehood, sense and nonsense.

We can clearly see this principle at work in Western civilization at the end of the twentieth century and the beginning of the twenty-first century. Those who have used relativism as an excuse for abandoning the absolutes of Scripture, turn around and openly embrace every superstition imaginable, from reincarnation to astrology to crystal power. A similar criticism can be made of Feyerabend. At the same time that he was pointing out the tyranny of science, he was also characterizing Christianity

Feyerabond

as being the "bloodthirsty religion of brotherly love . . ." (1978, 299). He argued that Western civilization should cast off the shackles of science, even as it had previously cast off the shackles of the "One True Religion!"—Christianity (307). Nevertheless, Feyerabend advocated that we "re-examine our attitude towards myth, religion [other than Christianity], magic, witchcraft . . ." (298).

Merely because Feyerabend has been castigated as "the worst enemy of science" (Theocharis and Psimopoulos 1987; Horgan 1993) does not necessarily make him a friend of Christianity. The same could be said for the other so-called enemies of science that we discussed earlier: Thomas Kuhn, Karl Popper, and Imre Lakatos. Their antipathy, though, actually makes their critiques on the weaknesses of science all the more powerful. They certainly cannot be accused of attacking science on the basis of a positive bias toward the truths of Christianity. Their attack on scientific truth is largely an attack from within, philosophers of science probing the logical and mathematical limitations of their own discipline.

At the outset of this part 3, the following questions were posed: Why is scientific truth not absolute? Why is scientific knowledge in a constant state of flux? Why do we see a steady progression of scientific paradigms marching across the pages of human history? There is but one answer to these questions: The foundation of scientific knowledge is faulty; it is built on the shifting sands of the inductive method and mathematical probability. Neither of these foundations has the logical integrity necessary to support the scientific claims of absolute truth that have been erected upon them.

For more than two thousand years, science was dominated by Aristotle's philosophical approach with its emphasis on deduction. In the early 1600s, Francis Bacon introduced the modern experimental approach to science by stressing the superiority of induction over deduction. By the late 1600s, scientists such as John Locke were so enthralled with the experimental approach that they came to follow empiricism, believing that empirical observations were the only source of truth. In the 1700s, however, David Hume showed that inductive observations in the past or present couldn't logically be projected into the future. In other words, no logical basis exists for believing that a finite number of observations can ever be used to generate universal statements about other things that have not yet been examined empirically.

At the beginning of the twentieth century, the Vienna Circle attempted to circumvent Hume's Problem of Induction by speaking only in terms of mathematical probabilities. Kurt Gödel, however, with his First and Second Incompleteness Theorems, proved that mathematical systems themselves are neither complete nor consistent. Karl Popper attempted to solve Hume's Problem by simply abandoning induction as a necessary prerequisite of the scientific method. Although scientific theories could not be verified, as the logical positivists had believed, Popper showed that they could be falsified. Subsequently, one of Popper's students, Imre Lakatos, argued that, in the real world, most scientists defend their theories rather than attempt to falsify them. He suggested that science is actually composed of a series of scientific research programs that actively protect their core theories from attack. Lakatos had difficulty, however, showing that scientific truth differs from religion or metaphysics because his only criterion for a progressive, scientific program was that it should produce novel facts about the world.

In light of all of these failures to show that science is superior to religion or metaphysics, Paul Feyerabend came to the opposite conclusion. In fact, he believed that the scientific method is itself a myth and that modern science is little more than a specialized form of religion. His conclusions led many philosophers and scientists in the latter half of the twentieth century into cynicism (absolute truth, if it exists, cannot be found) or relativism (there is no such thing as absolute truth).

Despite the facts that, even today, Hume's Problem of Induction has never been resolved and Gödel's Incompleteness Theorems have never been disproved, and although scientists cannot logically justify or prove hypotheses that are based on induction and mathematical probabilities, scientists have continued to advocate and practice the scientific method. As Imre Lakatos has commented, "One can today easily demonstrate that there can be no valid derivation of a law of nature from any finite number of facts; but we still keep reading about scientific theories being proven from facts. Why this stubborn resistance to elementary logic?" (1978, 1:2).

In light of the futility of science's ever finding absolute truth, one alternative is simply to give up hope of ever finding truth and descend into the darkness of cynicism and relativism. Not liking either of these alternatives, most scientists continue to believe in the scientific method, even though they realize that it is seriously flawed—better a leaky boat than no boat at all. As Hume himself noted, "Thus the skeptic still continues to reason and believe, even tho' he asserts, that he cannot defend his reason by reason . . ." (1978, 187). Similarly, A. J. Ayer, after stating that "the most important of the defects [of logical positivism] was that nearly all of it was false," went on to admit that he still believed in "the general rightness of the approach" (1978, 131). Such reluctance to abandon falsehood in the brilliant light of truth becomes both an intellectual and a spiritual sin:

> In them is fulfilled the prophecy of Isaiah: "You will be ever hearing but never understanding; you will be ever seeing but never perceiving. For this people's heart has become calloused; they hardly hear with their ears, and they have closed their eyes. Otherwise they might see with their eyes, hear with their ears, understand with their hearts and turn, and I would heal them." (Matt. 13:14–15)

PART 4

BIASED METHODS:
THE CULTURAL LIMITATIONS
OF SCIENTIFIC TRUTH

"What is truth?" Pilate asked.
—John 18:38

CHAPTER 8

SCIENCE AS HISTORY

As THOMAS KUHN HAS SHOWN, the absolute truths of science are not absolute. Rather, they continue to change through time. Old theories and paradigms, like children's sand castles, are regularly swept away by the advancing and retreating tide of human understanding. Attempts by Hume, Comte, and the Vienna Circle to ground the scientific method on a solid foundation of logic or mathematics all failed. As Karl Popper has noted,

> The empirical basis of objective science has thus nothing "absolute" about it. Science does not rest upon solid bedrock. The bold structure of its theories rises, as it were, above a swamp. It is like a building erected on piles. The piles are driven down from above into the swamp, but not down to any natural or "given" base; and if we stop driving the piles deeper, it is not because we have reached firm ground. We simply stop when we are satisfied that the piles are firm enough to carry the structure, at least for the time being. (1968, 111)

It is a self-fulfilling prophesy that Popper's own principle of falsification, as well as Lakatos's scientific research programs, also sank into this same swamp of subjectivism, leading Feyerabend to conclude that "anything goes" in the search for truth (1978, 23).

Because of the setbacks discussed earlier in this book, science at the beginning of the twenty-first century is going through a rare period of self-examination. Scientists are attempting to look beyond the limits of their own particular disciplines to examine the very nature of truth itself. One of the tools that has aided them in this quest is epistemology, the study of the nature and grounds of knowledge (how we know what we know). Epistemology was once a very specialized field within the realm of philosophy but has now become an important element in many scientific disciplines. Astronomers, geologists, and anthropologists alike are attempting to explain how they arrive at truth. During this process, questions have arisen not only about how we find truth but also the nature of truth. The answers to these questions have often been surprising and disturbing. Indeed, the conclusions derived from this research have been the source of considerable discomfort to those scientists who have built their lives on the premise that scientific truth should be equated with absolute truth.

Cultural Influence on Science

One of the most important discoveries arising from the recent emphasis on epistemology has been the strong interaction between scientific truth and culture. In 1871, the British anthropologist Sir Edward Tylor (1832–1917) defined culture as "that complex whole which includes knowledge, belief, art, law, morals, custom and any other capabilities and habits acquired by man as a member of society" (Haviland 1999, 36). According to modern anthropology, when a human is born, he or she has certain basic instincts (such as breathing, eating, and crying) that do not need to be learned. Everything else, however—talking, reading, writing, wearing clothes, making friends, driving a car, building a house—must be learned. All of the beliefs, behavior patterns, and material possessions that we acquire as a result of learning from others are what anthropologists call "culture."

Scientists often picture themselves as being completely objective, dispassionate observers of nature; they are interested in only "the facts." Recent studies in epistemology have shown, however, that culture plays a very important role in determining how scientists actually perceive and define truth. First, for instance, the very language—be it German, English, Russian, etc.—that a scientist uses to describe the natural world is derived from the scientist's culture. Second, the quantifications that a

scientist uses to study nature—minutes, grams, volts—are not instinc-
tual; they are ways of measuring the world that are also learned in the
context of a culture. Third, and perhaps most importantly, the scientist's
very perception of reality is strongly colored by the philosophical orientation of the surrounding culture. In a culture dominated by, for example, the belief that natural events are governed by the whims of a
multitude of gods and goddesses, the search for natural laws may be perceived as irrational behavior. Conversely, in a totally materialistic society, any allusions to the supernatural may be considered superstitious
nonsense. Therefore, the way a culture interprets reality will be of fundamental importance in determining how members of that culture perceive and explain the world around them. A scientist can never completely
escape the influence of the culture into which he or she was born, or the
culture in which he or she now lives.

Culture not only preconditions the minds of scientists to see the world
in a certain way but also plays an active role in providing the motivation
to conduct scientific research. The very questions that scientists ask are
determined, in part, by their culture. Scientists need funding to conduct
their research. If they attempt to answer questions that are highly relevant to their culture or government, they will have much greater success at fundraising than if they attempt to answer questions that are of
interest to only themselves or a small group of fellow scientists. Moreover, scientists, like all other human beings, need recognition and praise
for their work. Again, there are severe cultural restraints as to what type
of work is most visible and appreciated by the general public. Some of
the most successful scientists have been those who were highly adept at
touching cultural hot buttons that would win them fame and fortune.
Therefore, a scientist's perception and pursuit of truth is very closely
bound to the culture within which he or she conducts research. Part 4 of
this book examines a number of instances that exemplify this interplay
between culture and science.

Hard Science Becomes Soft Science

As noted in part 3, the sciences are usually divided into the hard and
the soft sciences, the natural sciences verses the social sciences. The *natural*

sciences (such as astronomy, geology, and biology) are often described as being "hard sciences" because, as you will recall, they deal with material objects—stars, rocks, plants, and animals—that can be studied through experimentation and/or quantification. On the other hand, the *social sciences* (such as anthropology, history, and psychology) deal with human behavior. Some types of experimentation on human subjects is generally considered, of course, to be unethical. Moreover, the complexity of human behavior has frequently defied the quantification required of hard sciences, thus foiling attempts to predict future behavior.

What is usually ignored, however, is that many of the hard sciences have a soft underbelly—history. The theories generated by the hard sciences to explain how natural phenomena originated (e.g., the dinosaurs, the continents, or the planets) are largely historical, rather than experimental. The focus is upon unique, one time events that can't be duplicated in the laboratory.

Historical Events in Astronomy

Once astronomers have built a catalog of the different types of stars and galaxies that can be observed in outer space, the question naturally arises, how did the universe come to be? The study of the present universe naturally leads to the study of the past universe: How did stars develop (stellar evolution)? How did the galaxies originate (galactic formation)? Where did the universe come from (cosmology)? Because astronomers looking out into space are also looking back in time—because the universe is so large, it takes great amounts of time for light from distant stars and galaxies to travel to the earth—it is possible to study stars and galaxies at different time periods. It is clearly impossible, however, to look beyond the beginning of time to see how the universe came into existence. Therefore, the creation of the visible universe is a one-time event that is not continuing to happen today. Astronomers who are studying cosmology are very much like historians who are studying human history; both are dealing with one-time events; both are trying to reconstruct what happened in the past based on the fragmentary evidence that still exists in the present.

Historical Events in Geology

Geologists study not only the earth as it is today but also attempt to study the earth as it was in the past: ancient climates, land structures, extinct animals, etc. Natural history museums are filled with reconstructions of what the world was like during the Ice Age, during the Age of Dinosaurs, during the Age of Plants, or during the Age of Invertebrates. Paleontology textbooks contain numerous illustrations of how animals evolved from one form to another during the Paleozoic, Mesozoic, and Cenozoic eras. These are all historical events, however, happening but once in the past, and are not available for experimental analysis or quantification today. We can never experimentally replicate how dinosaurs evolved, for instance, unless we recreate dinosaurs (a la *Jurassic Park*) and then study them for vast periods of time to see what happens. We can never replicate (nor would we want to replicate) how an asteroid may have struck the earth at the end of the Cretaceous Period, causing the large-scale extinction of many species (including the dinosaurs). We can never experimentally replicate how vast ice sheets moved southward across North America and Europe during the height of the last Ice Age.

Scientists as Historians

Many of the most interesting things that astronomers, geologists, and biologists can tell us about the physical universe, then, are about historical events that occurred but once in the past and can not be reconstructed or replicated through experiment. Therefore, although these scientists may publicly proclaim the superiority of the hard sciences, much of their most interesting work revolves around history, which they often castigate as being a "soft science." As Stephen Jay Gould (1941–2002) has noted,

> Beyond a platitudinous appeal to open-mindedness, the "scientific method" involves a set of concepts and procedures tailored to the image of a man in a white coat twirling dials in a laboratory—experiment, quantification, repetition, prediction, and restriction of complexity to a few variables that can be controlled and manipulated. These procedures are powerful, but they do not encompass

all of nature's variety. How should scientists operate when they must try to explain the results of history, those inordinately complex events that can occur but once in detailed glory? Many large domains of nature—cosmology, geology, and evolution among them—must be studied with the tools of history. The appropriate methods focus on narrative, not experiment as usually conceived. (1989, 277)

Thus, when scientists attempt to explain the present by looking into the past, they have entered the realm of history. When they attempt to reconstruct what the world or the universe was like in earlier periods, they are not conducting experiments or quantifying, they are in actuality writing history. It is an unfortunate circumstance, though, that the writing of history is influenced strongly by the culture in which that writing occurs. In the twentieth century, we saw a number of groups attempt to rewrite history based on their political, racial, or sexual orientations. The Communists, for instance, attempted to rewrite all of Russian history in terms of the ideas of Marx and Engels. Nazi sympathizers have attempted to remove the Holocaust from histories of World War II. Some Native American groups—rejecting the archaeological evidence that indicate their ancestors originated in Siberia and entered North America by traveling across the Bering Strait land bridge during the Ice Age—are rewriting their history in terms of their ancient myths and legends which state that their ancestors "originated" in the Americas. Some feminist theologians—believing that the Bible has been corrupted by the "patriarchal chauvinism" of its male writers—are attempting to rewrite portions of the Bible, changing the male pronouns for God from *he* to *she* and removing those portions teaching what they believe has contributed to the "oppression of women." In light of all of these potentially biased points of view, deconstructionists are currently having a wonderful time rewriting history. Whether anything of substance will be left when they are finished is an open question.

An Example from Archaeology

To illustrate the interplay between culture and the writing of history in relation to science, we might examine the discipline of archaeology.

Many historians are drawn to the field of archaeology because of the opportunity it provides them to participate actively in *creating* history rather than just writing about it. Archaeologists frequently divide the past into two major periods: the historic and the prehistoric. The historic period for any culture begins with the introduction of writing. The oldest writing in the world is cuneiform, which the Sumerians developed in the Near East about five thousand years ago. In other regions of the world, however, writing developed much later. Writing was not introduced in North America, for instance, until the arrival of the Europeans some five hundred years ago. Without writing, it is very difficult through oral traditions, drawings, and paintings to retain more than a few centuries worth of accurate information about previous generations. Therefore, the only factual history we have for most "prehistoric cultures" that are more than a few hundred years old is that created by archaeologists through the study of material remains—clay pots, flint tools, stone foundations. Archaeologists are literally creating a history of earlier peoples and time periods where none previously existed.

Many archaeologists, however, have come to realize that these reconstructions of past times and cultures can be influenced strongly by the biases of their own time and culture. Providing a vivid example of the way in which historical bias may influence the interpretation of archaeological data is the ancient Minoan site of Knossos, which was constructed around 2000 B.C. on the island of Crete. At the very beginning of the twentieth century, British archaeologist Sir Arthur Evans (1851–1941) discovered and excavated Knossos. Extensive excavations of the site revealed a central court surrounded by a maze of rooms, courtyards, staircases, and corridors that covered an area of approximately six acres. Beautiful frescoes and murals covered some of the walls of this multistoried structure, and an elaborate drainage system ran throughout the building.

Sir Arthur Evans believed that Knossos was the palace of a hitherto undiscovered civilization that he named Minoan, after the legendary King Minos. Based on the scenes depicted in the murals and frescoes, the diversity of exotic trade items found at the site, and the complexity of the structure itself, Evans envisioned that the Minoan civilization represented a golden age of antiquity, an age that was characterized by a devotion to the peaceful pursuits of art, sport, and religion rather than warfare.

In the early 1970s, however, a German geologist named Hans Georg Wunderlich (1928–1974) wrote a book titled *The Secret of Crete* (1974), in which he challenged Evans's belief that the Minoan civilization represented a high point of ancient culture and civilization. Instead of being a palace of light and beauty, Wunderlich argued that Knossos was actually the source of one of Greece's darkest tales—the myth of Theseus and the Minotaur.

According to Greek mythology, King Minos of Crete had a wonderful bull that went mad. One of the "twelve labors" that Heracles had to perform for the king of Mycenai was to capture this bull and bring it to Greece. The bull left an offspring on Crete that was half man and half bull—the Minotaur (the bull of Minos). King Minos made the Minotaur his pet and built an elaborate, many-roomed house for him called the Labyrinth. When King Minos's son was killed in Athens, Minos made war on Athens. After defeating King Aigeus of Athens, King Minos forced the Athenians to pay him a yearly tribute of seven young men and seven young women. These unfortunate youths were taken on a black-sailed ship to Crete and released into the Labyrinth, where they soon became lost in the maze of rooms and passages. The Minotaur then hunted down each of these victims for sport and ate them. This practice ended only when Theseus, son of King Aigeus, volunteered to go as one of the victims and succeeded in slaying the Minotaur (Rouse 1957, 62, 117–24).

Wunderlich pointed out that Greek myths firmly place King Minos, the Minotaur, and the Labyrinth on the island of Crete. He suggested that the complex of rooms, passage ways, and courts at Knossos could have easily given rise to the story of the Labyrinth. The association of this site with bulls is also much in evidence in the artwork of the murals, frescoes, and shrines. As Wunderlich noted, "The monster of legend could be seen again in innumerable images of bulls, in bas-reliefs, small sculptures, bull-shaped vessels, seals and imprints of seals, and stylized bulls' horns" (1974, 9–10). He also argued that many of the rooms, as well as the furniture within them, were not utilitarian but were meant to serve ritual purposes. Likewise, the numerous vessels found in many of the rooms were not meant to store food for the living but grave goods for the dead. Wunderlich even argued that Evans's palace plumbing—which included drains, basins, and tub—was actually used for "preparing the corpse for embalming" (141). Therefore, according to Wunderlich, Evans's many-roomed palace of light and life was actually a mausoleum of darkness, death, and human sacrifice (as were many other so-called Minoan palaces on Crete):

> The palaces of Knossos, Phaistos, Hagia Triada, Mallia and Kato Zakro, therefore, were not the gay residences of peaceful and artistic rulers, as the imaginations of Sir Arthur and his successors have made them. In reality they were highly involved cult structures built for the veneration and burial of the dead. (Wunderlich 1974, 135)

The difference in perception between Evans and Wunderlich drives home the point that was made earlier: *facts do not speak for themselves; they are given meaning only through our interpretations.* The archaeological facts in this case are as follows: stone walls and pavements, clay pots and seals, and the painted murals and frescoes that make up the site of Knossos. One scholar interpreted the site as the palace of an enlightened civilization; another scholar saw the site as a mausoleum built by a society preoccupied with death. How can two scientists examining the same evidence arrive at such opposite conclusions?

Sir Arthur Evans was the son of a wealthy industrialist who lived in England at the turn of the century. Evans, however, had little interest in industry or the modern world. He longed for a coming golden age in which art and religion, rather than economics and business, would dominate. He found the prototype of his dreams in the Minoan civilization. Europe had once lived in the golden time of Minoan civilization; perhaps it would do so again. In an article titled "Structuralism and Myth in Minoan Studies" (1984), John Bintliff (1949–) notes that

> Evans's revitalization of a wondrous world of peaceful prosperity, stable divine autocrats and a benevolent aristocracy, owes a great deal to the general political, social and emotional "Angst" in Europe of his time. He succeeded brilliantly in conjuring up both a physical and imaginative world of the lost civilization that dominates our vision of the Minoans even today. (Bintliff 1984, 35)

It is not difficult, then, given the circumstances of Evans's era, to understand the way in which he interpreted the facts.

Wunderlich, on the other hand, came from Germany, a nation that recently had been at the fiery center of both World Wars I and II. In the 1970s, when Wunderlich's book was published, Germany was a divided country, situated at the frontier between Western and Eastern Europe. Armies were poised on either side of this border in anticipation of a possible third world war between the superpowers—the United States and the Soviet Union. Such a war threatened to unleash nuclear, chemical, and biological weapons that could drive humanity back to the Stone Age, if not obliterate it altogether. The future was not bright. Wunderlich saw the Minoans as a barbaric civilization obsessed with death, very much like the Cold War Europe of the late twentieth century.

In a sense, the way Evans and Wunderlich interpreted the site of Knossos was highly reflective of the historical bias of the time and the culture in which each lived. Both men were looking at the past through glasses tinted by the present.

To archaeologists, the realization that their reconstructions of past cultures can be so strongly distorted by the historical biases of their own time and culture is a rather disturbing revelation. As Ian Hodder (1949–), a professor of archaeology at the University of Cambridge, has noted,

> The notion that the past is an active product of the present, however, raises problems and dilemmas of its own. In particular, if archaeologists cannot be seen as providing neutral information for the public, what social responsibilities are involved? The questions that come to the fore include: what type of past do people want, should archaeologists provide a past that supports (legitimates) or disturbs present outlooks, which sections of society do archaeologists write for, and what are the implications of Western archaeologists working in developing countries? (1984, 28)

From Hodder's perspective, the writing of history ceases to be a neutral endeavor in which the only goal is the accurate collection and presentation of the facts. Instead the historians/archaeologists must consider the cultural context within which they are working, as well as the moral impact of the "story" they are creating.

Previous generations of archaeologists had assumed that they were simply using archaeological facts to discover the truth about the past. If, however, archaeology is not simply reconstructing the past but, instead, creating the past in terms of current ideals and expectations, the moral implications are much different. Instead of a single-minded pursuit of the truth, no matter where it leads, archaeologists, like Hodder, begin to ask, "What kind of truth should we be creating?" The idea that archaeology could be actively involved in not only creating a history of the past but also creating the past itself was a rather frightening idea.

Throughout the ages, dictators and totalitarian governments have been tempted to manipulate the past to achieve future ends. In George Orwell's classic antiutopian novel *1984*, Big Brother and the Party are heavily involved in reinterpreting the past:

> And if all others accepted the lie which the Party imposed—if all records told the same tale—then the lie passed into history and became truth. "Who controls the past," ran the Party slogan, "controls the future: who controls the present controls the past." And yet the past, though of its nature alterable, never had been altered. Whatever was true now was true from everlasting to everlasting. It was quite simple. All that was needed was an unending series of victories over your own memory. "Reality control" they called it; in Newspeak, "doublethink." (1977, 32)

Although Orwell created a totalitarian society in the future that was engaged in rewriting the past, Bintliff and Hodder believe that archaeologists in the present are already rewriting the past in terms of modern values and beliefs. Hodder went on to suggest that archaeological reconstructions of the past should be seen "as a cultural and social product" of the present, instead of a fully objective depiction of human antiquity (1984, 28). Given the cultural bias that often intrudes into the writing of history, the same criticism might also be leveled at the other historical reconstructions that scientists create.

The Myth of Objectivity

In a universe that science tells us is approximately 15 billion years old, the present makes up an extremely small subset of the whole. Although scientists are justifiably proud of the various laws, rules, principles, and processes that they have discovered in nature, and which can be replicated and experimentally verified in the laboratory, this is not the whole show. Much of what there is to know about the universe concerns events that happened in the past. Indeed, some of the most interesting information that science can give us is about historical events: the Big Bang, the formation of galaxies and solar systems, the appearance of life, Snowball Earth, the Cambrian Explosion, supercontinents, dinosaurs, asteroid impacts, mammoths and mastodons, early civilizations, and so on. However, these are all unique, one-time events that can not be reduced to laws or replicated in the laboratory. Scientists who are studying these events are not only doing science, they are also doing history.

When scientists write historical narratives about the past, they are subject to the same cultural constraints and limitations as other historians. Their reconstructions of the past may easily be distorted by the cultural biases and expectations of the present. *Facts do not speak for themselves*, they must be interpreted. As Hodder and Bintliff have pointed out, we often interpret the past in terms of present fears and expectations. Consequently, there is little doubt that scientists of tomorrow may find that their interpretations of past events differ drastically from those of today. Such are the historical limitations of scientific truth.

The popular belief that scientists can be completely objective about the past is an obvious falsehood. Scientists can no more escape the influence of culture than they can escape the confines of their own bodies. In acknowledging this weakness, however, scientists should not throw their hands up in despair. Instead, they should recognize the limitations that culture and historical bias impose upon their work, and attempt to take these factors into account rather than delude themselves with the belief that they are being totally objective. What scientists must strive for is a clearer view of reality, not just of events in the past, but of their own work in the present.

CHAPTER 9

SCIENCE AS LITERATURE

WHEN, AS CHAPTER 8 demonstrates, scientists selectively create reconstructions of the past to meet certain cultural needs, they are not only writing history but also telling stories. In *The Literary Mind* (1996), Mark Turner argues, in fact, that the human mind constantly makes use of stories to process and interpret information: "Narrative imagining—story—is the fundamental instrument of thought. Rational capacities depend upon it. It is our chief means of looking into the future, of predicting, of planning, and of explaining. It is a literary capacity indispensable to human cognition generally" (4–5). The scientist who makes use of stories to explain data is simply doing what all humans do when they try to make sense of the world around them—they arrange information into logical narratives.

Stories, however, like all forms of literature, follow certain culturally prescribed patterns or templates. Whether one is writing a poem, a novel, or a textbook, certain rules must be followed if the end product is going to be understood and appreciated by the reading public. To be a good historian, for example, one must not only have an excellent control of the facts but must also be able to weave the facts together into a meaningful, pleasing narrative. This narrative must address issues and concerns that are relevant to the people reading the history. Therefore, scientific writing, historical narrative, and storytelling have much in common in terms of both their strengths and their weaknesses. Like history, all forms of literature are subject to cultural bias.

Stephen Jay Gould: Storytelling in Science

It is, in fact, a scientist who has frequently called attention to the historical and literary biases in scientific writing. Stephen Jay Gould taught biology, geology, and the history of science at Harvard University. He is well known for his work with Niles Eldredge on the theory of punctuated equilibrium, an evolutionary model that challenges some of the basic concepts of classical Darwinian evolution. Gould is also one of the most influential and prolific scientific essayists in the late twentieth century and the early twenty-first century. In addition to writing three hundred articles for the monthly *Natural History Magazine,* he has published more than a dozen books.

In an essay titled "Literary Bias on the Slippery Slope," Gould notes,

> So much of science proceeds by telling stories—and we are especially vulnerable to constraints of this medium because we so rarely recognize what we are doing. We think that we are reading nature by applying rules of logic and laws of matter to our observations. But we are often telling stories—in the good sense, but stories nonetheless. (1991, 251)

In his article, Gould suggests a reason for the storytelling. Much of the time science, like life, is not very exciting. The scientist may spend months or years accumulating and analyzing data without making any significant discoveries. Therefore, the scientific writer must often embellish his subject matter to catch the attention of the reader. Scientific writing, like the stage, must be larger than life if it is to be successful, and this is where the storytelling element comes into play (250–52).

One of the most common storytelling elements in folklore is the motif. A motif is like a building block in a child's toy set. At one time, the block may be used to build a fort; at another time, the same block may be part of a robot or an airplane. Similarly, motifs are the building blocks of stories. The same motif may be used repeatedly to create many different stories.

The three common types of motifs are (1) actor, (2) item, and (3) incident (Clifton 1968, 125). Examples of actor motifs are the bad wolf

("The Three Little Pigs," "Little Red Riding Hood," and "Peter and the Wolf") and miniature humans ("Thumbelina," "Tom Thumb," and "Indian in the Cupboard"). Item motifs are like the stage props in a theater that help provide the setting for the play. Common item motifs include magic pots ("The Swineherd"), magic spinning wheels ("Rumpelstiltskin" and "The Princess and the Goblin"), and magic harps ("Jack and the Beanstalk"). Incident motifs include such events as reversal of fortune ("Puss in Boots," "Cinderella," and "The Golden Goose") and magic enchantments ("The Frog Prince," "Beauty and the Beast," and "Sleeping Beauty").

It is interesting that anthropologists have discovered that their accounts of—that is, writings of—human evolution also contain folklorelike motifs. Richard Leakey (1944–) is one of the best-known physical anthropologists of the late twentieth century. He is most famous for his work around Lake Turkana in Kenya, where he and his team members discovered a number of very important fossil hominids, including *Homo rudolphensis* (KNM-ER 1470), *Homo ergaster* (KNM-WT 15000), *Australopithecus aethiopicus* (KNM-WT 17000), *Australopithecus anamensis*, and *Kenyathropus platyops*. Richard Leakey has also published a number of books on human evolution, including *Origins: What New Discoveries Reveal About the Emergence of Our Species and Its Possible Future* (1977), *People of the Lake: Mankind and Its Beginnings* (1978), *Origins Reconsidered: In Search of What Makes Us Human* (1992), and *The Sixth Extinction: Patterns of Life and the Future of Humankind* (1995)—all of these titles were coauthored with Roger Lewin.

Roger Lewin: Storytelling in Anthropology

In 1987, Roger Lewin (1946–) produced his own groundbreaking work, *Bones of Contention: Controversies in the Search for Human Origins.* In that book, Lewin uses his unique vantage point in anthropology to go behind the scenes of modern evolutionary theory and chronicle some of the major controversies that have occurred in the search for ancient human fossils. One of his most provocative chapters is titled "The Storytellers," in which he discusses the work of Misia Landau.

Scientific Motifs

During the late 1970s and early 1980s, Misia Landau was a doctoral student in the anthropology program at Yale University. While searching for a topic for her doctoral dissertation, she happened to read Vladimir Propp's book *Morphology of the Folk Tale* (1968). Propp (1895–1970) had discovered that hero myths in Russia and elsewhere contained a certain literary technique, that is, standardized elements—motifs—arranged in standardized plots: "The hero enters, is challenged by and overcomes a series of tests, and finally triumphs" (Lewin 1987, 32). Landau had a sudden insight that the literary techniques of which Propp wrote could be applied to the study of human evolution. She demonstrated that similar standardized elements and plots could also be found in anthropological accounts of human evolution.

By analyzing many of the books on human evolution written over the past one hundred years, Landau was able to identify four primary motifs that had repeatedly been used to explain the evolution of humankind:

> The main events in these stories are four, and they represent the evolutionary transformation of some kind of primitive primate ancestor into a civilized human being. They are as follows: the shift from the trees to the ground—terrestriality; the change of posture from walking on four legs to balancing on two—bipedalism; the expansion of the brain, with flowering of intelligence and language—encephalization; and the emergence of technology, morals, and society—civilization. (Lewin 1987, 32–33)

Landau was able to show that these four evolutionary motifs—terrestriality, bipedalism, encephalization, and civilization—were used repeatedly in the writings of anthropologists for more than a century. Some anthropologists had championed the belief that terrestriality came first, followed by the development of bipedalism and encephalization. Other scientists thought that bipedalism or encephalization was the causal factor in human evolution. Nonetheless, although anthropologists over the decades had disagreed about which element came first in human evolution, the motifs that made up the story had not changed—they had simply been rearranged.

In addition to recurring motifs, Landau also noted that the story of human evolution was quite similar in structure to stories that our ancestors had been telling for centuries, perhaps millennia. Vladimir Propp had identified thirty-one separate elements in hero myths. Landau chose to use nine of these elements in her analysis, equating them with elements of human evolutionary stories (Lewin 1987, 33–34):

1. A "humble hero" = ancestral primate
2. Hero lives "in an initially stable environment" = primates live in the rainforests of equatorial Africa
3. Hero is forced to leave the safety of his home = Pliocene climate change causes the forest to die back
4. Hero must go on a "hazardous journey" = primates move out of the trees and onto the ground
5. Hero's merit is tested by a series of events = primates must survive in the terrestrial environment
6. Hero overcomes challenges by developing new skills = primates develop intelligence, bipedalism, etc.
7. Hero develops further talents that display his worth = primates create tools, reasoning, etc.
8. Hero's merit is tested by a new series of events = Pleistocene climate change at beginning of Ice Age
9. Hero ultimately triumphs over all adversities = modern humanity develops civilization

Told in this manner, the story of human evolution has great literary appeal because we've been telling the same type of stories to our children for generations. This basic plot is found in folktales around the world. Other humble heroes who have—like the ancestral primate—followed a similar path to success include, for instance, Niels the shepherd's son in "Niels and the Giants" (Lang 1967, 284–94), Aladdin the tailor's son in "Aladdin and the Wonderful Lamp" (Lang 1969, 80–93), Curdie the miner's son in *The Princess and the Goblin* (MacDonald 1964), Shasta the fisherman's boy in *The Horse and His Boy* (Lewis 1954), and Bilbo the Hobbit in *The Hobbit: Or There and Back Again* (Tolkien 1966). Both children and adults can read and enjoy these stories because they follow similar, culturally prescribed patterns. Anthropologists, perhaps subconsciously, have used these same literary patterns in telling the story of how humans evolved from primates.

The appearance of these common story motifs and plots in scientific accounts of human evolution should warn us that we are not being given "just the facts." The "facts" in these evolutionary reconstructions have been selected and standardized from a much larger body of data and have been organized in such a way that they tell a logical, pleasing story. Discrepancies or missing data are often ignored in the interest of telling a story that is complete and that flows smoothly from one point to the next.

Scientific Myths

The end result of using "evolutionary motifs" and a "humble hero plot" is the creation of a full-blown "myth" about human evolution. "The word *myth*, in popular usage, refers to something that is widely believed to be true but probably is not" (Haviland 1999, 419). In most people's minds, a myth is a story that is imaginary or untrue. We tend to categorize the beliefs of other people and cultures as "myths" when we don't share those same beliefs or outlooks on life. Many scientists and some theologians are fond of speaking about the myths found in the Bible. In the disciplines of anthropology and folklore, however, the term *myth* has a second, much more restrictive definition than that found in popular usage: "A traditional narrative in which people explain the nature of the world and their place in it; a myth deals with the ultimate questions of human existence" (Haviland 1999, 419). *Myth*, when defined in this more restrictive manner, eliminates judgment as to whether any particular story or idea is true or false; accounts are simply categorized as attempting to answer an ultimate question.

By studying genetics, fossils, and modern primates, anthropologists attempted to answer the ultimate question, *Where did I come from?* They may have believed that they were conducting objective, analytical research on human origins but, according to Lewin, "they had in fact been telling stories. Scientific stories, to be sure, but stories nevertheless" (Lewin 1987, 32). It is not surprising that anthropologists, in attempting to explain human origins, should resort to the use of literary motifs, plots, and myths. These are the standard means through which humans have always sought to answer the ultimate questions. "John Durant, a researcher at Oxford University, England, put it this way: 'Like the Judaeo-Christian myths they so largely replaced, theories of human evolution are first and foremost stories about the appearance of man on earth and the institution of society'"(Lewin 1987, 46).

If we define the term *myth* in the context of answering ultimate questions, many of the accounts in the Bible are indeed myths. The Bible gives very explicit answers to such questions as the following:

- Where did I come from? "In the beginning God created the heavens and the earth" (Gen. 1:1).
- Who am I? "So God created man in his own image" (Gen. 1:27).
- What is the purpose of life? "Fear God and keep his commandments, for this is the whole duty of man" (Eccl. 12:13).
- What happens after I die? "Just as man is destined to die once, and after that to face judgment . . ." (Heb. 9:27).

Because science also attempts to answer ultimate questions, it also contains myths. The question, *Where did I come from?* for instance, may be answered by

1. biologists using their knowledge of fertilization and cellular division;
2. anthropologists examining the fossil record;
3. archaeologists discussing prehistoric artifacts;
4. geologists analyzing rocks and minerals; and
5. astronomers studying the light from distant galaxies.

As noted in chapter 1 of this book, religion, science, and philosophy are all seeking truth. The most important truths to which each of these disciplines seek answers are the ultimate questions. Myths are the literary genre that attempt to answer ultimate questions. We should not be surprised, therefore, to find that there are scientific and philosophical myths, as well as religious myths. Moreover, as with any literary genre, myths are subject to the biases of the cultures in which they are formulated.

The "Story" of Ramapithecus

In 1934, a Yale graduate student (G. Edward Lewis) found two fragments of an upper jaw in India that he believed represented a new species. He named this new species *Ramapithecus*. In 1960, Lewis Leakey found similar tooth and jaw fragments in Africa. (Other fragments were later recovered from China and Europe.) Based on the shapes of these teeth and jaw fragments, anthropologists in the 1960s concluded that *Ramapithecus* was a direct ancestor of human beings. Indeed, with an estimated age of 9 to 14 million years, *Ramapithecus* was believed to be the earliest fossil representative of the hominid (humanlike) line.

David Pilbeam (1940–), a young British anthropologist at Yale University, was Misia Landau's advisor when she did her doctoral dissertation on folklore elements in evolutionary accounts. Pilbeam had already developed a strong interest in comparative studies because of his own involvement in creating evolutionary "stories." During the 1960s and 1970s, David Pilbeam and his Yale colleague, Elwyn Simons, had become the leading experts on *Ramapithecus*. Based on their reconstructions of the jaw fragments that G. Edward Lewis had found in the 1930s, Simons and Pilbeam not only argued that *Ramapithecus* was humanity's earliest ancestor but also speculated about its appearance and behavior: "*Ramapithecus* probably walked about on two legs, not four; used tools to prepare its food; hunted, and had a social life more complex than any ape" (Lewin 1987, 87). Pictures appeared in anthropology textbooks, depicting a hair-covered, slightly stooping creature that was half human, half ape. Such details were remarkable given the fact that only a few fragments of the upper jaw had been recovered. Nevertheless, such reconstructions became standard fare in anthropology classes across the country, and a whole generation of enlightened students came to believe that humans could directly trace their ancestry back some 14 million years ago to *Ramapithecus*.

The evidence supporting *Ramapithecus*'s position in the hominid line began to unravel with the introduction of molecular biology into the study of human evolution. In 1967, Vincent Sarich and Allan Wilson published in the journal *Science* a groundbreaking article titled "Immunological Time Scale for Hominid Evolution." Based on their studies of the differences and similarities of blood proteins between humans and other primates, Sarich and Wilson concluded that man and African apes had shared a common ancestor as recently as 5 million years ago. Although these early immunological studies were themselves highly suspect because of the newness of the technique, subsequent studies over the next decade, including the use of DNA analysis, tended to convince many scientists that there had been a relatively late divergence between apes and humans. This new theory of a late divergence left *Ramapithecus* as the odd man—ape—out.

Even more decisive, however, was the discovery in the 1980s of two more nearly complete skulls of a closely related species called *Sivapithecus*. Although the upper jaws and teeth of *Sivapithecus* were very similar to those of *Ramapithecus*, the *Sivapithecus* skulls were not hominid-like at all. Instead, the skulls were much more similar to orangutans than humans, suggesting that both *Sivapithecus* and *Ramapithecus* were distant ancestors of orangutans, rather than of humans.

As a result of both molecular and fossil evidence, *Ramapithecus* has been dropped quietly from the anthropology textbooks and some ten million years have disappeared from the human ancestral line.

After spending the better part of two decades championing the cause of *Ramapithecus*, the subsequent collapse of this hominid line left Pilbeam somewhat skeptical about the absoluteness of any scientific pronouncement:

"I will never again cling so firmly to one particular evolutionary scheme," announced David Pilbeam at the beginning of 1978. "I have come to believe that many statements we make about the hows and whys of human evolution say as much about us, the paleoanthropologists and the larger society in which we live, as about anything that 'really' happened." (Lewin 1987, 85)

Pilbeam had learned the same lesson about anthropology that Hodder had learned about archaeology—the literary and historical reconstructions of scientists are influenced as much by the culture within which they work as by the facts with which they work.

In retrospect, Pilbeam could see how "virtually all our theories about human origins were relatively unconstrained by fossil data" (Lewin 1987, 43). Indeed, the theories about *Ramapithecus* had assumed a life of their own; the fragmentary fossils were interpreted in a manner that would not contradict the theories. Once again it had been shown that *facts do not speak for themselves*; facts must be analyzed and interpreted by human beings before they have any significance or meaning. It is not difficult to manipulate scientific facts to support the intellectual outcomes one desires. Cultural bias and the love of a good, logical story often overwhelm the efforts of scientists to remain objective during the process. Misia Landau might have been the first scientist to identify literary elements in modern accounts of human evolution, but her advisor, David Pilbeam, already had firsthand experience at myth making.

Timothy Ferris: Storytelling in Astronomy

Anthropologists, though, are not the only scientists who have incorporated storytelling into their work. As Harvard paleontologist Stephen Jay Gould has noted,

> This [storytelling] constraint does not apply only to something so clearly ripe for narration and close to home as "the rise of man from the apes" (to choose a storylike description that enfolds biases of gender and progress into its conventionality). Even the most distant and abstract subjects, like the formation of the universe or the principles of evolution, fall within the bounds of necessary narrative. (1991, 251)

Timothy Ferris (1942–) is an astronomer at the University of California in Berkeley. He has written several popular accounts of astronomy for the general public, including *The Red Limit: The Search for the Edge of the Universe* (1983), *Coming of Age in the Milky Way* (1988), *The Mind's Sky: Human Intelligence in a Cosmic Context* (1992), and *The Whole Shebang: A State-of-the-Universe(s) Report* (1997).

In *The Red Limit* (1983), Ferris calls attention to the storytelling element in accounts of modern astronomy:

Reports of scientific discovery, this book included, I'm afraid, tend to give a spurious impression of great progress recently attained. They suggest that humankind labored in ignorance for centuries until a few years ago, when the light of wisdom dawned. I think this tendency comes about because discoveries, by their nature, make good stories, while enduring bafflement does not; the storyteller concentrates on what has been learned and ignores what has resisted comprehension. In any event, it is a distortion. (219)

Human understanding can easily become buried in facts, especially if some of the facts contradict each other. As Ferris notes in the above excerpt, a good scientist (or teacher, or storyteller) always picks and chooses his or her facts in order to get certain points across. Consequently, a certain amount of distortion and oversimplification always occurs in any presentations—unless the presenter has an infinite amount of time and the listener has an infinite amount of patience.

After discussing the great progress that has been made in astronomy over the past few decades, Ferris goes on to lament how little astronomers still know about the universe as a whole. The rapidly changing theories in the science of astronomy provide clear evidence that absolute truth has not been obtained; the search for astronomical truth is still very much a work in progress. Despite the current limitations of our knowledge, Ferris nonetheless proclaims his "faith of science," that "the seamless weave of nature will reveal itself to our reasoned inquiry" (1983, 244).

In his conclusion to *Coming of Age in the Milky Way*, Ferris further reiterates how limited is our knowledge of the universe. Astronomers have made remarkable progress in the last one hundred years in providing humanity with a breathtaking perspective of earth's place in the cosmos. It is now known that earth is the third planet from the sun, located in an outer arm of a spiral galaxy called the Milky Way, in a vast universe composed of billions of other galaxies. In accomplishing this feat, Ferris suggests that astronomy, as a science, has "come of age" (1988, 382). Astronomy's greatest accomplishment, though, according to Ferris, has been to show that "we will never understand the universe in detail; it is just too big and varied for that" (383). Indeed, more stars are in our

Milky Way Galaxy alone than an individual could count physically over the course of many lifetimes. Beyond our galaxy are billions of other galaxies, each composed of billions or trillions of stars. Ferris cites the work of both Karl Popper, on the limitations of human knowledge, and Kurt Gödel's Second Incompleteness Theorem, arguing that our knowledge of the universe is permanently incomplete: "In short, there is not and never will be a complete and comprehensive scientific account of the universe that can be proved valid. The Creator must have been fond of uncertainty, for He (or She) has given it to us for keeps" (384).

In *The Mind's Sky*, Ferris explores more deeply the topic of what we can actually know about the universe. In writing of the interaction between the human mind and the universe it perceives, he compares the relationship between the human mind and the universe to a tree. The roots of a tree give rise to the leaves and branches, and also provide them with water and nutrients; in turn, the leaves and branches provide energy for the roots. In other words, the flow of energy is moving in both directions at the same time. Similarly, the universe gives rise to the human mind and also influences it, but the human mind creates an image of the universe. As Ferris notes,

> Sense data are conveyed to the brain from the wider world, but the eye and the rest of the brain, rather than passively recording images, actively select and manipulate them. Perception is an *act*; as the English neuroanatomist J. Z. Young notes, we "go around actively searching for things to see and . . . 'see' mainly those things that were expected." We act, in turn, *on* the outer world, projecting our concepts and theories and manipulating nature in accordance with our models of her. (1992, 201)

What we see is based, in part, on our expectations. It is difficult to see things for which we have no explanations. On the rare occasions when we do see something totally new (perhaps it is a UFO, or a ghost, or a living fossil—like pictures we have seen), we immediately begin the process of trying to fit it into the universe of things with which we are familiar. To truly see, is to see within some type of cultural context.

It is therefore impossible to attain complete objectivity about the uni-

SCIENCE AS LITERATURE   115

verse, even as it is impossible to attain complete objectivity about one's own culture or personality. We are intimately tied to each of these things, and they, in part, shape our very being. Thus, it cannot be hoped totally to separate the astronomer from the universe that he or she studies. "We are confronted, then, not with *the* universe, which remains an eternal riddle, but with whatever model of the universe we can build within the mind" (Ferris 1992, 15).

Balancing Truth and Fiction

A scientist's understanding about nature and the universe will always be tinged with subjectivity. And because scientists in fields as diverse as anthropology and astronomy need to attract the attention of their colleagues as well as to make their theories and discoveries interesting, understandable, and attractive to the general public, scientific theories often incorporate literary elements—motifs, plots, myths—into their writings. Thus, those theories will always contain a mixture of truth and fiction— as do all good stories: "The known universe is and always will be in some sense a creation of our (hopefully creative) minds" (Ferris 1992, 5–6).

In the balance between truth and fiction, however, the need to tell a good story—as Roger Lewin, David Pilbeam, and Timothy Ferris have shown—often outweighs a scientist's commitment to adhere strictly to the facts. Facts are often embellished and anomalies are frequently ignored as the scientist attempts to present his or her findings in a pleasing, logical, and understandable format.

Thus, science becomes literature, and literature (like history) is easily influenced by culture. Culture frequently dictates how stories are written and what questions these stories should answer. As Michael Dames has noted in *Mythic Ireland*,

> The recent appreciation by Popper and others that "scientific discovery is akin to explanatory story-telling, to myth-making, and to the poetic imagination" places science in the broad mythic field where, in any case, it was born and nurtured. There, the idea of objectivity appears as one among many story-telling techniques. The nineteenth-century conviction that the modern

world had entered a post-mythic state now appears to be a delusion. Instead . . . we inhabit a commonwealth of interacting mythic states which includes modern science among its number. (1992, 10)

For thousands of years, humans have been trying to make sense of the world around them by arranging their observations and experiences into stories. As Dames notes in the preceding quote, science is a part of that long and honorable tradition. It is a tradition that has, however, its cultural limitations and biases. Stories, by their very nature, must contain a mixture of fact and fiction, otherwise they are not stories.

SCIENCE AS PROPAGANDA

WHO WE ARE AS HUMAN beings is determined by both our genetic background (nature) and our cultural background (nurture). Much of what preoccupies our daily lives is derived from our cultural background: the language we speak, the foods we eat, the clothes we wear, the houses in which we live, and the jobs at which we work. Scientists can no more escape their cultural background than they can escape their genetic background. Chapters 8 and 9 demonstrated how cultural bias influences the accuracy of scientific truth when those truths are conveyed through history or literature. This chapter examines an even more disturbing form of cultural bias in which scientific truths are sometimes conveyed—racial bias.

Over the years, one very important aspect of Stephen Jay Gould's writing has been his attempt to show that scientific truth is not always objective truth; it is often colored by the personal biases of a scientist and his or her culture. Of the various types of cultural intolerance that may influence the work of a scientist, racial bias has been one of the most prevalent. Repeatedly during the past two centuries, scientists have allowed racial prejudices to influence the outcome of their scientific research. Gould has written a number of essays and an entire book highlighting this problem.

Stephen Jay Gould: Biological Determinism

In *The Mismeasure of Man*, Gould attempts to document the dark history of scientific racism by drawing examples from the work of some of the most prominent scientists of the nineteenth and early twentieth centuries (1981, 27). Gould suggests that much of their racial bias was grounded in the idea of "biological determinism." This theory "holds that shared behavioral norms, and the social and economic differences between human groups—primarily races, classes, and sexes—arise from inherited, inborn distinctions and that society, in this sense, is an accurate reflection of biology" (20). In other words, men have the right to dominate women because men are stronger and smarter; people in the upper classes have more wealth and power because they are mentally superior to people in the lower classes; Western civilization has the right to dominate the Chinese, the Polynesians, or the Africans because white people are more evolutionarily advanced than these other races. Therefore, according to the theory, the social and political inequalities we see in the world are simply a reflection of the underlying biological differences between sexes, social classes, and races. Societal inequalities are simply a reflection of biological differences.

As Gould points out, ideas similar to biological determinism had been used to justify social inequalities since the time of Plato. Biological determinism itself, however, dressed up these old racial prejudices in the white garments of "pure" science: "Determinists have often invoked the traditional prestige of science as objective knowledge, free from social and political taint. They portray themselves as purveyors of harsh truth and their opponents as sentimentalists, ideologues, and wishful thinkers" (1981, 20). With biological determinism, racist beliefs that had previously been justified on the basis of philosophical arguments or religious interpretations now were explained in terms of scientific theories and discoveries.

Europeans and Americans in the nineteenth century were particularly interested in proving the inequality of the races and the sexes as a means of justifying their current activities. The Italians, Portuguese, Spanish, French, Germans, Dutch, and British, following the voyages of discovery during the Renaissance, had gone on to establish colonies in Africa, the Far East, Indonesia, Australia, the South Pacific, and the Americas. Europeans not only took over lands belonging to indigenous peoples but also dominated the native populations. This domination included not only colonization and exploitation but also slavery and even genocide.

Consequently, Europeans and their descendants needed to justify their right to rule over other cultures. They did so by using the same argument that oppressive cultures had used down through the ages—racial superiority. Empire-builders—such as the Sumerians, Akkadians, Assyrians, Babylonians, Persians, Greeks, Romans, Mongols, Vikings, and others—had also justified their domination of other cultures on the basis of their "obvious" physical and mental superiority.

Scientists who had been reared in European and American cultures of the nineteenth century would, quite naturally, share their fellow citizens' perspective on colonization, slavery, and biological determinism. Indeed, many scientists of that time were interested in finding a way to prove the validity of biological determinism. This theory was a popular topic that had generated widespread interest among the peoples of both Europe and America. Scientists who addressed this issue could count on both public and governmental support for their work. Scientists who could prove the truthfulness of biological determinism would win fame and honor. As a result of these cultural enticements, it is not surprising that some of the most famous scientists of the nineteenth century were in-volved in research that today would be considered extremely racist. Such is the influence of culture on scientists and scientific research.

Nineteenth-century scientists, in their efforts to prove the validity of biological determinism, needed to isolate a specific human trait that could be used to rank the various races into the more-advanced or less-advanced. God has given mankind dominion "over the fish of the sea and the birds of the air, over the livestock, over all the earth, and over all the creatures that move along the ground" (Gen. 1:26). We exercise this dominion, not through our physical prowess, but through our mental abilities. Thus, many people would argue that the distinguish-ing characteristic of the human species is our intellect. Biological de-terminists believed that the differences between social classes and races should also be manifested most clearly in terms of mental capacity. Consequently, scientists needed to find a way of measuring human in-telligence. Two types of measurement were devised: (a) craniometry (measuring the shape and size of the skull) and (b) psychological test-ing (IQ and other tests).

Samuel George Morton and Paul Broca: Craniometry

During the nineteenth century, craniometry was the most popular means for measuring intelligence. Scientists reasoned that intelligence obviously resides in the brain. Because the skull houses the brain, the size and shape of the skull should be an accurate reflection of the size and shape of the brain. Therefore, the skull could be used to measure human intelligence. One of the most famous craniometricians of the nineteenth century was a Philadelphia physician named Samuel George Morton (1799–1851).

> Morton, a Philadelphia patrician with two medical degrees—one from fashionable Edinburgh—provided the "facts" that won worldwide respect for the "American school" of polygeny. Morton began his collection of human skulls in the 1820s; he had more than one thousand when he died in 1851. Friends (and enemies) referred to his great charnel house as "the American Golgotha." (Gould 1981, 51)

To promote his scientific "facts," Mortin devised a method for measuring cranial capacity of the skulls in his collection. His first technique involved filling the brain case of each skull with white mustard seeds. Once the brain case had been filled with seeds, Morton poured the seeds into a container and measured the volume of seeds used to fill the skull. Mustard seeds, however, could be packed into the skull at various densities, giving inconsistent results. Therefore, Morton eventually settled on BB-sized lead shot for his measurements. Thus, he was able to determine how many cubic inches of cranial capacity the brain case of each skull contained (Gould 1981, 53).

Morton was particularly interested in Native Americans. In 1839 he published his famous *Crania Americana*, which was based on a study of some 144 skulls. He found that the mean cranial capacity of Native American skulls was five cubic inches less than that of Caucasian skulls. Because of their smaller cranial capacity, Morton concluded that Native Americans were intellectually incapable of obtaining the same level of civilization that Europeans had achieved.

Later, in a book titled *Crania Aegyptiaca* (1844), Morton examined some one hundred skulls from the tombs of ancient Egypt. He separated these skulls into five categories: Greeks, Jews, and Egyptians (all Caucasians), as well as "Negroid" (mixed Caucasian and Negro), and "Negro." In that study, Morton found that the cranial capacity of Negroid and Negro skulls was below that of Native Americans. Therefore, Morton thought that he had proven scientifically that Caucasians had larger brains than Native Americans and that Native Americans had larger brains than Negroes (blacks) (Gould 1981, 53–61). Consequently, Morton's studies of cranial capacity were thought to prove the validity of biological determinism and thereby to vindicate the social order of pre–Civil War America. Whites, with their larger cranial capacity, were the ruling class. Native Americans, with their somewhat smaller cranial capacity, were "savages." But blacks, with their small cranial capacity, were destined to be slaves.

Today, we recognize that Morton's conclusions were totally false. Because of the influence of cultural bias, however, neither Morton, his fellow scientists, nor the general public at that time recognized that Morton's work was badly flawed. By reanalyzing Morton's work, Gould has shown that Morton had (apparently unconsciously) manipulated his data to arrive at culturally acceptable conclusions. Among the errors that Gould (1981, 68–69) identified in Morton's work are the following:

1. He omitted skulls that ran counter to his theories;
2. He failed to take into account the correlation between body size and brain size (people with larger bodies have larger brains);
3. He failed to take into account the fact that males have larger bodies (and, thus, larger brains) than do females;
4. He rounded numbers upward when they favored Caucasians;
5. He rounded numbers downward when they favored non-Caucasians.

Despite the glaring nature of these mistakes to modern eyes, Gould believes that Morton (as well as his fellow scientists and countrymen) was largely unaware of these omissions and miscalculations:

> I detect no sign of fraud or conscious manipulation. Morton made no attempt to cover his tracks and I must presume that he

was unaware he had left them. He explained all his procedures
and published all his raw data. All I can discern is an *a priori*
conviction about racial ranking so powerful that it directed his
tabulations along preestablished lines. Yet Morton was widely
hailed as the objectivist of his age, the man who would rescue
American science from the mire of unsupported speculation.
(1981, 69)

Racism was so much a part of European and American culture that
Morton and his contemporaries were apparently unaware that they were
juggling the data in order to get the expected results. They were so blinded
by their cultural biases that they could only see what everyone expected
them to see.

The life and work of Paul Broca (1824–1880) provided Gould with
another classic example of the manner in which cultural intolerance can
influence scientific research. Broca was a famous French physician. In
1859, he founded the Anthropological Society of Paris. Like Morton, Broca
was interested in ranking the races of the world in terms of intelligence.
He had followed Morton's work carefully and also adopted the use of
lead shot for measuring the cranial capacity of skulls. When possible,
however, Broca much preferred to weigh the brain itself rather than simply to determine the volume of the area that the brain had originally
filled. This procedure obviously entailed an autopsy of the body soon
after death. It should come as no surprise, though, that many people
were not interested in having the brains of their recently deceased loved
ones removed from the skull and weighed. Fortunately for Broca and his
associates, many European academics were interested in craniometry and
were willing to donate their bodies for scientific research. As Gould notes,
"The dissection of dead colleagues became something of a cottage industry among nineteenth-century craniometricians" (1981, 92).

Broca's extensive studies on brain weight led to pretty much the same
conclusions that Morton had reached by measuring cranial capacity:
whites had the largest brains; blacks had the smallest brains. Broca used
these studies to justify his own racial biases. Gould cites, for example, an
1866 article on anthropology by Broca in which the latter states,

A prognathous [forward-jutting] face, more or less black color
of the skin, woolly hair and intellectual and social inferiority are
often associated, while more or less white skin, straight hair and
an orthognathous [straight] face are the ordinary equipment of
the highest groups in the human series. (1981, 83–84)

Broca's racial biases are clearly evident in the preceding citation. Thus,
it is apparent that Broca, like Morton, had reached "scientific" conclusions that were more closely tied to the racial biases of his time and culture than to any hard evidence he could find in his scientific data.

On the other hand, Broca was meticulous in his data collection. He
did not make the same obvious mistakes that Morton had made in his
calculations. How, then, did Broca reach the same erroneous conclusions?
Gould suggests that Broca's approach to science was "advocacy masquer-
ading as objectivity" (1981, 85). In other words, "Broca did not fudge
numbers; he merely selected among them or interpreted his way around
them to favored conclusions" (87). It was assumed, for instance, that professors would have larger brains than common folk. Broca and his colleagues found that the modern human brain weighed from 1,000 to 2,000
grams. The average brain was a little less than 1,400 grams. When it was
discovered that several professors at Göttingen had brains that weighed
less than average, Broca did not come to the obvious conclusion that
brain size is not necessarily a determinant of high intelligence. Instead,
he explained away the anomaly by suggesting that perhaps some of the
professors at Göttingen may not have been as intelligent as many people
had thought (92–94). Another common assumption was that criminals
were less intelligent than law-abiding citizens and, therefore, often displayed uncontrolled, animal-like behavior. When subsequent studies
showed that some criminals had larger brains than average, the presumed
correlation between criminality and small brains was not abandoned.
Instead, an exception to the rule was created by Paul Topinard (1830–
1911) to explain away this anomaly: "Too much of a good thing [brain
size] is bad for some people" (Gould 1981, 94).

Given Morton's, Broca's, and Topinard's problems with collecting and
interpreting data, it is not hard to see why cultural bias is often impervious to scientific research. In the grip of their culture's racial biases, many

scientists will (often unconsciously) make omissions or miscalculations that adjust the facts to fit the theory (such as Morton did). Other scientists, while avoiding errors in their data collection, will simply reinterpret the facts to conform to their personal and cultural expectations (such as Broca and Topinard did). Here can be seen another clear example of *facts do not speak for themselves*. Facts must be interpreted before they have any meaning. Unfortunately, cultural bias can easily influence how scientists interpret the facts.

Theory of Recapitulation

In 1859, the same year that Paul Broca founded the Anthropological Society of Paris, Charles Darwin published his groundbreaking work on evolution, *On The Origin of Species*. Before the introduction of Darwinian evolution, biological determinists generally held one of two theories concerning the development of the races: (1) "Monogenists," citing the book of Genesis, believed that all human beings were descendants of Adam and Eve, but after sin entered the world, humanity lost its sinless state. Some of Adam and Eve's offspring (Cain) fell farther away from God than did others (Abel). Monogenists believed that differences between the races are a measure of how far each group had degenerated from God's original creation. The most savage races (such as Africans or Native Americans) had obviously degenerated the farthest from a godlike character; Europeans had deviated the least. (2) "Polygenists" abandoned a strictly literal interpretation of the biblical account. They argued that God had created separate species (races) in various parts of the world. Therefore, each race had been created with its own unique character—some more intelligent, others less so (Gould 1981, 39–42).

With the introduction of Darwin's theory of evolution, biological determinists were free to abandon the biblical account of creation and seek justification for their biases through natural processes rather than divine revelation. In attempting to explain how life had arisen through random events—rather than Creation—evolutionists built evolutionary trees that were meant to show how primitive organisms had slowly evolved into more complex creatures. To buttress this theory, they suggested that the human embryo follows a similar evolutionary pathway, displaying in its early stages primitive forms that subsequently developed into more advanced forms and finally into the human form. In the case of the embryo, however, this entire process takes a mere nine months, rather than millions of years. This idea was called recapitulation.

> This theory, often expressed by the mouthful "ontogeny recapitulates phylogeny," held that higher animals, in their embryonic development, pass through a series of stages representing, in proper sequence, the adult forms of ancestral, lower creatures. Thus, the human embryo first develops gill slits, like a fish, later a three-chambered heart, like a reptile, still later a mammalian tail. (Gould 1980, 163)

Biological determinists used this theory of speeded up evolution to explain the differences between the human races. According to evolution, humans had evolved from lower forms of life—such as the apes. Biological determinists used these ideas to argue that some races were more evolved than others. Those races whose evolutionary progress had been prematurely halted or arrested were more like their primitive animal forebears than were the more evolutionary advanced races—the "true humans." Not surprisingly, in the latter half of the nineteenth century most peoples of European ancestry believed that Caucasians were the most evolutionarily advanced of the races. European and American scientists concurred.

John Down: Racism as Recapitulation *How far people have Evolved by their standing in life*

In an article titled "Dr. Down's Syndrome," Gould documents how recapitulation was subsequently used to rank the races. Dr. John Down (1828–1896) was a contemporary of Broca. He was also the superintendent at the Earlswood Asylum for Idiots in Surrey, England. Down is most famous for identifying a genetic disorder that came to be known as Mongolian idiocy, mongolism, or Down's syndrome. Nearly one hundred years later, in 1959, researchers discovered that this disorder arises because of an extra twenty-first chromosome at inception. In the 1800s, however, all that Dr. Down and his colleagues could do was describe the physical and mental manifestations of this disorder:

These unfortunate children suffer mild to severe mental retardation and have a reduced life expectancy. They exhibit, in addition, a suite of distinctive features, including short and broad
hands, a narrow high palate, rounded face and broad head, a
small nose with a flattened root, and a thick and furrowed tongue.
(Gould 1980, 161)

Because of the mental retardation that frequently accompanies this
disorder, Dr. Down had a number of patients with "mongolism" in his
asylum at Surrey.

John Down was not only a specialist in mental disorders but also a
firm believer in the theory that "ontogeny recapitulates phylogeny." In
his professional life, he attempted to explain mental retardation by suggesting that people with this disorder were "throwbacks" to an earlier
evolutionary stage. In other words, because of poor health or other envi-
ronmental factors, parents might occasionally produce a baby who was
only partially "evolved." Such an infant would exhibit the physical features and mental capacities of a more primitive stage of human development. Thus, mentally retarded children with Down's syndrome were not
merely flawed modern humans, they were primitive throwbacks whose
evolutionary development had been arrested before birth.

Down also believed that entire races presently living on the earth—
such as Africans, Native Americans, and Orientals—also exhibited arrested evolutionary development. Indeed, he attempted to classify the
various levels of mental retardation in terms of different ethnic groups
whose members best exemplified these stages of evolutionary stagna-
tion. In his 1866 article "Observations on an Ethnic Classification of Idiots," Down noted that many congenital idiots look very much like
Mongols (Gould 1980, 165). Indeed, as Gould points out, some
mongoloids, "to be sure, have a small but perceptible epicanthic fold, the
characteristic feature of an oriental eye, and some have slightly yellowish
skin" (161). Given these superficial similarities, as well as his relatively
low opinion of Orientals, Down assumed that Mongoloid idiots born
into English families were simply throwbacks to a more primitive evolutionary stage through which Caucasians—but not Orientals—had already passed. Therefore, Down's identification and interpretation of

Down's syndrome was firmly tied to the racial bias that characterized the Victorian era in which Down lived and worked.

Gould showed how peoples of African descent had fared even worse than Orientals at the hands of early evolutionary scientists. Indeed, many biological determinists used recapitulation to argue that blacks are the least evolved of the races and are, therefore, more like apes than humans. To illustrate this point, in "Racism and Recapitulation" Gould reproduces an illustration from the 1874 edition of Ernst Haeckel's (1834–1919) *Anthropogenie oder Entwickelungsgeschichte des menschen* (1874), which actually shows blacks occupying an evolutionary branch beneath that of gorillas and chimpanzees (Gould 1977a, 215).

Although in the latter half of the nineteenth century a number of scientists had abandoned their religious beliefs and embraced the evolutionary teachings of Charles Darwin, this had little impact on their racial biases. They simply transferred the justification for their biases from religion to science. Indeed, scientific facts and theories had almost no impact on racial bias. Gould clearly illustrates this disturbing fact by quoting two eminent scientists, D. G. Brinton (1837–1899) and L. Bolk (1866–1930), who were studying race in the late 1800s and early 1900s. In his book *Races and Peoples: Lectures on the Science of Ethnography* (1890), anthropologist D. G. Brinton uses recapitulation to argue,

> The adult who retains the more numerous fetal, infantile or simian traits, is unquestionably inferior to him whose development has progressed beyond them, nearer to the ideal form of the species, as revealed by a study of the symmetry of the parts of the body, and their relation to the erect stature. (Brinton 1890, 48)

In relation to this physical symmetry and stature, Brinton then goes on to state, "Measured by these criteria, the European or white race stands at the head of the list, the African or Negro at its foot" (1890, 48). In other words, Africans are less evolved than Europeans because Africans often have rounded heads and large eyes—like children. Therefore, as a race, they should be treated like children because they are not as evolutionarily evolved as the white race; recapitulation justifies the slave/master relationship.

In the early twentieth century, however, Europeans and Americans changed their minds about which races had the more adult traits and which races had the more infantile traits. This shift occurred, in part, because a less mature look became popular among European and American women in the 1920s. According to this new style, true beauty was exemplified not by the woman who looked the most mature, but by the woman who retained her girlish features and figure. It is apparent that European and American scientists were not immune to this shift in style because they soon began to modify their theories accordingly. Scientists began to argue that it is the Europeans and Americans who maintain the most infantile traits—not Africans. This did not mean, however, that Africans were superior to Europeans and Americans. No . . . without missing a beat, scientists now began to argue that the most advanced races are those who retain the most infantile features. To prove this point, Gould cites the Dutch anatomist Louis Bolk, who, in his 1926 book *Das Problem der Menschwerdung* stated,

> On the basis of my theory, I am obviously a believer in the inequality of races. . . . In his fetal development the Negro passes through a stage that has already become the final [and more preferable infantile] stage for the white man. (Gould 1977a, 214)

These shifting theories discussed above provide a classic example of the influence that culture exerts on scientific truth. Both the scientific "facts" (blacks have infantile traits/whites have infantile traits) and the scientific theories (infantile traits are inferior/infantile traits are superior) changed, but the cultural biases remained the same (whites are superior/blacks are inferior). Facts and theories were both altered to meet the expectations of the scientist and culture.

Edward Binet and Robert Yerkes: Intelligence Tests

In the twentieth century, intelligence testing replaced craniology as the preferred means for ranking people according to their mental abilities. Edward Binet (1857–1911), creator of the IQ test, became disillusioned with craniology after recognizing in his own work the strong impact of personal bias on the collection and interpretation of data on cranial capacity. As director of the psychology laboratory at the Sorbonne in France, Binet decided to devise a series of tests that would provide a more objective method of determining human intelligence than measuring skulls and weighing brains (Gould 1981, 146–48). Binet's primary objective in creating an intelligence test was to help teachers identify children who needed special help in the classroom. His approach to this problem, however, was unique:

> Unlike previous tests designed to measure specific and independent "faculties" of mind, Binet's scale was a hodgepodge of diverse activities. He hoped that by mixing together enough tests of different abilities he would be able to abstract a child's general potential with a single score. (Gould 1981, 149)

Binet developed this intelligence test for the specific purpose of identifying and helping those children whose mental development was behind that of their classmates. Other scientists, however, had different goals in mind. After Binet's death, many scientists used his intelligence test to determine the intellectual development of both children and adults. Their ultimate purpose, like that of the craniologists, was to rank social classes and races according to their intellectual development. This approach was most fully developed and applied by Robert Mearns Yerkes (1876–1956), a professor of psychology at Harvard University.

Yerkes gained prominence when in 1915 the United States was beginning to mobilize for war. World War I had begun in Europe, and the United States would eventually join Britain and France in that struggle. Thousands upon thousands of new recruits were entering camps across the country to become soldiers. Yerkes persuaded the U.S. government to allow him to develop a program of intelligence testing for these new recruits. He argued that the military could use such testing to assign soldiers to the tasks for which they were best qualified. Eventually, Yerkes and his associates tested some 1.75 million recruits. The results of this massive database would have repercussions throughout the rest of the twentieth century (Gould 1981, 192–95).

Perhaps one of the most disturbing findings extracted from Yerkes's data was that the average IQ of a military recruit was astonishingly low. This conclusion would have far reaching ramifications. The previous century had seen a large increase in immigration, and for decades Yerkes's findings would be used as proof that America's basic level of intelligence was being diluted by the massive influx of feeble-minded refugees from Eastern Europe and elsewhere. Indeed, many of the new recruits were recent arrivals to America who were ready to fight for their newly adopted country. Many of these new immigrants, however, could neither read nor write, nor speak English. Consequently, Yerkes developed two different intelligence tests: Alpha—for those who could read—and Beta—using pictures and symbols rather than questions—for those who could not read.

One of the most influential studies of Yerkes's data was made by one of his lieutenants, E. G. Boring. Using information from some 160,000 cases, Boring reached the following conclusions (Gould 1981, 196–97):

1. The average mental age of white American adults was 13.08;
2. Eastern European immigrants had lower mental ages than Western European immigrants;
3. Blacks had the lowest scores of all, with an average mental age of 10.41.

For reasons that shall soon become apparent, these findings of the Alpha and Beta tests were badly flawed.

Jews were among the groups of recent immigrants who were singled out as quite low in intelligence. C. C. Brigham, a professor of psychology at Princeton University and disciple of Yerkes, believed that the army study had dispelled the myth of Jewish genius, which had arisen as a result of such famous scholars as Sigmund Freud and Albert Einstein. As Brigham noted, "The able Jew is popularly recognized not only because of his ability, but because he is able and a Jew" (1922, 190). In other words, an able Jew was a "credit to his race" and consequently stood out from the feeble-minded Jewish masses.

Gould points out in an article titled "Racist Arguments and IQ" that the work of men such as Yerkes, Boring, and Brigham had a significant impact on the legislators who drafted the Immigration Restriction Act of 1924. This act placed severe restrictions upon the number of immigrants who would be allowed into the United States each year. Among the groups singled out were eastern Europeans, southern Europeans, and people of non-European descent—all groups that had been identified by Yerkes as having significantly lower IQs than did northern Europeans (1977b, 243–44). Jews were particularly singled out as an undesirable class of immigrants based largely on the work of Yerkes and Brigham.

Indeed, it has been estimated that between 1925 and the beginning of World War II (1939), the Immigration Restriction Act prevented more than six million people in southern, central, and eastern Europe from immigrating to the United States. Many of those peoples were Jews, Poles, and other nationalities who were later singled out by the Nazis for extermination during the Holocaust (Chase 1976, 300–1). By severely restricting the immigration of people who were attempting to flee from Europe before the outbreak of World War II, America left them to their fate. America's justification for closing her doors to the "poor and oppressed" of Europe during this critical period was the so-called scientific work on IQ by Yerkes and his associates. As Gould notes in an article titled "Science and Jewish Immigration," "The pathways to destruction are often indirect, but ideas can be agents as surely as guns and bombs" (1983, 302).

Today, nearly a century later, Americans no longer believe that Italians, Greeks, Slavs, and Jews are mentally inferior to people of northern European descent. To our culturally sensitive minds, such an idea is preposterous. This new cultural perspective allows us to recognize many glaring errors in the work of Yerkes and his associates. These errors were much less obvious, however, to the people of Yerkes's time because they shared the same collective cultural biases. In regard to the Army Mental Tests of World War I, Gould (1981, 199–222) identifies the following problems which Yerkes and his followers had conveniently overlooked or explained away.

1. *Content of the test.* Although Yerkes's Alpha and Beta intelligence tests were supposedly meant to measure "native intellectual ability" of people from any country, they contained many questions that only people who were quite familiar with American culture

could answer. Thus, recent immigrants naturally did poorly on these questions.

2. *Conditions of the test.* Tests were often given in locations that lacked adequate lighting or were so large that some of the recruits could not hear the explanations of how to take the test. For those who could hear and see, the instructions were often confusing, especially for recent immigrants who could speak very little English. Adding to this confusion, recruits were not given enough time to complete all of the questions on the tests—nor were they expected to do so. Nevertheless, during the course of the exam, they were frequently admonished to hurry.

3. *Standardization of the test.* For the tests to have any statistical significance, they would have to be standardized so that each recruit had the same opportunity to do well. In reality, however, pretest instructions varied widely from one examination to the next. Moreover, people taking the Alpha test generally received much more extensive instructions than did people taking the Beta test. Therefore, although both tests were supposed to measure basic intelligence, the people who took the Alpha test usually scored better than those who took the Beta test.

4. *Interpretation of the test.* An examination of the scores from those tests show an abnormally high incidence of 0 scores, which provides clear evidence that many recruits simply did not understand the instructions for taking the test. Instead of factoring out these 0 scores, however, Boring assigned them even greater significance, thereby dropping the scores of some recruits who scored 0 on several of the tests into the negative range. Moreover, the test gave clear evidence that native intelligence was not the only element affecting test scores. Other factors—such as health, amount of formal schooling, and length of time in America—played a significant role in how well a recruit did on the test. These factors, however, were completely ignored.

Despite these blatant flaws in the Army Mental Testing Program during World War I, the results of these tests were widely accepted by both the scientific community and the general public. Scientists and citizens alike wanted to believe that their racial prejudices rested on hard scientific data. The results of the Alpha and Beta tests would continue to influence public policy and immigration for years to come.

Indeed, Yerkes's legacy is still with us today in the form of IQ tests and college entrance exams. It is not surprising that such tests can still become the center of racial controversy. In 1994, for instance, two American professors published a highly controversial book, *The Bell Curve: Intelligence and Class Structure in American Life*. Drawing on modern statistical studies of IQ tests, the authors of this book concluded, "A substantial difference in cognitive ability distributions separates whites from blacks, and a smaller one separates East Asians from whites" (Herrnstein and Murray 1994, 315). Moreover, they also note, "Perhaps our central thought about immigration is that present policy assumes an indifference to the individual characteristics of immigrants that no society can indefinitely maintain without danger" (549). When people who were familiar with the work of Yerkes, Boring, and Brigham, first read the preceding claim, they likely felt a sense of déjá vu, or, in current parlance, "We've already been there and done that!"

Cultural Bias in the Twenty-first Century

Through his books and articles, Stephen Jay Gould has shown that a number of famous scientists over the past two hundred years have used "scientific data" drawn from biological determinism—craniology, evolutionary recapitulation, and intelligence tests—to "prove" the inferiority of Orientals, Africans, Native Americans, eastern and central Europeans, and Jews. There is little reason to believe that scientists today are any less vulnerable to the subtle influences of cultural bias than were nineteenth- and early twentieth-century scientists such as Morton, Broca, Down, Brinton, Bolk, Yerkes, Boring, and Brigham. Indeed, it is extremely likely that scientists of the twenty-first century have their own unique set of cultural biases and expectations. Like their predecessors, modern scientists may also be (unconsciously) omitting, manipulating, or reinterpreting data to justify the cultural biases of their own particular time and culture.

The old belief, then, that scientists can be completely objective in their research is an obvious falsehood. Cultural beliefs and biases shape the minds of individuals long before those individuals even dream of becoming scientists. Cultural ideas and patterns are woven into the very warp and woof of an individual's thinking processes. Even as our perception of the physical universe is constrained by our senses, so our interpretation of the physical universe is constrained by our cultural background—the ideas, theories, and biases that we are taught. An awareness of this truth—as well as the growing flux in scientific knowledge that is occurring today—has, in fact, shaken the faith of many scientists in the absoluteness of their discoveries.

That the racial biases of culture can play a significant role in the outcome of scientific research has been clearly shown. Scientists are no more immune to such prejudices than the average person in the street. Scientists, who would win fame and fortune from their work, can ill afford to contradict the prejudices of their own culture. Even if scientists desired to avoid such cultural bias, could they? Gould has stated that, "Astute scientists understand that political and cultural bias must impact their ideas, and they strive to recognize these inevitable influences" (1991, 251). If scientists could predict the future, they could identify which theories and ideas in the present are flawed or culturally biased and discard them. Such is, of course, impossible. Confined to the present, it is very difficult to even guess what those prejudices might be since everyone in the culture shares those same blind spots. Therefore, the only practical approach for scientists to take is to recognize the limitations that culture imposes on scientific truth.

PART 5

UNDISCOVERED COUNTRIES:

THE SPATIAL LIMITATIONS OF SCIENTIFIC TRUTH

They exchanged the truth of God for a lie,
and worshiped and served created things
rather than the Creator—
who is forever praised. Amen.
—Romans 1:25

CHAPTER 11

THE MICROUNIVERSE

CHAPTERS 5 THROUGH 7 discussed some of the profound upheavals in scientific thought that have occurred during the twentieth century. These upheavals have arisen not solely out of theoretical studies in philosophy, mathematics, and epistemology. A number of important discoveries in the physical sciences have been made that have shaken scientists' belief that the physical universe is entirely knowable. Scientists have discovered spatial boundaries that can never be crossed. Indeed, it might easily be argued that discoveries in the physical sciences inspired the growing role of uncertainty in epistemology, logic, and mathematics.

Creation of the Clockwork Universe

As discussed in chapter 3, Newtonian physics had a profound impact on the philosophy of Western science for some two hundred years. So powerful were Newton's mathematical descriptions of gravity and motion that many people came to believe that science would eventually develop rational explanations for everything in the physical universe. This belief, in turn, led to a mechanistic, that is, clocklike model of the universe, a universe that could be explained rationally and manipulated, just like any other machine. In a totally mechanistic universe, the need for supernatural explanations of natural phenomena would gradually disappear, and the idea of a creating, sustaining God would become irrelevant.

This mechanistic view of the universe began to unravel at the end of the nineteenth century and completely collapsed in the twentieth century.

The collapse has largely been due to several important twentieth-century discoveries in the physical sciences. This chapter documents some of those discoveries and traces their impact. First, however, to lay the groundwork for understanding how the clockwork universe theory came undone, the mechanistic model that came to be known as the "Newtonian universe" will be considered in more detail.

Isaac Newton: Universal Laws

Isaac Newton (1642–1721) was born in Lincolnshire, England. He entered Trinity College at Cambridge in 1661 and received his Bachelor of Arts degree in 1665. In the summer that he graduated from Cambridge, the University closed its doors because of the spreading epidemic of bubonic plague. Newton returned to his mother's country home at Woolsthorpe Manor in Lincolnshire to avoid the growing risk of contracting the plague in the densely populated cities. During his time of relative isolation at Woolsthorpe Manor, Newton experienced what has become known as his "miracle year." In a single year, 1666, Newton "produced an explanation for the spectral nature of sunlight, invented differential and integral calculus, and devised the universal theory of gravitation" (Sagan 1979, 27–28). After the plague in England slackened, Cambridge reopened its doors, and Newton returned to his official studies in late 1666. In 1667, he became a Fellow of Trinity College, and in 1668 he was appointed to the Lucasian Chair of Mathematics at Cambridge.

Although Newton had made his initial discovery of the law of gravity in 1666, not until 1687 did he formally publish his findings in his most famous work, *Philosophiae Naturalis Principia Mathematica (Mathematical Principles of Natural Philosophy)*. John Gribbin has commented,

> The *Principia* is the most important scientific book ever published (even more influential than [Steven Hawking's] *A Brief History of Time* [1988]), and influenced the course of science over the next three centuries. As well as setting out the law of gravity and the laws of motion, it laid the foundations of the modern scientific method. (1996, 291)

Newton's work was so important, Isaac Asimov (1920–1992) believed that Newton's *Principia* "represented the culmination of the Scientific Revolution that had begun with Copernicus a century and a half earlier" (1972, 139). *Principia* was originally written in Latin and was distributed widely and read by scholars and scientists throughout Europe.

Perhaps the most revolutionary aspect of *Principia* was Newton's introduction of "universal laws." Up to Newton's time, European scholars had continued to follow the old Aristotelian idea that the heavens and the earth were two completely different realms. Aristotle believed that the sun, moon, planets, and stars were attached to crystalline spheres that rotated around the earth in perfect, eternal circles. On the other hand, the earth and the things upon it were temporal and corruptible. Rather than moving in perfect circles, things on the earth moved in a linear fashion through the application of force (Burke 1985, 132). In *Principia*, Newton argued that the heavens and the earth were not of different character or substance. Moreover, he was able to prove mathematically that the same law of gravity that governed the falling of apples on the earth also governed the orbits of the planets around the sun. Newton thereby demonstrated that science had the power to make rational statements about not only the physical character of things on the earth but also the physical character of things in the heavens. Newton's law of gravity and his laws of motion were universal laws.

> Newton's ultimate motive for identifying the laws of motion and gravity was not to refute the biblical account of God's creation. Instead, he believed that his discovery of these universal laws simply confirmed the existence of a divine being who had created, and now governed, the universe.

As subsequent events would prove, Newton was perhaps too successful in his endeavor to show the orderly structure of God's creation. As noted in earlier chapters, scientific *facts do not speak for themselves;* they must be interpreted. Although Newton, through his discovery of the laws of gravity and motion, found strong confirmation of his beliefs in God, other scientists used these same facts in regard to the laws of gravity and motion to arrive at totally different conclusions. Two other early scientists, who also believed in God, had similar experiences: René Descartes—a predecessor of Newton—and Robert Boyle—Newton's contemporary.

René Descartes: Mechanistic Approach

The French philosopher and mathematician René Descartes (1596–1650) died some eight years after Newton's birth. Having been educated by the Jesuits, Descartes, like Newton, had deep religious convictions. During the course of his research, Descartes had concluded that all physical things in the world are composed of invisible particles of matter that are in constant motion. He reasoned that if one wants to understand the workings of a man-made machine—such as a watch—one must first understand the movement and interaction of the various components found within the machine. Similarly, if a scientist wants to understand the workings of a natural object in the physical universe, he must first understand the movements and interactions of those invisible particles that make up the object.

According to Descartes' "mechanistic approach," if the movement and interaction of these invisible particles could be discerned and mapped accurately, one should be able to explain the workings of natural objects as easily as one explains the workings of man-made machines. To facilitate the study of these invisible particles, Descartes invented analytic geometry by fusing algebra and geometry. Thereafter, "Cartesian coordinates" could be used to delineate a particle's exact position in space.

Robert Boyle: Clockwork Approach

The Irish physicist and chemist Robert Boyle (1627–1691) was a contemporary of Isaac Newton, and was strongly influenced by the mechanistic approach of Descartes. Moreover, his experiments with compressed gasses helped validate the existence of Descartes' "invisible particles." Boyle, however, went one step further than Descartes; he not only suggested that the universe was *like* a machine, he said that the universe was a machine, "a great piece of clock work" (Boorstin 1983, 72)—albeit, a clock which had been fashioned by God.

Like Newton, Boyle became more religious as he grew older. He helped finance missionary work in the Orient, and in his will he set up the Boyle Lectures, the purpose of which was to provide for a defense of Christianity against the attacks of unbelievers (Asimov 1972, 123). Boyle's own scientific work, however, had made an unfortunate, if inadvertent, contribution to the growing rejection of faith. Although Boyle, like Descartes and Newton, saw the hand of God at work in the machinelike regularity of the physical universe, later generations would not retain this saving insight.

As scientists learned more and more about the elaborate workings of nature, they became increasingly enamored with the regularity and predictability of natural law. They ceased gradually to be concerned with the ultimate source of those laws; theologians could debate that issue. The physical universe, not its Creator, became the focus of modern scientific thought; they "worshiped and served created things rather than the Creator" (Rom. 1:25). As scientists turned their eyes away from their Creator, their philosophy of life shifted gradually from theism—the belief that God made and governs the universe—to deism—the belief that God made the universe but no longer intervenes in its clocklike regularity—to atheism—the belief that the universe arose through natural processes; there is no God. The face of the natural world had not changed, nor had the facts that man could derive from studying the physical universe. What had changed was the manner in which scientists chose to interpret these facts. Therefore, despite Newton's religious beliefs, his discovery of the universal laws of gravity and motion caused an acceleration in the drift of science toward a totally mechanistic perspective of the physical universe:

> The fact that Newton demonstrated that the same laws hold for celestial and terrestrial phenomena, did not merely heap further scorn on the old Aristotelian division of the universe by the sphere of the moon, it also constituted a potent justification for the scientific credo in the idea of natural laws, and, moreover, on a universal scale. Boyle's comparison of the universe with a great clock was now seen, not as a fanciful literary flourish, but as a symbol of terrible appropriateness. If indeed the universe functioned entirely according to predetermined laws, if in principle all physical events were entirely predictable, whatever was the role of God? (C. Russell 1985, 90)

Popularity of the Clockwork Universe

The clockwork model of the universe became so popular that, by the time of David Hume (1711–1776), many scientists were uncomfortable with even mentioning God in the context of their studies. Natural law was becoming so all-pervasive that there was no longer any need (or room) for God to act in the physical universe. The stars followed their courses through the heavens in precisely defined orbits, night followed day as the earth spun upon its axis, and generation followed generation as life waxed and waned. A similar view of nature will be held by "scoffers" in the last days, who will say, "Ever since our fathers died, everything goes on as it has since the beginning of creation" (2 Peter 3:4). Indeed, in *An Essay on Miracles* (1845), Hume argued that the miraculous intervention of God into the physical world was actually precluded by natural law. Moreover, if God should attempt to intervene in space and time, such an event could never be proven through historical evidence. Therefore, as far as Hume was concerned, to speak of God or miracles was to speak of nonsense because such things could not be proven empirically. Thus, there was simply no longer any room for God in the mechanistic, Newtonian universe. "God, who had set the clocks to ticking, was now an anomaly in his own universe" (Eiseley 1960, 15).

Three hundred years after the time of Newton, many scientists are still enamored by the clocklike precision of the universe. Some of them are quite adamant in their belief that science can completely explain the physical universe without reference to a divine creator. Carl Sagan, for example, states at the very beginning of his book *Cosmos*, "THE COSMOS IS ALL THAT IS OR EVER WAS OR EVER WILL BE" (1980, 4). Richard Dawkins (1941–), in his book *The Blind Watchmaker* (1987), argues that natural selection, not God, is responsible for the appearance of life on the earth. Stephen Hawking (1942–), in his popular book *A Brief History of Time: From the Big Bang to Black Holes*, states the following:

> The idea that space and time may form a closed surface without boundary also has profound implications for the role of God in the affairs of the universe. . . . So long as the universe had a beginning, we could suppose it had a creator. But if the universe is

really completely self-contained, having no boundary or edge, it would have neither beginning nor end: it would simply be. What place, then, for a creator? (1988, 140–41)

To Hawking, then, as well as Sagan and Dawkins, the mechanistic structure of the universe makes the role of God negligible or nonexistent—God has *no* role.

The fundamental premise of the mechanistic approach to science is the belief that every aspect of the universe is ultimately knowable; like any man-made machine, the universe has a logical structure that is understandable. Through the application of the scientific method, scientists could force nature gradually to reveal its secrets until, at last, all laws, particles, and forces would be identified, cataloged, and understood. Moreover, this knowledge of the universe could be expanded from the present into both the past and the future. Newtonian physics, for instance, allowed astronomers to identify precisely the past and future motions of the planets around the sun, thereby making it possible to identify past or future eclipses of the moon. Expanding upon this idea, the French scientist Pierre Simon, Marquis de Laplace (1749–1827), "maintained that the entire history of the universe, past and future, could be calculated if the position and velocity of every particle in it were known for any one instant of time" (Asimov 1972, 687).

Consequently, in the clockwork model of the universe, it is believed that no truth can ultimately escape the all-pervasive eye of science. As science comes to fruition, humanity will no longer need to rely on religion and superstition to explain the mysteries of life; science will answer all these questions for us. According to Carl Sagan in one of the last books he wrote before he died, *The Demon-Haunted World: Science as a Candle in the Dark*, this is the great hope that science holds out to humanity:

Science teaches us about the deepest issues of origins, natures, and fates—of our species, of life, of our planet, of the Universe. For the first time in human history we are able to secure a real understanding of some of these matters. Every culture on Earth has addressed such issues and valued their importance. All of us feel goose bumps when we approach these grand questions. In the long run, the greatest gift of science may be in teaching us, in ways no other human endeavor has been able, something about our cosmic context, about where, when, and who we are. (1996, 38)

Down through the centuries the Newton universe provided a cozy setting for the pet ideologies of many scientists. The grandest assumption of these scientists was that all of the secrets of nature would be gradually unlocked. Given enough time, funding, and data, scientists would break down the walls of ignorance and erect in their place a palace of absolute truth.

Collapse of the Clockwork Universe

Despite the continued dominance of the mechanistic belief, the underpinnings for this mechanistic philosophy would be utterly destroyed. The early part of the twentieth century witnessed a devastating impact on the mechanistic model of the universe in the rise of two new scientific theories: the theory of relativity and quantum mechanics. These two theories resulted in some of the most important scientific discoveries made during the twentieth century, discoveries that revealed clearly the limitations of scientific knowledge about the universe. Simply stated, scientists discovered areas in the physical universe that seem to be permanently beyond their reach. Thus, scientific knowledge of these areas must remain forever tentative and provisional. Therefore, science seems likely to be denied forever its ultimate dream—the dream of finding absolute truth. The rest of this chapter examines several regions of the physical universe that apparently will remain "undiscovered country" despite the best efforts of science.

Albert Einstein: Relativity and Simultaneous Time

As noted in chapter 3, Newton's seventeenth-century paradigm of the universe was swept away in the twentieth century by Einstein's theory of relativity. Einstein's relativistic universe not only replaced the Newtonian universe but also destroyed many of our fundamental certainties about the nature of the physical universe. Since the time of Francis Bacon, scientists have believed that the only proper way to conduct scientific research is through the inductive method; scientists must first make observations of nature before attempting to develop hypotheses to explain nature. Auguste Comte later argued that all truly scientific observations must be mathematically quantifiable. Today, scientists quantify their observations in terms of such physical characteristics as length, mass, and time; they measure such entities as the diameter of an atomic nucleus, the mass of a neutron star, or the half-life of the uranium-238 isotope—all measurements determined by mathematics.

Einstein's theory of relativity proved conclusively that, despite their fundamental importance to the scientific method, physical characteristics such as length, mass, and time are relative to the velocity or gravity of the system in which they are being measured. In other words, a twelve-inch ruler on the space shuttle traveling at eighteen thousand miles per hour would be slightly shorter than a twelve-inch ruler in a car traveling at a hundred miles per hour. A man or woman who weighs one hundred fifty pounds on the earth would not weigh one hundred fifty pounds on the moon, on the planet Jupiter, or on any other planet that had stronger or weaker gravity than that of the earth. Even time itself can run at different speeds. If a spaceship could be accelerated to the speed of light, time would literally stop for occupants traveling on that ship. The same would be true for a person caught in the gigantic gravitational attraction of a black hole. Length, mass, and time vary according to the speed or gravity of the reference system. Indeed, scientists now believe that the gravitational forces are so strong in a black hole that all of the fundamental laws of matter and energy are suspended. The same is believed to hold true for the moment of creation when all of the matter of the universe was compressed into a single point of space-time during the big bang. Therefore, the prospect of making absolute spatial measurements in the Einsteinian universe has become much more problematic than making absolute spatial measurements in the Newtonian universe. Not only do these characteristics change from one reference point to another but also at some places and times in the history of the universe the natural laws governing these concepts cease even to exist.

Barrow summarizes the difference between time in Newton's universe and time in Einstein's universe:

Isaac Newton's seventeenth-century picture of the world gave time a transcendental status. Time just passed, inexorably and uniformly, entirely unaffected by the events and contents of the universe. Einstein's picture of time was radically different. The geometry of space and the rate of flow of time were both determined by the material contents of the universe. (1994, 94)

If time, then, is affected by velocity and gravity, one of the implications of Einstein's theory of relativity is that Laplace's dream of knowing simultaneously the position and velocity of every particle in the universe for a single instant of time is quite impossible. Time itself runs at different rates in different places. In a black hole or on a rocket ship traveling at the speed of light, time stands still. Each planet, star, and galaxy has its own unique velocity through space and its own unique gravity. Therefore, time on each of the billions of planets, stars, and galaxies that make up the universe is running at different rates than that which we experience here on earth. According to the theory of relativity, Laplace's idea of scientists one day being able to know what is happening simultaneously throughout the universe at any one instance of time is not only impossible but also irrational. Martin Gardner, in his book *Relativity for the Millions*, discusses the problem of absolute simultaneity:

It is important to understand that this is not just a question of being unable to learn the truth of the matter. *There is no actual truth of the matter.* There is no absolute time throughout the universe by which absolute simultaneity can be measured. Absolute simultaneity of distant events is a meaningless concept. (1962, 43)

Despite the impossibility of simultaneity, and the impact of Einstein's theory of relativity on our understanding of the nature of reality, it was but the first crack to appear in the edifice of the clockwork universe.

Max Planck: Quantum Mechanics and Quantum Weirdness

At the same time that Albert Einstein was developing his General and Special Theories of Relativity to explain the macrouniverse (the movements of stars, planets, and galaxies), other scientists—such as Max Planck (1858–1947), Niels Bohr, and Werner Heisenberg—were attempting to study the microuniverse, that is, the atoms and subatomic particles out of which the universe is built. This field of study became known as quantum mechanics. Quantum mechanics would have an even more devastating impact on the clockwork model of the universe than did Einstein's theory of relativity. As John Casti has pointed out, "The implications of this work drove the last nail into the coffin of Newtonian reality" (Casti 1989, 419).

At the beginning of the twentieth century, when scientists set out to delineate the atomic structure of matter, they assumed that they would find an orderly microcosm within the atom that would operate by the same principles and laws that governed the stars and the planets. Once these rules had been identified and quantified, science would have fulfilled Descartes' and Laplace's dreams of mapping the movement and interaction of the invisible particles out of which the universe was built. Science would then be at the very doorstep of absolute truth, ready to advance to that final and complete explanation for the workings of this vast, clocklike universe. Quantum mechanics, however, transformed this dream into a nightmare, and by the end of the twentieth century, most scientists had given up hope of ever fully understanding the nature of reality.

Max Karl Ernst Ludwig Planck is recognized as the founder of quantum mechanics. Born in Kiel, Germany, Planck while still a boy moved with his family to Munich and attended college in both Munich and Berlin, eventually receiving his doctorate in thermodynamics from the University of Berlin in 1887. Two years later, he became a professor at that university. In 1900, he laid the groundwork for quantum mechanics, and in 1918 he received the Nobel Prize in Physics for this work.

The problem that led Planck to the discovery of quantum mechanics was that of "black body radiation." When sunlight is passed through a prism, it is split into the familiar colors of the rainbow: red, orange, yellow, green, blue, indigo, and violet. These colors are the result of the different wavelengths of electromagnetic energy that are present in the light; red has the longest wavelengths and the least amount of energy, and violet has the shortest wavelengths and the greatest amount of energy. Because

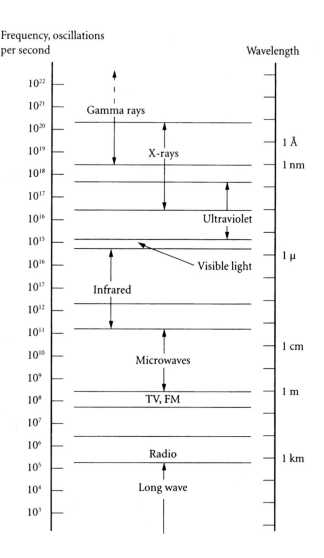

Frequency, oscillations
per second

Wavelength

10^{22}	
10^{21}	Gamma rays
10^{20}	
10^{19}	X-rays — 1 Å
10^{18}	— 1 nm
10^{17}	
10^{16}	
10^{15}	Ultraviolet
10^{16}	Visible light — 1 μ
10^{17}	Infrared
10^{12}	
10^{11}	
10^{10}	Microwaves — 1 cm
10^{9}	
10^{8}	TV, FM — 1 m
10^{7}	
10^{6}	Radio
10^{5}	— 1 km
10^{4}	Long wave
10^{3}	

Electromagnetic Spectrum

Energy travels as waves (as well as particles). Shorter waves (such as gamma-rays) have more energy; longer waves (such as radio waves) have less energy. Light is the only form of electromagnetic radiation that is visible to the human eye. When white light passes through a glass prism (or raindrop), it will separate into the various colors of the rainbow—the shortest waves of light are purple and blue, intermediate length waves are yellow and green, the longest waves are orange and red.

black absorbs all of these wavelengths and thus reflects no light, it has no color.

It was assumed that black bodies should also radiate all wavelengths of energy because the atoms in the black body have absorbed all wavelengths of light. When an atom absorbs light, one or more of the electrons in orbit around the nucleus of the atom will move to a new, higher energy shell with a larger orbit. This condition is only temporary however, since atoms cannot continue to absorb energy indefinitely. If they did, the electrons would eventually gain so much energy and occupy such large orbits, they would escape from the atom. Therefore, atoms not only absorb energy, they also release energy. When an electron eventually drops back to its original lower energy shell with a smaller orbit, it releases the energy it had previously absorbed. Thus, black bodies that absorb light, eventually release radiation.

Because most wavelengths of light fall in the upper, shorter ranges, however, it was theorized that a black body should radiate most of its energy in the violet/ultraviolet range. Moreover, because short-wave violet light has a higher frequency (more energy) than long-wave red light, it was also assumed that a black body should rapidly radiate away its energy in what was termed a "violet catastrophe." Such catastrophes, however, did not actually occur—and no one could explain why they didn't.

In attempting to solve the mystery of black body radiation, Planck was forced to abandon the constraints of classical mechanics. One of the assumptions of classical mechanics was that atoms could absorb or radiate energy in a continuous flow. Even as the amount of water in a stream can vary from a trickle to a mighty torrent, so the amount of energy passing into or out of an individual atom was thought to vary across an infinite range of possibilities, that is, the electromagnetic stream of energy could vary by infinitesimal amounts. Planck discovered, however, that the only mathematical model that could explain the behavior of black body radiation also required that energy be absorbed or emitted in discrete lumps or packages rather than in a continuous flow. Planck called these packages of energy "quanta" (singular, "quantum"), because *quanta* in Latin means "how much."

Quantum mechanics resolved the theoretical problem of the violet catastrophe. Because energy can be absorbed or emitted only in discrete

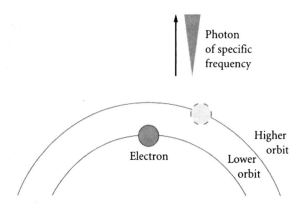

Planck's Quanta

When an atom absorbs a quantum of energy, an electron is forced to "jump" to a higher energy shell. An electron that absorbs a small packet (or quantum) of energy will only have to jump to the next highest energy level. Electrons that absorb larger packets of energy will be forced to jump two or more energy levels. When the electron drops back to its original ground state, the packet of energy that it previously absorbed is released as radiation (heat a piece of iron and it will radiate red light).

packages, it cannot easily drain away from a black body by the emission of short-wave, high-frequency electromagnetic radiation. Planck showed that a direct mathematical correlation exists between the size of quanta— or package—and their wavelength (Planck's constant). Large packages of radiation (quanta) require high inputs of energy (short-wave). There-fore, atoms tend to radiate most of their energy in smaller quanta at longer wavelengths rather than in larger quanta at shorter wavelengths.

A piece of iron when heated in a fire provides an illustration. Most of the energy absorbed by the iron is radiated back into the room in the form of invisible (long-wave) infrared radiation. If the intensity of the fire is increased, the iron may become "red hot," now emitting some of its radiation in the form of red light waves. At even higher temperatures, the iron may release orange or yellow light waves. It will take a very hot fire indeed, however, for the iron to begin to radiate energy in the form of blue or violet light waves. With very massive inputs of energy, we can induce iron to release invisible ultraviolet radiation or even X-rays, but it is not an easy procedure. Because of this same difficulty, atoms most commonly radiate away excess energy in the form of smaller quanta at longer (red) wavelengths, and don't usually build up sufficient energy to radiate energy at the shorter (blue/purple) wavelengths. Thus, no violet catastrophe occurs.

Planck's resolution of the violet catastrophe problem and his recognition of the quantum character of energy, laid the foundation for a revolution in physics that would sweep away the staid certainties and common-sense assumptions of classical mechanics. "In fact, all of physics before 1900 is now called classical physics and after 1900 it is modern physics" (Asimov 1972, 502). In place of the clocklike regularity of Descartes' and Newton's classical mechanics, the quantum mechanics of Planck would eventually lead to the discovery of quantum leaps, the uncertainty principle, and wave-particle duality (discussion commences below). Some scientists have aptly called this new understanding of the subatomic world, "quantum weirdness":

> The longer you look at it, the stranger it gets. The colloquial term is *quantum weirdness,* and it's not just a matter of getting used to the Alice-in-Wonderland oddities of a world in which particles are also waves [i.e., wave-particle duality] and can leap from one place to another without traversing the intervening space [i.e., quantum leaps]. Quantum weirdness goes deeper: It implies that the logical foundations of classical science are violated in the quantum realm [i.e., the uncertainty principle], and it opens up a glimpse of an unfamiliar and perhaps older aspect of nature that some call the *implicate* universe. (Ferris 1997, 265)

Since the era of Newton, Descartes, and Boyle, science had itself made a "quantum leap." The clockwork universe, recall, was built upon the work of these scientists, all of whom believed in God. Subsequently, based on the work of Hume and many others, this model of the universe became so mechanistic and deterministic that many scientists came to believe that it had effectively eliminated any need for the existence of God or a supernatural realm.

The last two authors discussed above—Einstein and Planck—reversed this trend and largely discredited the clockwork model.

Einstein's theory of relativity undercut the placid assumption that the world is as we see it. He showed that even such fundamental concepts as length, mass, and time are not absolute—they change under the influence of acceleration or gravity. Laplace's dream of predicting the past or future state of the universe—based on the position of all the particles of matter at any one moment in time—was shown to be not just impossible, but irrational. Because of the relativity of time, there can be no "one moment of time" for the entire universe. Relativity thus imposes severe spatial limitations on what scientists can do or know.

Planck, in order to explain black body radiation, was forced to abandon the classic mechanics of Newton, upon which the clockwork model of the universe was built. Planck's quantum mechanics gave a very different picture of reality, a reality best described as "quantum weirdness," where uncertainty, rather than certainty, is the ruling principle. At spatial scales typically found inside the atom, is encountered a world of uncertainty that defies many common scientific assumptions.

The next stage in the development of quantum mechanics occurred in 1913, when, as shall be seen, Niels Bohr merged Planck's quantum theory with Rutherford's nuclear model of the atom.

Niels Bohr: Quantum Leaps and the Collapse of Causality

Niels Henrik David Bohr (1885–1962) was born in Copenhagen, Denmark. The son of a physiology professor, Bohr began studying physics at the University of Copenhagen in 1903 and received his doctorate in 1911. After graduating from Copenhagen, he moved to England to continue his research in physics, first studying under J. J. Thompson at Cambridge and then moving on to Manchester to study under Ernest Rutherford. While working at Manchester in 1913, Bohr proposed his now-famous theory of "quantum leaps." In 1916, he accepted an appointment as professor of physics at the University of Copenhagen and in 1922 received the Nobel Prize in Physics for his application of quantum theory to the structure of the atom.

While Planck had focused on the actual energy that is absorbed and emitted by the atom, Bohr was concerned with the internal structure of the atom itself, that is, *how* the atom absorbs and emits quanta of energy.

Recall the relationship between energy and light. Isaac Newton had discovered that when white light is passed through a glass prism, the prism separates the different wavelengths of light into a band of colors called a spectrum (plural, spectra). We see a similar phenomenon when sunlight passes through raindrops to create a rainbow. The longest wavelengths with the lowest energy (red light) are at one end of the spectrum and the shortest wavelengths with the highest energy (blue/purple light) are at the other end of the spectrum.

Subsequent work in spectroscopy (the study of light spectra) had shown that each element absorbs or emits light at certain characteristic wavelengths. When an atom of a particular element *absorbs* energy, it leaves dark "absorption lines" in the spectrum for those wavelengths it has absorbed; when an atom of a particular element *emits* energy, it creates bright lines in the spectrum for those wavelengths it has emitted. Although spectral lines had been observed throughout the nineteenth century, no one had yet attempted to explain the atomic processes within the atom that govern the exact positioning of these absorption and emission lines in the spectrum. Bohr set out to resolve this problem.

In Rutherford's nuclear model of the atom, electrons orbit a small, massive nucleus at the center of the atom, similar to the way the planets orbit the sun. Although most of the mass of the atom lies within its nucleus, that nucleus represents an extremely small portion of the atom's total volume. Indeed, if the nucleus of an atom were expanded to the size of a grain of sand and placed on the fifty-yard line of a football field, the orbits of the electrons that surround the nucleus would fill the entire football stadium. Nevertheless, the electrons themselves are also extremely small, so small, in fact that the kinetic energy each electron possesses is in the same range as the quanta that Planck identified. Therefore, scientists at the beginning of the twentieth century assumed that when electrons absorb quanta, they accelerate, and their orbits, of necessity, become larger. On the other hand, when electrons emit energy, they decelerate and their orbits become smaller. According to classical mechanics, when these orbiting electrons emit energy, they should slow down and begin to spiral in toward the nucleus. Therefore, how can electrons that are continuously absorbing and emitting energy maintain their orbits indefinitely? Why don't all atoms eventually collapse into their nuclei?

In 1913, Niels Bohr theorized that the electrons orbiting the nucleus of an atom are not free to assume an infinite range of orbits. Instead, only certain highly prescribed orbits, or shells, exist within which electrons are able to move. Bohr was able by Planck's constant to delineate mathematically the size of these orbits, thereby merging quantum mechanics with Rutherford's nuclear model of the atom. Moreover, Bohr found that when an electron within these "quantized" orbits absorbed energy, it didn't spiral out to a larger orbit, nor did it spiral into a smaller orbit when it emitted energy. Instead, the electron "jumped" instantaneously from one orbit to another. Therefore, an electron in orbit around the nucleus of an atom is not continuously gaining or losing energy. As long as the electron remains within its orbit, it is neither absorbing nor emitting energy. Only when the electron jumps between orbits does it gain or release energy. Moreover, the size of the quantum package that the electron absorbs when it jumps to a higher energy shell is exactly the same size as the quantum package that it releases when it drops back to a lower energy shell. In addition, the sizes of these quanta correlate exactly with the wavelengths found in the spectral lines of the atom. Thus, by merging quantum theory with Rutherford's nuclear model of the atom, Bohr succeeded in explaining the mechanism responsible for the spectral lines in spectroscopy, as well as advancing our understanding of how the atom maintains its energy balance and stability.

The quantum jumps or leaps that Bohr first hypothesized are unlike anything scientists had ever imagined. When an electron absorbs a quantum of energy, it doesn't simply move across the space from one orbit to another orbit. Instead, the electron exists either in one shell or another but is never in transition between two shells. Thus, at the subatomic level, electrons are defying the common logic that, to get from point A to point B, one has to move across the intervening space. The basic rules of cause and effect that govern events in the macroworld apparently do not apply in the microworld. In his book *Taking the Quantum Leap*, Fred Wolf notes that quantum mechanics has introduced several paradoxes into modern science with which scientists have great difficulty dealing:

> The first paradox was that things [in the microworld] moved without following a law of mechanical motion. Physicists had

grown accustomed to certain basic ideas concerning the way things move. There was an invested "faith" in the Newtonian or classical mechanical picture of matter in motion. This picture described motion as a continuous "blend" of changing positions. The object moved in a "flow" from one point to another.

Quantum mechanics failed to reinforce that picture. In fact, it indicated that motion could not take place [in the microworld] in that way. Instead, things moved in a disjointed or discontinuous manner. They "jumped" from one place to another, seemingly without effort and without bothering to go between the two places. (1981, 3)

After centuries of relying on causality to explain the physical universe, scientists studying quantum mechanics at the beginning of the twentieth century made the startling discovery that "strict causality [i.e., for all things] is fundamentally and intrinsically undemonstrable" (Hoffmann 1959, 179).

With the work of Einstein, Planck, and Bohr, then, the safe, predictable, and understandable clockwork model of the universe began to dissolve like snow in a fire. Those scientists who had sought shelter under this clockwork model in order to justify their agnosticism or atheism found they were in danger of being buried under its collapsing structure.

The work of Werner Heisenberg however, had, if anything, an even more devastating impact upon the clockwork model.

Werner Heisenberg: Quantum Uncertainty and the Collapse of Reality

The solid reality of the Newtonian universe was warping and cracking under the growing weight of the quantum mechanics theories that had been advanced by Max Planck in 1900 and Niels Bohr in 1913. That solid reality ruptured and collapsed with the additional discoveries of Werner Heisenberg in 1927. Werner Karl Heisenberg (1901–1976) was born in Duisburg, Germany. Although his father was a professor of Byzantine history, Werner chose to pursue physics. He studied the structure of the atom under Arnold Sommerfield at the University of Munich and received his Ph.D. from that institution in 1923. Heisenberg then went on to work as an assistant with Max Born at the University of Göttingen and Niels Bohr at the University of Copenhagen. In 1925, Heisenberg developed a complex technique for studying the atom, which he called "matrix mechanics." This technique could be used to study the light emissions from electrons that orbited nuclei. As a result of his observation, Heisenberg published in 1927 his famous "uncertainty principle." In 1927, Heisenberg also accepted an appointment as chair of theoretical physics at the University of Leipzig, thereby becoming Germany's youngest full professor. In 1933, he shared the Nobel Prize in Physics for his discovery of the uncertainty principle.

Heisenberg was strongly influenced by Niels Bohr. He took to heart Bohr's statement that the study of quantum mechanics necessitates "a final renunciation of the classical ideal of causality and a radical revision of our attitude towards the problem of physical reality" (Bohr 1958, 60). Heisenberg renounced all efforts to create mental pictures of how the internal structure of the atom must look. Instead, he focused on analyzing the hard data that could be extracted from atoms through visual observations. Using his matrix mechanics, Heisenberg plotted these observations on square tabulation charts. These observations of light emissions from electrons orbiting nuclei ultimately led Heisenberg to an astonishing conclusion. He found that it is impossible to simultaneously know both the position and the momentum of an electron within the atom. This discovery became known as Heisenberg's "uncertainty principle." Lindley gives a concise summation of the implications:

> This was the true revolution of quantum theory—not the idea that light came in packages, that energy came in quanta; not the odd fact that photons and electrons sometimes behaved as waves, sometimes as particles; but the principle that physics, at this subatomic level, possessed an irreducible element of uncertainty. (1993, 74–75)

As noted earlier in this chapter, the theory of a mechanistic universe

had reached its ultimate expression in the work of the French astronomer Pierre Simon, Marquis de Laplace. Laplace had argued that scientists might one day reconstruct the entire history of the universe (both
past and present) if they could but determine the position and momentum of every particle in the universe for a single instance of time (Asimov
1972, 687). Although it could certainly be argued, even in Laplace's day,
that it would ultimately prove impossible for scientists to plot the position and momentum of *every* particle in the universe for even a single
instance of time, Heisenberg's uncertainty principle showed that it was
impossible for scientists to plot the position and momentum of even *one*
particle in the universe for a single instance of time. This was a great
shock to scientists. Here was an undiscovered country, a realm into which
science could probe no deeper, a permanent barrier to the advancement
of scientific knowledge, a limitation that future technological advances
could not overcome. As Cassidy points out, Heisenberg's discovery had
stunning implications:

> The indeterminacy is not the fault of the experimenter: it is a
> fundamental consequence of quantum equations and a feature
> of every quantum experiment. Furthermore, Heisenberg de-
> clared, the uncertainty principle will never be overcome when-
> ever and as long as quantum mechanics is valid. For the first
> time since the Scientific Revolution, a leading physicist had pro-
> claimed a limitation to scientific understanding. (1992, 106)

Science, then, had come up against a limitation in discovering the secrets of the physical universe. Since antiquity, humans had been plotting
the location and movement of the sun, the moon, and the planets as they
moved across the sky. Humans had subsequently learned to determine
the location and movement of armies on land, of ships in the ocean, of
planes in the sky, and of satellites in space. Position and momentum were
two fundamental aspects of reality that humans could use to understand
the physical universe around them. When Heisenberg attempted to ob-
tain this same type of information about an electron, however, he was
unsuccessful. Based on his analysis of the radiation being absorbed and
emitted from atoms, Heisenberg found that it was impossible to know

simultaneously the exact position and momentum of an electron as it moved about an atom. Whenever he sharpened his resolution of the position of the electron, he lost clarity regarding its momentum, and whenever he increased the precision of his measurements on the momentum of an electron, he lost information about its position. It was as though the electron's position and momentum had been stamped on opposite sides of a coin, and both sides of the coin can never, of course, be seen clearly at the same time.

Causes of Quantum Uncertainty

Subatomic particles stubbornly refuse to play by the rules of cause and effect. Moreover, they have a proclivity for assuming different guises to match our expectations (wave or particle). Scientists, though, have nonetheless made progress in their attempt to explain the cause(s) of quantum uncertainty. Given that subatomic particles themselves seem to be indecisive as to whether they are particles or waves, perhaps it is only natural that we need more than one explanation to describe such dualistic entities. Thus, not just one, but two popular explanations have been offered: *Uncertainty as a Function of Scale* and *Uncertainty as a Function of Wave-Particle Duality*.

The first explanation—*uncertainty as a function of scale*—centers on the problem of scale. As was noted earlier, electrons are so tiny that the amount of kinetic energy they carry is similar in magnitude to the energy in Planck's quantum. Therefore, when an electron absorbs electromagnetic radiation, a significant change occurs in its momentum. To "see" an electron, however, it must be "illuminated" with some type of electromagnetic radiation. Illuminating with long-wave forms of radiation that have low-energy content (light waves, infrared waves, or radio waves), will not disrupt badly the momentum of the electron. Unfortunately, such low-energy radiation has wavelengths that are longer than the diameter of an electron. Consequently, these long waves tend to arch over the electron and are not reflected back to the instruments, making it difficult to determine the exact position of the electron. Illuminating with short-wave forms of radiation that have high-energy content (ultraviolet rays, X-rays, or gamma rays), can pinpoint the location of the electron much more successfully. When such high-energy radiation strikes an electron, though, it alters the electron's momentum radically. Because of these unfortunate physical constraints, uncertainty will always exist about either an electron's exact position or its precise momentum. An attempt to gain precision in one of these measurements always results in a loss of precision in the other measurement.

The second explanation of Heisenberg's uncertainty principle—*uncertainty as a function of wave-particle duality*—arises from the wave-particle duality of matter at the subatomic scale. As scientists probed ever deeper into the world of subatomic particles, they were perplexed to discover that electrons sometimes behave as particles, and sometimes as waves. For many years scientists argued over which observation was correct, until Niels Bohr advanced his Principle of Complementarity, which stated that subatomic particles are *both* waves and particles. Which aspect manifests itself is dependent on the observer. If a scientist sets up experiments to observe particles, he or she sees particles; if a scientist sets up experiments to observe waves, he or she see waves. Many scientists have resigned themselves to this odd state of affairs. In any event, following this reasoning, when attempting to determine the exact position of an electron, the focus is on the particle aspect of the electron; when attempting to determine its momentum, the focus is on its wave aspect. Consequently, the exact position of the electron can be determined only when it is treated as a particle; the exact momentum of an electron can be determined only when it is treated as a wave. Because the electron can't be treated as both a particle and a wave simultaneously, its exact position and momentum can never be determined simultaneously.

Through the development of quantum mechanics, science has probed beneath the surface of the visible universe and into the very essence of matter and energy. At the beginning of the twentieth century, most scientists assumed that this search eventually would reveal a hard bedrock of reality out of which the universe is constructed. What has been discovered, however, is a realm in which cause and effect are no longer connected, where subatomic particles are flickering back and forth between energy and matter, and where uncertainty is one of the few certainties (Asimov 1976, 213). What has been found is a parallel universe more akin to the world depicted in Lewis Carroll's *Through the Looking Glass: And What*

Alice Found There than to the normal everyday world of experience. Indeed, the discovery of quantum leaps, the wave-particle duality of matter, and the uncertainty principle has raised disturbing questions concerning the very nature of physical reality. As Niels Bohr once said, "Anyone who is not shocked by quantum theory has not understood it" (Davies 1983, 100).

Interpretations of Quantum Uncertainty

What, then, are the implications of quantum uncertainty? How do these discoveries about the strange goings on in the microuniverse impact our understanding of the macrouniverse? One thing is certain, quantum uncertainty has shattered the old assumptions about the predictability of subatomic particles that once undergirded the clockwork model of the universe. But are deeper issues afoot? Are these ideas threatening to undercut our very perceptions of reality? That depends, in part, on which interpretation of quantum uncertainty one accepts.

Niels Bohr: The Copenhagen Interpretation

The most popular of these interpretations is called the Copenhagen Interpretation. This interpretation was developed in 1927 and was influenced strongly by Niels Bohr and his Principle of Complementarity. According to this approach, no absolute reality underlies the visible universe: "The implication of such a claim is that quantum objects in their unmeasured state literally have no dynamic attributes" (Casti 1989, 442). In other words, subatomic particles (such as electrons) are neither particles nor waves until someone attempts to measure them. Moreover, the type of measurement the researcher attempts to make on an electron determines the type of attribute the electron manifests. Therefore, according to the Copenhagen Interpretation, at the quantum level of the universe, the act of measurement determines the nature of reality, that is, we create reality by making observations (442–43). This concept, observes Lindley, is directly opposed to the old Newton/Descartes/Boyle model:

> The founding principle of classical physics is that a real, objective world exists, a world the scientist can understand in limit-

less detail. Quantum theory takes away this certainty, asserting that scientists cannot hope to discover the "real" world in infinite detail, not because there is any limit to their intellectual ingenuity or technical expertise, nor even because there are laws of physics preventing the attainment of perfect knowledge. The basis of quantum theory is more revolutionary yet: it asserts that perfect objective knowledge of the world cannot be had because there is no objective world. (1993, 62)

Hugh Everett: The Many-Worlds Interpretation

Other physicists have advanced a number of other, less popular, interpretations of quantum mechanics than that of Niels Bohr. One of the most interesting of these alternative approaches is the Many-Worlds Interpretation, developed in 1957 by Hugh Everett III (1930–1982) while he was still a graduate student at Princeton University. Everett disagreed strongly with the Copenhagen Interpretation of reality. Everett argued that instead of there being no absolute reality, there are multiple realities. He suggested that every time a measurement that has several possible outcomes is made, the universe will split into parallel universes, each manifesting one of those possible outcomes. Therefore, the act of measurement does not determine the nature of reality; instead, reality bifurcates into all of its possible forms. Because the researcher performing the experiment can occupy, of course, only one of those parallel universes, he or she sees only one of the possible outcomes. "The future is not altered by consciousness. Rather, *all* possible futures really happen!" (Wolf 1981, 211).

Albert Einstein: Naive Realism Interpretation

Albert Einstein would not have been impressed by any of the preceding interpretations of quantum uncertainty:

Einstein found the concept of quantum indeterminism so shocking that he dismissed it with the retort that "God does not play dice with the Universe!" and spent much of the rest of his life looking for the deterministic clockwork that he thought must lie hidden beneath the apparently haphazard world of quantum mechanics. (Davies and Gribbin 1992, 209)

Einstein championed an approach to explaining quantum mechanics that Casti has called "naive realism" (1989, 415). Einstein believed that quantum leaps and Heisenberg's uncertainty principle merely "appeared" to defy the laws of cause and effect. Still undiscovered were "hidden variables," which would eventually reconcile these quantum observations with common sense. For instance, Einstein believed that the electron has attributes regardless of whether anyone is measuring them, even as a tree that falls in the forest makes a noise regardless of whether anyone is there to hear it. Einstein never found these hidden variables, however, and the bulk of experimental and mathematical work over the past few decades still strongly supports the Copenhagen Interpretation (Casti 1989, 457–58).

The Unknowable Universe

Quantum mechanics has caused scientists to question not only the nature of physical reality but also their ability to objectively study the physical universe. Compare this state of affairs to the dream built upon the clockwork model of the universe. At the beginning of the twentieth century, many scientists were optimistic that science would ultimately be successful in its quest for absolute truth. They believed that as our scientific knowledge of the physical universe continued to grow, science would be able to piece together the facts, one by one, until a complete picture of the universe and humanity's place within it could be assembled. This clockwork model projected that the visible universe represented the totality of reality and that all aspects of this reality were amenable to scientific measurement and testing.

The early part of the twentieth century, however, saw the rise of two new scientific theories—relativity and quantum theory—that would have a devastating impact on the mechanistic model of the universe:

It was a time for revolutions; not one revolution but two, coming directly on top of each other. First there was the quantum theory, which provided novel insights into the bizarre workings of the micro-world, and then there was the theory of relativity, which cast space and time into the melting pot. The old world view of a rational and mechanistic universe ordered by rigid laws of cause and effect, collapsed into oblivion, to be replaced by a mystical world of paradox and surrealism. (Davies 1984, 23)

With the development of Einstein's general theory of relativity, it became evident that the very units of measurement that science commonly uses to study the universe (mass, length, and time) are themselves not absolute. These units of measurement vary according to the gravity or velocity of the system in which they are being measured. More importantly, relativity destroyed Laplace's mechanistic dream that "the entire history of the universe, past and future, could be calculated if the position and velocity of every particle in it were known for any one instance of time" (Asimov 1972, 687). Because time runs at different rates in different places, making measurements simultaneously across the universe is simply impossible.

Furthermore, with the development of Max Planck's quantum mechanics, scientists discovered that, at the fundamental level of natural phenomena, they couldn't determine the simultaneous location and velocity of even one single subatomic particle; electrons cannot be observed without altering their behavior. Depending on how the scientific observer sets up the experiments, subatomic particles flicker back and forth between matter and energy. Thus, the observer is connected intimately with the thing that he or she is attempting to observe. Even worse, the very methods of observation predetermine the outcome of the observation. When experiments are set up to detect waves, the electron appears as a wave; when experiments are set up to detect particles, the electron appears as a particle. At the quantum level the fundamental dichotomies between matter and energy, cause and effect, and the observer and the observed all broke down; the walls between subjectivity and objectivity seemed to collapse. Thus, scientists, instead of finding solid bedrock underlying the physical universe, seem to have fallen into a quicksand of subjectivism and illusion.

The real universe, then, is far more unknowable than the imaginary clockwork universe envisioned by Newton, Descartes, Boyle, and Hume. At the very foundations of the real universe, the entire microworld of atoms and subatomic particles lies hidden in the darkness of quantum uncertainty, beyond the ken of scientific observation. Indeed, as J. B. S. Haldane once noted, "The universe is not only queerer than we imagine, but it is queerer than we can imagine" (Wolf 1981, 100).

THE MACROUNIVERSE

AFTER THE QUANTUM MECHANICS revolution, science became more circumspect about its abilities and potential. In one of the older popular accounts on quantum mechanics, *The Strange Story of the Quantum* (first published in 1947), the author notes, "Science has suddenly become more humble. In the good old days, it could predict the future boldly. But what of now? To predict the future we must know the present, and the present is not knowable, for in trying to know it we inevitably alter it" (Hoffmann 1959, 151–52).

Science would find ever more limitations in the decades that followed. Heisenberg's 1927 uncertainty principle had identified a severe limitation concerning how deeply science could penetrate into the microuniverse. Two years later, a discovery in astronomy by Edwin Hubble would set a limit on how deeply science could penetrate into the macrouniverse.

Edwin Hubble:
Cosmological Constant and the Edge of Space

Edwin Powell Hubble (1889–1953) was born in Marshfield, Missouri. The son of an insurance agent, Hubble initially set out for a career in law. While at the University of Chicago, he excelled in athletics, the sciences, and languages. Graduating in 1910, he continued his studies as a Rhodes scholar at Queens College in Oxford. After three years at Oxford, Hubble returned to the United States and set out to pursue his real love—

astronomy. In 1914, he returned to the University of Chicago and began to work as a research assistant for George Hale at the Yerkes Observatory in Williams Bay, Wisconsin. Following his graduation in 1917 with a Ph.D. in astronomy, Hubble volunteered for military duty in France during World War I. In 1919, after the war, Hubble accepted a position at the Mount Wilson Observatory in California and remained there for the rest of his career.

In 1918, the largest telescope in the world, the one hundred-inch Hooker telescope, went into operation at the Mount Wilson Observatory. When Hubble arrived at the observatory the following year, he already had an application in mind for this powerful new instrument of science. For more than one hundred fifty years, astronomers had been aware of the presence of nebulae in the night skies. Many astronomers believed that these hazy clouds of light were nothing more than dust and gas that were being illuminated by neighboring stars. Others, including Immanuel Kant (philosopher, 1724–1804), believed that some of these clouds were composed of stars, "island universes" that lay beyond our own Milky Way Galaxy. While still at the Yerkes Observatory, Hubble had studied many of these nebulae with the twenty-four-inch telescope there, and had written his dissertation on "Photographic Investigations of Faint Nebulae." At Mount Wilson, he could continue his studies of nebulae with the most powerful telescope in the world.

By the time Hubble was ready to begin his professional career at Mount Wilson, astronomers had accumulated a good deal of evidence to support the theory that some nebulae are indeed composed of stars. They offered three main lines of evidence: (1) absorption lines in nebulae spectra; (2) Doppler shifts; (3) novae.

Regarding the first line of evidence, each star has a unique absorption line–fingerprint based on the elements that are present in the star. The light collected from nebulae frequently have absorption lines for a variety of different elements suggesting that the light is emitted by a large number of stars rather than just a few neighboring stars in the vicinity of the nebulae.

Second, the absorption lines in the spectra from many of the nebulae are shifted away from their natural positions. Such shifts are caused by the motion of a light-emitting source, either toward or away from the observer. This phenomenon is called the Doppler effect and is commonly observed with sound waves. For example, as an ambulance approaches an observer, the sound waves produced by its siren are compressed and the pitch rises. Once the ambulance passes, the pitch drops because the sound waves begin to expand as the vehicle recedes from the observer. Similarly, light waves from stars or galaxies are compressed (shifted toward the shorter, blue end of the spectrum) when they are moving toward the earth. Light waves are expanded (shifted toward the longer, red end of the spectrum) when stars and galaxies are moving away from the earth. The amount of shift in the absorption lines of light from many of the nebulae suggests that these nebulae are moving at much higher speeds than has been observed for stars or clouds of dust near the earth.

Third, astronomers had been able to observe novae—which are exploding stars—in some of the nebulae. Novae are visible at great distances because the exploding star releases such massive amounts of energy. A really large star that explodes (a supernova) may release as much energy for a short time (a few days) as all the billions of stars in a galaxy. Therefore, although the nebula were so far away from the earth that individual stars could not be seen with telescopes smaller than the Mount Wilson telescope used by Hubble, these very bright novae and supernovae could be seen—thereby suggesting the presence of stars in the nebulae.

By 1924, Hubble, using the telescope at Mount Wilson, was able to distinguish individual stars in the Andromeda Nebulae. Before that time, no one had been able to distinguish individual stars within nebulae— except for the Large and Small Magellanic Clouds. These Clouds were also classified as nebulae, but they are located so close to our galaxy that many astronomers once thought they might simply be a part of our galaxy. The Andromeda Nebulae, however, is located some two million light-years from our galaxy, although it can be seen faintly with the naked eye in the constellation Andromeda. (A light-year is the distance light travels in one year; moving at 186,200 miles per second, light will travel 5,900,000,000,000 miles in one year).

Some of the stars that Hubble was able to resolve in the Andromeda Nebulae were Cepheid variables, large yellow stars that slowly increase and decrease in brightness, like a slow-motion caution light. From studies of Cepheid variables in our own galaxy, astronomers knew that the brightness (absolute luminosity) of these stars is in direct proportion to the rate at which they wax and wane; the longer the periodicity, the brighter the star. Because the long-period Cepheid variables in the Andromeda Nebulae are much dimmer than variables of the same periodicity in our galaxy, Hubble was able to (crudely) calculate their distance from earth as 930,000 light-years—clearly well beyond the borders of our Milky Way Galaxy.

Thus, 169 years after Immanuel Kant's island universes were first postulated, Hubble succeeded in validating their existence. These extragalactic clouds of stars were later named galaxies by Harlow Shapley (1885–1972), one of Hubble's colleagues at Mount Wilson. As Asimov (1972, 631) has noted, "Shapley later made the logical suggestion that the extragalactic nebulae be called galaxies, emphasizing the fact that our own galaxy (sometimes called the Milky Way Galaxy) was only one of many."

In the following years, Hubble located a number of other nebulae (galaxies) containing Cepheid variables. Using the periodicity-brightness yardstick, he was able to identify galaxies at greater and greater distances from the Milky Way. When the distances grew so great that the Cepheid variables were no longer visible within the galaxies, Hubble devised new measuring devices. These new techniques were also based on the relationship between distance and brightness (distant objects appear less bright than nearby objects). First, Hubble identified the brightest stars within galaxies of known distance and, by using these "highest magnitude stars" as his point of reference, continued measuring the distances to galaxies at even greater distances.

Second, he also classified galaxies into three types: spiral, barred spiral, and elliptical. Because spiral galaxies are the most common type, Hubble measured the collective brightness of all of the stars within a number of spiral galaxies of known distance. Then, using the average brightness of these spiral galaxies, he was able to measure the distance to even more remote spiral galaxies in which no individual stars could be resolved (even with the one hundred-inch Mount Wilson telescope).

As his database of extragalactic nebulae grew, however, Hubble began to see a strange pattern in the spectra of the absorption lines emitted from these galaxies. This pattern would result in Hubble's most famous discovery and would revolutionize our understanding of the physical universe.

As the focus of Hubble's research moved beyond the galaxies in the local group that lies fairly close to the Milky Way Galaxy (such as the Magellanic Clouds and Andromeda), he found that the absorption lines in the spectra of all galaxies beyond the local group were shifted toward the red end of the spectrum. The further these galaxies were from earth, the greater was their redshift. Moreover, none of the most distant galaxies have spectra that are blueshifted. Hubble came to realize that most of the galaxies he could observe (other than those in the local group) are moving away from us. Indeed, a direct correlation exists between the distance of a galaxy and its speed of recession; the farther away it is, the faster it is receding, and the greater is its redshift. This correlation between distance and speed of recession became known as Hubble's Law: "The recession velocity (indicated by *redshift*) of a distant *galaxy* (one outside the Local Group) is directly proportional to its distance from us" (Gribbin 1996, 212). Hubble announced his discovery about the macrouniverse in 1929, only two years after Heisenberg formulated his uncertainty principle regarding the microuniverse.

The most straightforward explanation for Hubble's Law is that the universe is expanding. In whatever direction Hubble and his colleagues looked in the night sky, they found galaxies that are moving away from us, as if in some huge explosion. This expansion should not, however, as Timothy Ferris points out, be visualized in terms of a bomb:

Classic Doppler shifts arise from motions *through* space. Cosmological redshifts result from the expansion of intergalactic space itself. By keeping this in mind we can avoid lapsing into the parochial notion that galaxies are flying through static space, like shards of a bomb. The universe should not be thought of as expanding "into" preexisting space. All the space the universe has ever had has been in the universe from the beginning, and the space is stretching. This perspective can also help us understand why the special-relativity rule that *nothing can be accelerated to a velocity greater than that of light* does not apply to galaxies in an expanding universe. That rule is true in static space, *but*

expanding cosmic space can carry galaxies away from one another
at velocities greater than that of light. (1997, 44; emphasis added)

Albert Einstein formulated his general theory of relativity in 1915 to explain the specific effects of gravity. To his dismay, he found that this theory, when applied to space-time, proved mathematically that the universe should be either expanding or contracting. Because of the all pervasive influence of gravity, stars and galaxies cannot remain stationary throughout time—their mutual gravitational attraction will cause them to collapse together, unless they are in motion, expanding away from each other. Einstein wanted to believe, however, that the universe was static and eternal. As a result, he committed what he would later describe as the "biggest blunder" of his career, adding to his formula what he called a "cosmological constant." This constant, when factored into the other equations of general relativity, allowed the universe to remain static. When, in 1929, Hubble announced his discovery of a law that was not an arbitrary construct but a pattern arising out of the observable universe, physicists and astronomers were quick to see an alternate solution to Einstein's earlier problem. The universe was indeed unstable; it was expanding, just as Einstein's original theory of general relativity had predicted.

Even before Hubble's discovery, however, many scientists were unhappy with Einstein's cosmological constant. In 1927, in an attempt to create a model of the universe that better matched Einstein's (unaltered) equations for general relativity, the Belgian astronomer Georges Lemaître (1894–1966) had advanced the first big bang model for the creation of the universe (Gribbin 1996, 53). Later, in the 1940s, the Russian physicist George Gamow (1904–1968), through his theoretical studies of how the elements might have come into existence, laid the basis for the modern big bang theory. This theory now dominates scientific thinking concerning the creation of the universe. The big bang theory postulates that some 10 to 20 billion years ago, the current physical universe came into existence. The earliest empirical evidence to support the big bang theory was Hubble's discovery of the expanding universe (Horgan 1996, 96).

Embedded within Hubble's discovery, though, is another interesting concept that is equally revolutionary. That concept is called "Hubble's radius" and may have implications as powerful for the macrouniverse as Heisenberg's uncertainty principle has for the microuniverse. Hubble's radius suggests that there might be a limit to what astronomers can learn about the physical universe. As previously stated, Hubble found that the farther away a galaxy is from the earth, the faster it is receding. Some of the most distant galaxies that Hubble recorded are moving away from us at speeds representing a significant percentage of the speed of light. By the end of the twentieth century, astronomers had identified remote galaxies that are moving away from our galaxy at more than 90 percent of the speed of light (Ferris 1983, 181). Consequently, if the Hubble constant remains valid, we will reach a point in our observations at which galaxies are so distant that they are receding at the speed of light or even faster. This point will denote the edge of the observable universe:

> From *Hubble's Law*, it follows that there must be a certain distance at which *galaxies* would be receding from us at the *speed of light*. We could never see anything from beyond this distance, known as the Hubble radius. The Hubble radius is equal to the distance that light could travel in the time since the *Big Bang*, so it is the same number in *light years* as the *age of the Universe* in years—roughly 20 billion light years, or 6,000 million *parsecs* [1 parsec = 3.2616 light-years (the distance from which the earth and the sun would appear to be separated by an angle of 1 arc second)]. (Gribbin 1996, 212).

Beyond the Hubble radius, myriad other galaxies may well exist, but astronomers will never be able to see them because they are receding from earth faster than their light is traveling toward earth. Thus, the universe may have a visible edge beyond which astronomers can never hope to see. If so, scientific knowledge of the universe will forever be limited to the "visible" portion of the universe within the Hubble radius:

> At some vast distance from ourselves, the velocity of recession should attain the speed of light and neither light nor any other form of communication could reach us from any of those galaxies or others still more distant. This distance would represent

the effective "Hubble radius" of that portion of the universe which we can come to know. (Asimov 1972, 631)

The only factor that could negate the limiting effect of Hubble's radius upon how much of the physical universe humans will actually be able to observe, would be a universe that is younger than twenty billion years old. Such a "younger" universe would not yet have had time to expand beyond the Hubble radius, so all parts of that universe would still be within the visual range of humans on earth. In other words, no galaxies in the expanding universe would have yet had time to reach the edge of the Hubble radius, beyond which, galaxies are receding away from us faster than their light is traveling toward us.

Recent attempts to date the origin of the universe more accurately suggest that the big bang occurred some fifteen billion years ago rather than twenty billion years ago. Moreover, recent observations of the most distant galaxies reveal that they are smaller and more "immature" (in terms of their development) than normal galaxies. Therefore, as astronomers peer ever deeper into space, it is possible that they may eventually be able to see the entire universe—not just the visible portion within the Hubble radius. As the universe continues to expand, however, the most distant galaxies will inevitably reach the edge of the Hubble radius and disappear forever from sight. There is a spatial boundary in space, then, beyond which science cannot probe. If that boundary has not yet been reached in the present, the expanding universe insures that it will be reached—in the future.

Max Planck: Planck Epoch and the Edge of Time

In addition to the visual boundary at the edge of space, twentieth-century science has also identified another boundary—this one at the edge of time. As has been noted, science, like religion and philosophy, is interested in answering ultimate questions. One of the ultimate questions mentioned in chapter 1 is *Where did we come from?* Cosmology is the specialized field within astronomy that attempts to provide the ultimate answer to this question by explaining how the universe itself came into existence. Cosmologists' answer to the question of origins lies in the big bang theory. This theory posits that the big bang marks the beginning of the universe, the point where space and time came into existence. According to modern cosmology, all matter and energy in the universe owes its existence to this event.

Today, it is theorized that we live in the aftermath of the big bang. The fabric of space continues to expand, and the galaxies grow ever more distant from each other. If, though, we could somehow reverse time and travel back toward the dawn of creation, we would find the galaxies all moving toward each other as space contracted. Light from the distant galaxies would be blueshifted rather than redshifted. Hubble's Law would have to be rewritten to read, "The *procession* velocity (indicated by *blueshift*) of a distant galaxy (one outside the Local Group) is directly proportional to its distance from us. Eventually all of the stars, planets, and galaxies, all of the matter and energy in the universe, will coalesce into a superdense, superhot ball of fire—the big bang itself."

Astronomers and physicists have been very interested in developing models that would allow them to reconstruct the conditions of the very early universe immediately after the big bang. In addition to the simple desire to answer that ultimate question of origins, though, scientists have another motive. One of the great dreams of Albert Einstein was to develop a "unified field theory" that would simplify our understanding of the forces at work in nature. Four known forces now exist: (1) gravity; (2) electromagnetism; (3) the strong nuclear force; (4) the weak nuclear force. Gravity and electromagnetism are infinite in range, and their effects are easily observed in our everyday activities (falling apples or electric lights); the strong and the weak nuclear forces are *finite* in range and their effects are manifested only at the subatomic scale. Einstein believed that he could find a way to combine electromagnetism and gravity into a single unified force, even as James Clerk Maxwell (Scottish mathematician and physicist, 1831–1879) had been able to merge electricity and magnetism into a single force—electromagnetism. We now use electricity in factories to make magnets, and we use magnets at dams to make electricity.

Although Einstein failed in his endeavor, his efforts gave future generations of physicists a worthy goal for which to shoot—to solve the problem that Einstein couldn't. Developing a unified field theory would fulfill, beyond the egotistical goal of being successful where Einstein had failed, a much deeper motivation. The desire for beauty and simplicity in their explanations of nature is for many scientists—as it was for Einstein—a fundamental motivation. Since the Middle Ages, many scientists have judged the worth of competing theories on the basis of Occam's Razor, which states that the more complex a theory is, the more likely it is to be wrong. It is unfortunate for scientists that our current models of the universe are often quite complex—including the necessity of enlisting at least four separate forces to explain the workings of the universe.

In the 1960s, a number of theories arose from the ashes of Einstein's failed attempt at a unified field theory. Known as "grand unification theories," or GUTs, these models temporally sidestepped the thorny problem of gravity in which Einstein had become entangled. Instead, they focused on merging the other three forces of nature: electromagnetism, the weak nuclear force, and the strong nuclear force.

During the 1970s, a new generation of even more ambitious theories were advanced under the rubric of "supersymmetry," or "theories of everything," or TOEs. What the theorists really wanted was a "superunified" theory that would identify symmetrical family relationships among all four forces (Ferris 1988, 328). Supersymmetry theories attempted to create a truly inclusive theory of the universe by explaining how all of the known forces in nature (including gravity) arose from a single force at the beginning of time. By the 1980s, however, supersymmetry was beginning to reach the limits of its explanatory power: "It could not generate all the known quarks, leptons [the two families of subatomic particles out of which all matter is made], and gauge particles [the family of subatomic particles that carries force], and it introduced even more unexplained terms than had grand unified theories and the standard model" (328).

By the late 1980s, a new approach was developing called "string theory" (discussed in chapter 13), which postulated that matter is not made of subatomic particles but strings. Through the simple vibration of these strings, one could account for all of the known quarks and leptons as well as gauge particles: "String theory proffered potential answers to some of the most troubling questions that had been confronting theorists concerned with unification" (Ferris 1988, 328).

One thing that all TOEs share is a heavy reliance on the big bang theory.

Only under the extreme conditions thought to exist during the early stages of the big bang can sufficiently high energy levels be found that would make possible the unification of the four basic forces. Thus, scientists who are searching for beauty and symmetry in the universe, as well as scientists who are searching for an answer to the ultimate question of origins, have both converged on the big bang in their quest for truth.

There, however, at the very doors of creation, they have found yet another spatial barrier—the Planck boundary at 10^{-43} second before the big bang. The big bang arose from what scientists call a "singularity," in which all of the matter and energy of our current universe was compressed into a tiny point in space no more than 10^{-33} cm across. (In a singularity, all values—such as pressure, density, and temperature—reach infinity.) Following the big bang, this unimaginably hot energy and matter were hurled outward in a violent explosion. As the universe expanded out of the singularity, however, its pressure dropped, its density began to fall, and its temperature began to cool. By 10^{-43} second after the big bang, the temperature already had dropped from infinity to 10^{32} Kelvin. (Temperatures in Kelvin measure degrees above absolute zero—the point at which matter possesses a minimum amount of energy.) In 1965—that is, ten to twenty billion years later—scientists at the Bell Research Laboratory found that remnant heat from this explosion still permeates the universe. This background radiation now stands at 2.7°K. Thus, in the past ten to twenty billion years, the universe has cooled from a temperature of 100,000,000,000,000,000,000,000,000,000,000°K, to the current temperature of 2.7°K.

Scientists reason that such a drastic reduction in temperature has likely had a significant impact on the physical character of the expanding universe. Despite its billions of galaxies filled with blazing stars, the current universe is said to be a frozen wasteland in contrast to the temperatures it experienced during its infancy. This is why the big bang theory plays such an important role in TOEs. Many physicists believe that as the universe began to cool, not only matter but also the forces governing matter began to freeze out of the early homogenous universe. Although all of the forces were at one time unified in the very early stages of the big bang, as the universe began to cool, these forces began to crystallize into the forms we see today. Even as water, depending on its temperature, can assume various forms (solid, liquid, gas), so the force governing matter broke into separate forces as the temperature of the universe began to cool. As a result—in a universe the ambient temperature of which now stands at 2.7°K, rather than 10^{32}°K—four forces govern nature, not one force. Barrow summarizes the relationship between temperature and unification:

> At first sight, these attempts at unification appear doomed, because we know that the fundamental forces of nature are of very different strengths and act upon different collections of particles. How could these disparate things be the same? The answer is that the strengths of the forces of nature vary with the temperature of the environment. So although they are very different from one another in the low-energy world in which we live, they will slowly change as we probe conditions of higher temperature. (1994, 56)

As has been stated, for scientists to attain such temperatures, it is necessary to replicate conditions that are thought to have existed during the early history of the universe. Physicists and astronomers have been amazingly successful at first theorizing and then replicating those conditions. By building particle accelerators to collide subatomic particles at velocities approaching the speed of light, physicists have, in fact, been able to replicate such conditions. Indeed, these accelerators can now generate tiny sparks that are vastly hotter than the interior of stars. Moreover, when these extreme temperatures are created, new subatomic particles appear that scientists believe have not existed since the universe began to expand and cool billions of years ago.

The existence of some of these particles was predicted accurately by unification theories long before accelerators large enough to bring these particles back into existence could be built. For example, in 1967, Steve Weinberg (1933–) and Aldus Salam (1926–1996) developed the electroweak theory, which showed mathematically that the electromagnetic force and the weak nuclear force could have coexisted during the early stages of the big bang. Moreover, they predicted that this early, hot universe would have contained massive particles, which they called W^+,

W-, and Z^0. These particles would have played a critical role in the inter-action of these two forces. Not until 1983, however, with the completion of the proton-antiproton collider at the European Center for Nuclear Research near Geneva, Switzerland, were scientists able to create tem-peratures hot enough to bring these particles back into existence, thus confirming the validity of the electroweak theory.

Physicists at the beginning of the twenty-first century believe they now have a fairly good theoretical understanding of the early universe. Traveling back in time toward the beginning of the big bang, tempera-tures, pressure, and density begin to climb. Within 10^{-12} second (one tril-lionth of a second) before the big bang, the temperature of the universe reaches 10^{15}°K, and the weak nuclear force merges with the electromag-netic force into the electroweak force. At 10^{-36} second before the big bang, the temperature of the universe rises to 10^{28}°K. and the strong nuclear force merges with the electroweak force. Finally, current theory suggests, at 10^{-43} second before the big bang, the temperature of the universe reaches 10^{32}°K, and gravity merges with the other three forces into perfect sym-metry. The four forces are now one (Gribbin 1996, 177). Bartusiak ex-plains the rarified condition under which this unification could take place:

> The climb toward a complete unification of the forces continues upward into a mathematical heaven called supersymmetry, where all the forces, including gravity, look and act the same. This uni-formity, of course, is no longer in place. Such a state of supersymmetry was maintained only during the first 10^{-43} second of the universe's existence, when cosmic temperatures were mon-strously high—high enough to maintain the symmetry (1993, 273).

Such conditions, however, cannot be replicated. First, temperatures of 10^{28}°K and 10^{32}°K present an experimental barrier that cannot be reached; second, the Planck boundary at 10^{-43} second before the big bang represents a time barrier beyond which we cannot go.

In regard to the first barrier, science can verify the accuracy of the electroweak theory because temperatures reaching 10^{15}°K can be gener-ated in particle accelerators. To generate, though, temperatures of 10^{28}°K to validate the predicted unification of the strong nuclear force with the electroweak force, science would need to build a particle accelerator larger than our entire solar system (Boslough 1992, 157). To reach temperatures of 10^{32}°K, at which point gravity is thought to merge with the other three forces, current particle accelerators would have to improve by a factor of 10,000 trillion (Gribbin 1996, 317). This latter improvement would require building an accelerator as large as a galaxy (Lederman and Schramm 1995, 160). Thus, scientists may theorize about what the early universe was like at a temperature of 10^{32}°K, but will probably never be able to use particle accelerators to experimentally test these theories. Boslough explains that conditions at the very beginning of the universe will always be out of reach:

> Beyond the particle physicists' first trillionth of a second [10^{-12}] lay a desert realm of time and energy, a terra incognita that would indefinitely remain beyond the capabilities of even the greatest of accelerators to explore. As more than one physicist has expressed it, "God has always seemed to be just around the corner." (Boslough 1992, 224–25)

Even more problematic than the temperature barrier, however, is the second barrier, the time barrier, or Planck boundary, that is encountered at 10^{-43} second before the big bang:

> The first minute or the first second or the first split second would persist as yet more corners were turned. But it is unlikely physicists will ever turn the last corner. There always would be another one just ahead, meaning that the trillionth of a second that particle physicists believe lies between them and revelation may just as well be a trillion years. (Boslough 1992, 224–25)

If scientists move beyond the Planck boundary, however, back toward the very beginning of the big bang, they enter the Planck epoch, "a brief but important instant, from time zero to only 10^{-43} second" (Ferris 1997, 102). The Planck epoch not only takes us back to the very point of creation but also encompasses Planck time (10^{-43} second), "the smallest measurement of time that has any meaning" (Gribbin 1996, 318). Planck time is how long it takes light, traveling at 186,200 miles per second, to cross a distance equal to one Planck length, that is, 10^{-33} of a centimeter—"the smallest measurement of length that has any meaning" (317). Thus, at 10^{-43} second after the big bang, the universe had expanded from a singularity with no dimensions, to a universe that was 10^{-33} centimeter across (one Planck length).

If the big bang represents the beginning of the universe, then in order to answer the ultimate question, *Where did the universe come from?* scientists must penetrate beyond the Planck boundary at 10^{-43} second, back to the very point of creation itself. Scientists must explain what brought the universe into existence. But, even as quantum mechanics introduces uncertainty into our understanding of subatomic particles, it also introduces uncertainty into our understanding of the beginning of the universe. Before 10^{-43} second, the universe was the same size as a subatomic particle. After 10^{-43} second the universe emerged from Planck length and Planck time and began to expand. Before that time, the entire universe was contained within an area no larger than 10^{-33} cm in diameter. This is the scale at which quantum mechanics dominates all physical interactions. Therefore, the Planck boundary is like a locked door through which scientists cannot pass in their quest for knowledge (Ferris 1988, 346). Beyond the Planck boundary, in the Planck epoch (0–10^{-43} second), the four forces of nature presumably merge in supersymmetry, the current laws of physics cease to function, and space and time lose their significance—the universe disappears into the darkness of quantum uncertainty. Dennis Overbye observes the ramifications of quantum uncertainty:

> Quantum uncertainty itself determined how close to the putative beginning—the singularity—you could slice time. At a ten-millionth of a trillionth of a trillionth of a trillionth of a second—a number written as 10^{-43}—after the big bang, an era known as the Planck time, quantum uncertainties in the geometry of space-time were the same size as the universe, which meant that space and time considered in chunks shorter than that were simply incomprehensible. They were in the same limbo land of probability as the electron before its place or motion had been measured. (1991, 234–35)

The Veiled Universe

Thus, in the macrouniverse—as in the microuniverse—there are severe spatial limitations to how much scientists can learn about nature. As scientists trained their telescopes on the night sky to study the macrouniverse, they found yet another barrier. According to Hubble's Law, the more distant a galaxy is from the earth, the faster it seems to be receding from us (due to the expansion of space itself following the big bang). Because astronomers have already identified galaxies that are receding from us at more than 90 percent of the speed of light, at some point in space (if the universe is old enough), astronomers may reach the limit of their ability to see because the galaxies will be moving away from us faster than their light is moving toward us. Thus, the universe has an edge beyond which astronomers cannot see (the Hubble radius). Indeed, according to inflationary theory, this universe quite likely is vastly larger than that portion that is visible to humans (Horgan 1996, 99).

Another spatial limitation was discovered when scientists attempted to look back in time to the beginning of the universe. As scientists approach to within 10^{-43} second of the emergence of the universe from a singularity, they come to the Planck boundary. Beyond this boundary, the entire universe was less than 10^{-33} centimeter in diameter (the Planck length). At this small scale, scientists enter the realm of quantum mechanics, and the birth of the universe is veiled in quantum uncertainty. Moreover, even if scientists should someday be able to cross the Planck boundary and reach the singularity itself, all measurements of pressure, density, and temperature would reach infinity, and the laws of space and time would themselves break down. Thus, at the very point of creation, scientists would lose the tools and laws they need for measuring and understanding physical reality.

Scientists, then, may come very close to grasping absolute truth (10^{-43} second), but no closer. Consequently, scientists have a great deal to say about what happened in the universe after the big bang but very little of substance to say about what happened at, or before, the big bang. It is as though God, like an artist, has hung a sheet over His work so we cannot see Him in the actual act of creation.

CHAPTER 13

THE HIDDEN UNIVERSE

IN THEIR SEARCH FOR BEAUTY and simplicity, scientists have not only had to contend with the asymmetry of the four forces in the current physical universe, but they also were confronted with asymmetry in their own theories. Modern physics is dominated by two theories that arose in the early part of the twentieth century: quantum mechanics and relativity. One theory explains the microworld of atoms and subatomic particles; the other theory explains the macroworld of stars and galaxies. Obvious questions arise. Why should physicists need two different theories to explain one universe? Why should stars and galaxies be governed by different laws than electrons and atoms?

> Thus the paradox: General relativity says that large objects—rocks, footballs, planets, stars—behave in a predictable manner, while quantum theory maintains that at the atomic level, matter behaves randomly. Clearly there cannot be separate rules for different parts of the universe. (Boslough 1981, 68, 70)

When Hubble discovered the expanding universe, Einstein was forced to abandon his cosmological constant. Once the cosmological constant had been removed from the equations of general relativity, the theory clearly predicted that the universe should either be expanding or collapsing. Hubble proved that the universe was expanding. If, however, physicists try to imagine the universe collapsing back into its initial state at the beginning of the big bang, they run into problems. In a collapsing universe, general relativity predicts that gravity will eventually compress all of the matter in the universe into a singularity. As the universe shrinks into a singularity, however, its diameter drops below the Planck length, and we enter the realm governed by quantum mechanics, not relativity: "Thus, general relativity brings about its own downfall by predicting singularities. In order to discuss the beginning of the universe, we need a theory that combines general relativity with quantum mechanics" (Hawking 1993, 92).

Quantum mechanics, however, can neither describe the conditions in a singularity nor merge gravity with the other four forces. When physicists attempt to use quantum mechanics to study singularities, their mathematical theories always end up giving nonsensical results in the form of infinities (Davies and Gribbin 1992, 253–54). Despite the introduction into theories of such exotic entities as supersymmetry and supergravity, gravity stubbornly resists all attempts at unification with the other forces (Barrow 1994, 130). Therefore, trying to merge quantum mechanics and general relativity is like trying to mix fire and water (Boslough 1981, 68).

One of the great scientific quests of the second half of the twentieth century was the search for a way to merge Planck's quantum mechanics with Einstein's relativity to produce a single theorem called "quantum gravity." Indeed, many scientists thought that "Unifying quantum theory and general relativity would remove the last barrier to understanding why the universe is the way it is" (Boslough 1981, 70). In the late 1960s, a new theory appeared on the scene that promised to make quantum gravity a reality; it was called "string theory."

John Schwartz:
Cosmic Strings and Multiple Dimensions

String theory was initially developed in 1968 by the Italian physicist Gabriele Veneziano (1942–). It was an attempt to explain how the strong nuclear force holds quarks together within the nucleus of the atom. He envisioned that "quarks were not particles but the ends of pieces of string" (Lindley 1993, 223). Although Veneziano's model was soon rejected as a means of explaining the strong nuclear force, the idea of "strings" was not abandoned. John Schwartz, a research associate at the California Institute of Technology, was fascinated by the idea that subatomic particles could be visualized as strings rather than points in space. In 1974, Schwartz and French theorist Joel Scherk showed that the idea of strings could much more effectively be applied to gravity (discussed below) than to the strong nuclear force.

String theory offered the possibility of resolving the paradox between quantum mechanics and general relativity. In 1974, John Schwartz and Joel Scherk were able to show, mathematically, that, if they pictured subatomic particles as tiny strings rather than tiny points in space, the infinities disappeared from their calculations. Perhaps even more importantly, inherent within the mathematics of string theory was the *requirement* for a particle with zero mass and a spin of two—Einstein's "graviton." Because of the curvature of space, Einstein's theory of relativity "requires the existence of gravity waves, ripples in the fabric of space-time, and the associated graviton, a particle with zero mass and spin 2" (Gribbin and Rees 1989, 177). With string theory, instead of scientists trying to incorporate gravity into their equations, gravity arose naturally out of the equations: "Indeed, string theory could not work *without* including gravity" (Ferris 1988, 330). Here was a mathematical theory, based on tiny strings in the microworld of quantum mechanics, that required the presence of gravity—the controlling factor in the macroworld. String theory seemed to offer a direct route to the Holy Grail of quantum gravity.

By 1984, John Schwartz, working with Michael Green of the Imperial College of London, had shown that string theory could resolve many of the difficulties encountered by the grand unification theories of the 1960s and the supersymmetry theories of the 1970s. String theory apparently had the potential to unify not only quantum mechanics and general relativity but also the four basic forces of nature; it was truly a "theory of everything," thereby, becoming known as "superstring theory" (Barrow 1994, 129). Thus, "by 1987 strings were the hottest topic in theoretical particle physics" (Ferris 1988, 330). It remained the hottest topic throughout the 1990s and, if Edward Witten (1951–) is correct, physicists will be working out the implications of string theory for the next couple of centuries:

> Ed Witten, a young Princeton physicist legendary for his bril-
> liance and quickness who rapidly became one of the ringleaders
> of the superstring revolution, called superstrings a piece of
> twenty-first-century physics that had fallen into the twentieth
> century, and would probably require twenty-second-century
> mathematics to understand. (Overbye 1991, 372)

String theorists postulate that strings are the fundamental building blocks out of which everything in the universe is made. Quantum uncertainty states that subatomic particles are neither matter nor energy—they are both (i.e., wave-particle duality). According to superstring theory, strings are neither matter nor energy but a different substance—the primeval ground of reality out of which matter and energy are made (Overbye 1991, 372). String theorists, however, are hard pressed to describe such a fundamental substance (Horgan 1996, 71). This substance has been described as "space," "self-contained pieces of space," "shards of space that splintered at the outset of cosmic expansion" (Ferris 1997, 220), "curved space" (224), and even "tiny one-dimensional rips in the smooth fabric of space" (Weinberg 1993, 213). Because no one has ever actually seen a string, or is likely ever to see one, the descriptions of strings are naturally quite abstract. Scientists are trying to touch the untouchable, to define that which is almost beyond definition. Only in mathematical calculations do strings offer hints as to their existence. As John Horgan has noted,

> The true meaning of superstring theory, of course, is embedded
> in the theory's austere mathematics. I once heard a professor of
> literature liken James Joyce's gobbleygookian tome *Finnegans
> Wake* to the gargoyles atop the cathedral of Notre Dame, built
> solely for God's amusement. I suspect that if Witten ever finds
> the theory he so desires, only he—and God, perhaps—will truly
> appreciate its beauty. (Horgan 1996, 71)

Appreciating this beauty takes, indeed, some imagination since the totality of our knowledge about strings is purely theoretical and mathematical. Strings are one-dimensional lines. Their length is 10^{-33} centimeter (the Planck length) but they have no measurable thickness—

"like an infinitely thin piece of string" (Hawking 1988, 159). An individual string can be either open or closed. A closed string forms a tiny loop because its two loose ends are attached to each other. Since they are so very small, closed loops appear as points in space (thus the long-standing belief that subatomic particles are points rather than lines). Strings can merge and split apart from each other, creating various geometric forms from crosses to circles. They are like "elastic bands" under various levels of tension based on the surrounding heat and pressure. Moreover, they can vibrate like the strings of a violin across an infinite range of modes, thereby creating all of the known subatomic particles, plus an infinite number of yet-to-be discovered particles:

> Always moving and oscillating, strings engaged one another in a free-for-all dance, swaying, bumping, sliding into one another in a process that Green and Schwartz showed mathematically could potentially create every type of subatomic particle—even the elusive and hypothetical little graviton. (Boslough 1992, 198)

Because strings can theoretically account for all of the particles that the theory of supersymmetry demands, they are now usually called "superstrings" (Overbye 1991, 372).

One of the interesting implications of superstring theory is that for each subatomic particle and force that we observe in nature a mirror image of that particle and force must exist (Davies and Gribbin 1992, 256–57). This is because the initial singularity out of which the universe expanded was perfect (super symmetry). Because all the matter and energy in the universe occupied a single point in space (a singularity) at the beginning of time, the infinite pressure and temperature of this unimaginably dense structure destroyed any trace of nonhomogeneity. The big bang broke that perfect symmetry and scattered the fragments (i.e., the resulting matter and energy) across the expanding universe (Ferris 1988, 334). Today, these mirror-image particles and forces do not interact with their counterparts, except through the force of gravity. Therefore, they are often described as "shadow matter" or "shadow forces." Matter and shadow matter coexist in the universe but interact only through the medium of gravity (Overbye 1991, 373).

For years, astronomers have noted that some galaxies exhibit stronger gravitation fields than can be accounted for by the visible stars within those galaxies (Boslough 1992, 70). The billions of stars in a galaxy are held together by their mutual gravitational attraction. One way that we can determine the strength of a galaxy's gravitational field is by observing the speed of the stars in the galaxy as they rotate around the galaxy's central nucleus. If a star moves fast enough, it will break loose from this gravitational attraction of the galaxy and be flung into intergalactic space (i.e., the space between the galaxies). Therefore, when we see stars in rapid rotation around a galactic nucleus, and these stars are not being ejected into intergalactic space—even though calculations suggest that the visible matter in the galaxy cannot generate a large enough gravitation field to hold them in place— we must assume that some type of "hidden matter" is present. This hidden matter generates enough additional gravitational attraction to hold the stars within the galaxy—despite their high speeds.

Astronomers have often explained these gravitational discrepancies by suggesting that galaxies contain large amounts of "dark matter" (dust, dead stars, free-ranging subatomic particles, etc.). Because this matter does not give off light, it is largely invisible in the blackness of space. Some superstring theorists have offered an alternate explanation: the missing matter could be shadow matter (Davies and Gribbin 1992, 257). According to these superstring theorists, a shadow universe composed of mirror-image particles and forces may lie embedded within the visible universe. This shadow universe, should it exist, will forever remain hidden from our view—unless it is discernable by its gravitational interaction with the visible universe. Shadow matter, however, is still a highly speculative topic, one that Davies and Gribbin describe as "extreme speculations on the fringes of superstring theory" (257).

A topic much more central to superstring theory and even more fascinating than shadow matter, is the possibility of hidden dimensions. One of the great attractions string theory holds for scientists is that it can provide a bridge between quantum mechanics and general relativity, and potentially create a unified theory that explains both the very large, and the very small. But, in order for the mathematical equations of string theory to work, it must be postulated that the universe has two, ten, or twenty-six dimensions (Ferris 1988, 332).

Scientists were presented with a sort of devil's bargain: Yes, string theory may allow you to merge quantum mechanics and general relativity into a unified theory—but in exchange you must give up your four-dimensional universe. Boslough presents a vivid analogy of this dilemma:

> Writing a unified theory is something of an ad hoc affair, like putting up a tent in a high wind; while one sets the pegs, the tent flaps free. Einstein's relativity required abandoning classical conceptions of space and time; quantum mechanics required abridging classical causality. The odd thing about string theory was very odd indeed: It required that the universe have at least ten dimensions. (1992, 330–31)

By the mid 1980s, most string theorists agreed that strings existed in ten-dimensional space rather than two- or twenty-six-dimensional space. There were five different theories, though, as to how supersymmetry could be incorporated into string theory: Type I, Type IIA, Type IIB, Heterotic type O(32), and Heterotic type E_8 x E_8. This unfortunate situation naturally presented a grave challenge to the hope that superstring theory could merge quantum mechanics and relativity into a "theory of everything" (TOE). How could a true TOE have five different manifestations (Greene 1999, 182–83)? In 1995, Edward Witten came to the rescue of string theory by showing that these five different supersymmetry theories could all be merged into a single theory called M-theory—if physicists added one additional spatial dimension to their calculations. But this new, more comprehensive theory also came with a price: M-theory has *eleven* dimensions, plus vibrating one-dimensional strings. "It also includes other objects: vibrating *two*-dimensional membranes, undulating *three*-dimensional blobs (called 'three-branes'), and a host of other ingredients as well" (Greene 1999, 287–88).

The universe in which we live, however, contains only three spatial dimensions (length, width, and thickness) and one temporal dimension (time). Where are the other seven spatial dimensions required by eleven-dimensional M-theory? Mathematicians have become quite accustomed to working with the idea of hyperdimensional space in their attempts to solve some of the more difficult problems of physics. Indeed, in 1919 the

German mathematician Theodor Kaluza (1885–1954) wrote to Einstein, suggesting that a solution to a unified field theory might be achieved if Einstein worked out his equations in five-dimensional space (Greene 1999, 332). Over the years, mathematicians were able to develop a theory called "compaction" to explain how extra dimensions could be present yet invisible. According to this theory, space within these dimensions becomes so curved that these dimensions roll up into tiny balls only 10^{-33} centimeter in diameter and become embedded in the very fabric of space-time. The dimensions are present but invisible. Hawking presents an apt analogy of how space-time containing these dimensions might appear:

> It is like the surface of an orange: if you look at it close up, it is all curved and wrinkled, but if you look at it from a distance, you don't see the bumps and it appears to be smooth. So it is with space-time: on a very small scale it is ten-dimensional and highly curved, but on bigger scales you don't see the curvature or the extra dimensions. (Hawking 1988, 163)

Some theorists have suggested that, at singularity, all eleven dimensions were of equal strength and size. Following the big bang, however, as the universe expanded beyond the Planck boundary at 10^{-43} second, only the three spatial dimensions and the one time dimension continued to expand. The other seven dimensions remain locked at their original size of 10^{-33} centimeter, still present but forever invisible (Davies and Gribbin 1992, 256; Barrow 1994, 130). Physicists cannot explain why only these four dimensions expanded while the others remained bound in their singularity state. Nonetheless, it was very fortuitous for us that this event did occur. Life would theoretically be impossible in a universe that contained more than three large spatial dimensions because everything from atoms to planetary orbits in such a universe would be unstable (Barrow 1994, 132).

Speculation about multiple dimensions and invisible universes carries a certain irony in regard to many scientists' dismissing Christianity. One of the principal objections that many scientists have to religion is its insistence that another reality underlies the world of everyday experience—the realm of the supernatural. The word *supernatural* implies a "super" realm that lies outside the "natural" realm. Consequently, such a realm, should it exist, would be impervious to scientific exploration and experimentation. Science can study only what it can measure and quantify in the physical universe. Therefore, science can neither prove nor disprove the existence of a supernatural realm; it can neither prove nor disprove the existence of the God who dwells in such a realm. This very dilemma led, of course, to the development and popularity of the clockwork model of the universe.

The clockwork model stated that the physical universe is completely self-contained—what you see is all that exists. By this definition, the supernatural simply does not exist. Physical laws acting within a physical universe can explain all things; neither need nor room exists for the supernatural. It is rather ironic, therefore, that, during the latter half of the twentieth century, work in physics and cosmology revealed that the structure of the physical universe is itself so porous that it is virtually impossible to exclude the possibility of supernatural realms.

In explaining these realms that are outside the natural realm, superstring theory is on the cutting edge of modern physics. Within this theory lies science's best hope of both unifying the four basic forces of nature and merging quantum mechanics and general relativity. The Nobel Prize–winning physicist Murry Gell-Mann (1929–) "felt that superstring theory would probably be confirmed as the final, fundamental theory of physics early in the next millennium" (Horgan 1996, 215). Yet, this achievement, if it comes, will not be without a steep price. Superstring theory will erode yet more scientific certainties about the universe in which we live; scientists will face even more stringent spatial limitations to our scientific knowledge. Superstring theory requires multiple dimensions, but these multiple dimensions cannot be studied empirically because they remain bound in their pre–big bang, singularity state. They may be embedded within the space-time structure of our physical universe, but they are "rolled-up" and hidden from our view. Multiple dimensions and shadow matter may lie as close as the air in front of our noses, but they are forever beyond the reach of our senses.

Hints of these invisible phenomena, these "other worlds" and "undiscovered countries," came seeping unbidden into physicists' theories in the guise of quantum uncertainty, shadow matter, and multiple dimensions. These leaks between the natural and supernatural realms became a torrent, however, with the introduction of Alan Guth's inflationary theory in the early 1980s.

Alan Guth: Inflation Theory and Multiple Universes

Alan Guth (1947–) was born in Brunswick, New Jersey. His father was a small-businessman, working in a variety of areas, such as groceries and dry-cleaning. Alan Guth, on the other hand, displayed an early talent for science and mathematics rather than business. In high school, he was attracted to physics because of his desire to "understand what the fundamental laws of nature are" (Overbye 1991, 218). He began his undergraduate work in 1964 with a full scholarship to the Massachusetts Institute of Technology (MIT), completing a Ph.D. in elementary particle physics in 1972. Following his graduation from MIT, Guth held a series of postdoctoral research positions at Princeton University, Columbia University, and Cornell University.

In October 1979, Guth left Cornell for a one-year research position at the Stanford Linear Accelerator Center in California. Shortly after he arrived in Stanford, Guth made a discovery about the origin of the universe that would change his life and revolutionize cosmology. In his notebook on December 6 he wrote, "SPECTACULAR REALIZATION: This kind of supercooling can explain why the universe today is so incredibly flat—and therefore resolve the fine-tuning paradox pointed out by Bob Dicke" (Guth 1997, 179). Guth called his spectacular realization "inflation." By January 1980, he had gone public with his idea, and in 1981, he published the first version of his inflationary model, "Inflationary Universe: A Possible Solution to the Horizon and Flatness Problems." The significance of Guth's work was not lost on other physicists, and a number of universities began to make job offers. In June 1981, Guth became a full assistant professor in the department of physics at his alma mater, MIT. Today, Guth holds the position of V. F. Weisskopf Professor of Physics at MIT.

Guth's inflationary theory (discussed below) was developed in the early 1980s in an attempt to resolve some of the major problems raised by the big bang theory. The big bang theory explains a number of puzzling aspects about the visible universe, including (1) the distribution of elements in the universe, (2) the expansion of the universe, and (3) the presence of background radiation. But the theory also raises some interesting problems. Perhaps the most intriguing question is, *How is it possible for humans to exist in an expanding universe?* Einstein's theory of relativity predicted an expanding universe, and Hubble's observations with the one-hundred-inch Mount Wilson telescope confirmed the existence of such a universe. For life, however, to appear and survive in an expanding universe, the rate of expansion must be neither too slow nor too fast. This issue is called the "flatness problem."

The rate at which the universe expands is determined by its density. If the density of the early universe had been too high, gravity would have quickly taken control, slowing the expansion of the universe and causing it eventually to collapse upon itself in a huge implosion—long before life had the chance to appear and develop. On the other hand, if the density of the early universe had been too low, the universe would have expanded too rapidly, and the force of gravity would have been completely overwhelmed by the outward momentum of the expansion. In this latter scenario, the planets, stars, and galaxies never would have formed; matter and energy would have been scattered across the universe in a thin, lifeless broth (Morris 1993, 84). Thus, if life is to be possible in an expanding universe the universe must have a certain critical density. It is, shall we say, fortunate that the actual density of matter in the universe today lies very close to this critical density. As a result, the expansion of the universe was neither too fast nor too slow; it was just right.

For the expansion rate of the universe to be amenable to life today, the actual density of the universe at the beginning of the big bang (at 10^{-43} second) could not have deviated from the critical density by more than one part in about 10^{59} parts (Krauss 1989, 137). In other words, the chance of the big bang creating an expanding universe where life is possible was only 1 in 10^{59} (a 1 followed by 59 zeros). To a Christian, such odds provide clear evidence that the universe was purposefully designed; it did not arise by chance. Indeed, in his book *The Fingerprint of God*, Hugh Ross includes the flatness problem as one of his evidences of divine creation (1991, 124). To many scientists, however, such evidence was not a revelation but an embarrassment, a problem requiring an alternative solution. Guth's inflationary theory seemed to provide a way out of this dilemma:

> The incredible smoothness of the background radiation and signs that the universe is "flat"—poised on a knife edge between being open (expanding forever) or closed (eventually collapsing in on itself)—seem like coincidences too good to be true. Some Christians take phenomena like smoothness and flatness as miracles. Better than the holy dirt of Chimayo, they provide evidence of a willful God, a master craftsman. But the point of science is to expel miracles, to explain the world through natural law. And so some cosmologists take a leap of faith in a different direction and embrace the doctrine of cosmological inflation. (Johnson 1995, 314)

Alan Guth developed his inflationary model to explain how the "flatness" of the universe could have arisen naturally out of the conditions that prevailed at the beginning of time. As has already been noted in this chapter, the theory of supersymmetry postulates that the four basic forces in nature were united into a single force at 10^{-43} second after creation when the universe was extremely hot (10^{32}°K). As the universe expanded and its temperature began to cool, this single force began to crystallize into the four basic forces we know today: gravity, electromagnetism, the strong nuclear force, and the weak nuclear force. Guth suggested that the universe went through a brief "phase transition" in which the four forces remained unified, even though the temperature of the universe had dropped below the critical point at which they should have splintered apart. In other words, the universe went through a period of "supercooling" in which the four forces remained united, even though they should have begun to separate. Similarly, water, if it is very pure and is stirred gently, can be supercooled below its normal freezing temperature of 32°F without becoming solid. This extremely short hiatus of phase transition, during which the forces remained together in uneasy unity, provided an excess of energy that allowed the young universe to balloon rapidly outward in a process that Guth called "inflation." Bartusiak explains how Guth came to name his theory:

The delay in its "crystallization" endowed the universe with tremendous potential energy, like a rock perched on the edge of a steep, high cliff about to fall. While in this odd state, the force of gravity actually became largely repulsive rather than attractive. Space-time, as a consequence, shot outward with an unbelievably explosive speed, but only for a brief moment. Inspired by the heady economic conditions of the times, Guth labeled this special epoch in the universe's history "inflation." (Bartusiak 1993, 246–47)

Guth projected that the universe had gone through an exceedingly brief period of very rapid expansion following its emergence from a singularity at 10^{-43} second. During this period of supercooling—which lasted from 10^{-35} to 10^{-32} seconds—the universe expanded 10^{30} times, from an invisible particle a trillionth the size of a proton, to a visible ball roughly ten meters across (Smoot and Davidson 1993, 180, 283–84). Immediately following this period of rapid inflation, the supercooled force crystallized into its modern manifestations, releasing a torrent of energy that reheated the universe and propelled it outward at a more leisurely pace, thereby inaugurating the big bang (Ferris 1988, 359).

Guth's inflationary model resolved the flatness problem by drastically expanding the size of the universe in a very short period of time. This rapid inflation would have evened out—as inflating a basketball to the size of the earth would make its surface become relatively flat—any differences between the actual mass of the early universe and the critical mass necessary for creating an expanding universe hospitable to life. Moreover, inflation provided a totally naturalistic explanation for what had seemed to be clear evidence of design: "Suddenly Guth understood everything. It was so simple. It had to be right. No outside force, no hand of God, no divine creative power was necessary. The universe had done it all by itself" (Boslough 1992, 63). Nevertheless, as Guth attempted to close a possible window into the supernatural realm, he unintentionally opened a door.

Despite the success of the inflationary model in explaining the flatness of the expanding universe, major questions still remained. Where did the universe come from? What lay beyond the Planck boundary at

10^{-43} second? What happened in the singularity itself? Guth thought he could answer these questions by merging his inflation model with an earlier (unsuccessful) theory called vacuum genesis. In 1973, Edward Tryon had attempted to explain the origin of the universe in an article titled "Is the Universe a Vacuum Fluctuation?" Tryon based his vacuum genesis theory on the uncertainty principle that is inherent in quantum mechanics.

John Wheeler (1911–), a student of Niles Bohr, once noted that, because of quantum uncertainty, even a vacuum is not really empty. Virtual particles of matter and antimatter can materialize spontaneously from nothingness, exist for a brief time, and then annihilate each other in a burst of energy. If one could examine a vacuum with fine enough detail, one would see that even empty space is actually boiling with what Wheeler called "quantum foam" (Wheeler and Ford 1998, 149; Gribbin 1996, 417–18). Johnson expands on these activities:

> It seems that nature not only abhors a vacuum, it doesn't allow one to exist. It is not just that space is filled with cosmic dust. According to quantum theory, the vacuum we once thought was empty actually seethes with energy, constantly creating pairs of "virtual particles"—matter and antimatter—that jump out and flash their tails for an instant before annihilating one another and returning to the void. (Johnson 1995, 82)

The first law of thermodynamics states that matter (at the present time in the history of the universe) can be neither created nor destroyed. Virtual particles do not violate this law because they arise from nothingness and return rapidly to nothingness, thereby having no lasting impact on the energy content of the vacuum. Tryon speculated that the universe itself might have come into existence as a virtual particle. Such a universe could persist for an indefinite period of time— as long as the energy balance of the vacuum remained neutral. He called this process "vacuum genesis." However, for vacuum genesis to have been possible, the force of gravity must exactly balance the amount of energy in the universe today. If gravity and energy are exactly balanced, they will cancel each other out—leaving the energy budget of the vacuum neutral. When scientists tested Tryon's prediction, they found that the force of gravity and the amount of energy in the universe are indeed evenly balanced.

Tryon's model of vacuum genesis, however, was not widely accepted in the 1970s because of "its failure to explain why the universe had become so large" (Guth 1997, 13). In the early 1980s, Guth realized that his inflationary model would also resolve Tryon's problem—a virtual particle could easily be "inflated" into a full-fledged universe. By merging vacuum genesis with his inflationary model, Guth argued that science could explain not only what happened after the universe emerged from a singularity but also the origin of the singularity itself. The universe arose by chance out of a quantum fluctuation; a virtual particle had inflated into the visible universe. God was no longer necessary, even at the moment of creation:

> Most important of all, the question of the origin of the matter in the universe is no longer thought to be beyond the range of science. After two thousand years of scientific research, it now seems likely that Lucretius was wrong. Conceivably, *everything* can be created from nothing. And "everything" might include a lot more than what we can see. In the context of inflationary cosmology, it is fair to say that the universe is the ultimate free lunch. (Guth 1997, 15)

As the old saying goes, however, there's no such thing as a free lunch. Guth's attempt to shut a possible window into the supernatural realm at the moment of creation by providing a totally naturalistic explanation for the Big Bang singularity, had inadvertently opened a door for the supernatural in the form of other universes. If our universe can arise out of nothingness because of the instability of a vacuum (Wheeler's "quantum foam"), what is to prohibit a multitude of other universes from coming into existence in the same manner? If one universe can arise through a vacuum fluctuation, why can't many universes thus arise? Shockingly, no scientific reason exists why other virtual particles cannot inflate into other, separate universes. "Perhaps we have become accustomed to particles popping spontaneously in and out of the vacuum, but any theory of 'quantum gravity' may force us to assimilate the notion of *universes* popping in and out of the vacuum" (Krauss 1989, 136).

Another interesting implication of inflationary theory is that the formation of new universes need not be restricted to the past. The Russian cosmologist Andrei Linde created a mathematical model of "chaotic inflationary" that predicts that new universes are being created regularly, even within our own universe. According to Linde, tiny regions of spacetime are constantly "budding off" from our universe and creating "baby universes" in a process he calls "eternal inflation." These baby universes then inflate into full-fledged universes in their own right but in a different place and a different time (Morris 1993, 141). Following this line of reasoning, trillions of other universes may exist, each with its own unique set of physical laws and conditions. Therefore, some writers have suggested that it would be more proper if, when attempting to address the whole of reality, we used terms such as *megaverse* (Johnson 1995, 80), *metauniverse* (Gribbin 1996, 38), or *multiverse* (Rees 1997, 3). From this perspective, our own universe may be only a tiny subset of a much larger entity. Gribbin and Rees comment on the possibility of our present universe being merely a drop in a vast cosmic bucket:

> "Many and strange are the universes that drift like bubbles in the foam upon the River of Time." When Arthur C. Clarke wrote those words, almost forty years ago, as the opening to a science fiction story called "The Wall of Darkness," he can have had no idea that in the late 1980s they would stand as an accurate description of modern cosmological thought. Theorists are now being led to consider the possibility that our Universe is indeed just one bubble among many in some greater meta-universe. (1989, 280)

This vastly broadened perspective of the possible nature of reality also unfortunately brings with it severe limitations on scientific knowledge. Most theorists believe that these universes, once they form, become forever disconnected from our own universe (Horgan 1996, 101; Rees 1997, 4). These universes literally exist in other places and other times, governed by different laws—perhaps built out of different numbers of dimensions—than our own universe. As such, these other universes represent the ultimate example of an "undiscovered country," a realm or realms totally separate from the everyday reality that we experience in this physical universe. In this sense, multiple universes are little different from the realm of the supernatural; their existence can never be proved or disproved since they lie outside the arena of scientific scrutiny.

Like multiple dimensions, multiple universes may lie just beyond our noses, but we will never be able to see or touch them. Consequently, scientific knowledge will be forever bound to the reality of but one universe—ours. This limitation is indeed limiting if one is genuinely interested in the pursuit of ultimate truth. Thus, three hundred years after Isaac Newton, we are still in a state of relative ignorance. As Newton described himself, we are still like children picking up pretty pebbles along the beach, while the great ocean of truth stretches away to the horizon.

The Universe Beyond Our Grasp

Thus, the attempt to explain how the current universe arose from a singularity and what came before that singularity has resulted in yet another irony. The amount of scientific knowledge potentially lying beyond the grasp of scientific scrutiny has drastically increased: First, while superstring theory will allow scientists to merge the four basic forces into a single force at the dawn of time, as well as combine the theories of quantum mechanics and general relativity into a theory of quantum gravity, it does so only at the expense of adding invisible dimensions to the universe. Second, the supersymmetry requirements of string theory and the critical density requirements of inflationary theory require the presence of large amounts of "dark matter" that can be detected only by its interaction with the rest of the physical universe through the force of gravity. Finally, inflationary theory, to explain how the universe could have arisen through quantum genesis, must acknowledge that this same process could have generated other universes. Such universes, if they exist, would lie forever beyond our reach and perception.

In light of the information presented in part 5, it is obvious that Hume's statement—anything we cannot prove empirically has no meaning—has little relevance in modern science. Strings, dark matter, multiple dimensions, and multiple universes are, mathematically, part and parcel of modern physics and cosmology, yet no scientist has ever observed these entities, let alone been able to prove them empirically. Today, ultimate reality itself seems to lie forever beyond the detection of the most sensitive scientific instruments. Therefore, if science at the beginning of the twenty-first century seems somewhat less sure of itself than it did at the beginning of the twentieth century, it is not without reasons.

The logical, philosophical, and epistemological problems with the scientific method—which have been raised by scholars such as Hume, Gödel, Popper, Gould, and Lewin—are not without their counterpoints in the scientific discoveries of Einstein, Planck, Hubble, Schwartz, and Guth. In addition to the temporal, logical, and cultural limitations discussed in preceding parts of this book, a number of major physical, that is, spatial, limitations may keep science from ever arriving at absolute truth.

Boundaries exist in space and time beyond which science apparently cannot go. Limits exist in the micro- and macroworlds beyond which science cannot see. Secrets to the universe exist that science may never be able to apprehend. As David Lindley noted in his book *The End of Physics,* "Will the end of physics be reached not because we have discovered all the answers but because the questions that remain are forever unanswerable, so that we must simply make do with what we have?" (1993, 20).

PART 6

FALSE INTERPRETATIONS:
THE EMPIRICAL LIMITATIONS OF SCIENTIFIC TRUTH

They will turn their ears away from
the truth and turn aside to myths.
—2 Timothy 4:4

CHAPTER 14

IGNORING THE ASTRONOMICAL EVIDENCE

SCIENTISTS NOW REALIZE THAT the universe is a much less certain place than they ever had imagined. There are things that science cannot know and places where science cannot go. The list of these things and places that lie beyond the reach of science seems to grow with each new scientific breakthrough.

These limitations have not, however, been accompanied by a mass conversion of scientists to Christianity. Although many scientists found their primary justification for rejecting God in the secure, machinelike regularity of the physical universe, the destruction of that model has had little impact on their religious views. To the minds of many scientists, there is no more room for God in a universe dominated by relativity and quantum uncertainty than there was in a universe dominated by Newton's laws of gravity and motion. The unthinkable (the supernatural) in the Newtonian universe is still the unthinkable in the Einsteinian universe. In light of this situation, it is not remiss to suggest that scientists, instead of being totally objective, often see what they want to see and hear what they want to hear. Thus, a final limitation of scientific truth is the subjective nature of the human senses.

It has been said that science is very much like a conversation between two people; scientists ask questions and nature provides answers. Part 2 examined the *temporal limitations* of both the questions and the answers. As scientists become more sophisticated in the questions they ask, nature

Review of limitations

provides more detailed and complex answers. Thus, the truths of science are constantly changing.

Part 3 examined the *logical limitations* of this dialogue. The answers that nature provides can never be absolutely proven because of the problem of induction. Statements about universal phenomenon cannot be proven from statements about particular instances because of scientists' finite data base.

Part 4 discussed the *cultural limitations* of this dialogue. Culture imposes limitations on the kind of questions that scientists ask, as well as how the answers that nature provides are interpreted.

Part 5 demonstrated the *spatial limitations* to this dialogue. There are places in the micro, macro, and hidden universe that are outside the scope of our empirical observations. We cannot even begin to ask intelligent questions about these areas because they are permanently beyond our reach.

Now, part 6 examines the greatest of all obstacles to a successful dialogue between science and nature—the *empirical limitations*. Modern science is built on empirical observations of nature but empirical observations must be interpreted by the human mind before they have any meaning. Therefore, the weakest links in this dialogue between scientists and nature is the human mind itself. Although scientists can strive for objectivity in their analysis and interpretation of empirical observations, they are never entirely free from the subjective influence of their backgrounds, experiences, educations, beliefs, hopes, fears, theories, and biases. The answers that nature provides to scientists' questions are in the form of raw data. How scientists interpret this data is the problem.

As stated, then, science is based on empirical evidence that is derived from the senses. Although scientists have devised various ways to greatly enhance the quality and quantity of sensory data (microscopes, telescopes, stethoscopes, etc.), all sensory data must still be interpreted to have any meaning. The interpretation of sensory data, however, is influenced strongly by the mental constructs of the human mind, and is thus not always objective. The explanatory models of the world that the human mind creates can act as filters, selectively including or excluding certain types of sensory data. Thus, the interpretation of sensory data may vary drastically from one individual to another, depending on the explanatory models that each is employing. A scientist who is, for instance, an atheist will see the big bang event as justification for belief that the universe arose by chance. A scientist who is a Christian and accepts the big bang theory will see it as a justification for belief that God created the universe.

Sometimes our beliefs are so discordant with our sense perceptions that we make statements such as, "I couldn't believe my eyes!" or "I couldn't believe my ears!" At other times, we alter our beliefs drastically to harmonize them with our sense perceptions. In this latter case, one is reminded of the old joke about a man who believed that he was dead. To dissuade him of this belief, the man's doctor got him to agree that dead men don't bleed. The doctor then pricked the man's finger with a pin, producing blood, whereupon the man exclaimed, "Doctor, we were both wrong; dead men do bleed!"

New facts or new models of the universe do not always result in new beliefs. As has often been pointed out in this book, *Facts do not speak for themselves;* they must be interpreted—and our beliefs often determine how we will interpret the facts. Our understanding of the universe may be faulty because of the empirical limitations of our senses: we see only what we want to see and we hear only what we want to hear.

Problems with Seeing

Stephen Hawking and Banesh Hoffmann: Different Perspectives

As pointed out in preceding chapters, modern science is an uneasy mixture of truth, conjecture, and falsehood. Its pronouncements have not attained the status of absolute truth, nor are they likely to achieve such perfection. Severe constraints on the scientific method arise from the very structure of the universe. Equally powerful constraints arise from the structure of the human mind. These constraints include temporal, logical, cultural, and physical limitations on what we can know about the universe or how clearly we can understand those aspects of the universe that are knowable. Because of these limitations, scientific knowledge remains in a state of flux, ever acquiring more information about the complexities of the physical universe but never actually arriving at fixed, unchanging, absolute truth. Consequently, scientific truth remains plastic and pliable.

Because scientific truth is temporal and relative rather than permanent and absolute, it can easily be molded to accommodate the philosophical orientation of its user. In other words, scientific truth can readily be shaped into configurations that defame religion, or support it. Scientists, like their fellow humans, see what they want to see. The scientist Stephen Hawking, for instance, may use scientific knowledge about quantum mechanics to validate his personal philosophy of atheism. In his famous book *A Brief History of Time: From the Big Bang to Black Holes* (1988), Hawking attempted to prove that the universe has neither spatial nor temporal boundaries. If this view is true, then the universe has no beginning or end. Consequently, Hawking argued that his model of quantum cosmology had eliminated the need for a God.

> "What place, then, for a creator?" Hawking asked. There is *no* place, was his reply. A final theory would exclude God from the universe, and with him all mystery. Like Steven Weinberg, Hawking hoped to rout mysticism, vitalism, and creationism from one of their last refuges, the origin of the universe. (Horgan 1996, 94)

On the other hand, scientist Banesh Hoffmann found in the workings of quantum mechanics strong support for his Christian faith. Hoffmann stood in awe of the fact that the entire physical universe, including our bodies and minds, is constructed of subatomic particles that constantly flicker back and forth between matter and energy (wave-particle duality) and can never be apprehended entirely by empirical means (quantum uncertainty). In the epilogue to his book *The Strange Story of the Quantum,* Hoffmann expresses his wonder:

> How much more, then, shall we marvel at the wondrous powers of God who created the heaven and the earth from a primal essence of such exquisite subtlety that with it he could fashion brains and minds afire with the divine gift of clairvoyance to penetrate his mysteries. If the mind of a mere Bohr or Einstein

astounds us with its power, how may we begin to extol the glory of God who created them? (Hoffmann 1959, 231)

Here we see two physicists, both of whom are using the facts of quantum mechanics, arriving at totally different conclusions about ultimate reality. According to Hawking, quantum mechanics can *eliminate* the need for a Creator; according to Hoffmann, quantum mechanics can *illuminate* the work of the Creator. Each scientist sees what he wants to see in the physical universe and interprets the facts accordingly. Does the quantum uncertainty, built into the very foundation of the universe, arise from divine prerogative, or is it evidence that the universe arose from chaos and is governed by random chance? What the scientist already believes about reality will determine how he or she answers this question.

Isaac Newton and David Hume provide another classic example of two scientists who saw the same facts through different eyes. Newton saw the handiwork of God behind the laws of gravity and motion that he discovered. In contrast, Hume, looking at these same laws, saw an impersonal, self-regulating machine that had no need for divine direction or control. It should come as no surprise, therefore, that paradigm changes in science usually have little impact upon the theism, agnosticism, or atheism of most scientists.

C. S. Lewis and Alan Guth: Blind to the Obvious

C. S. Lewis (1898–1963), famous for his work in Christian apologetics, was fond of discussing the variable character of human perception. In Lewis's first book, *The Pilgrim's Regress* (1943), the main character, John, is imprisoned by a giant called "The Spirit of the Age." During his imprisonment, John is forced to see the world as the giant sees it. Everything becomes transparent, and every time John looks at another human being, he sees beneath the skin to the blood, organs, and bone. John is freed from this gruesome vision, finally able to see his fellow humans normally, only when Reason slays the giant (58–64). In *The Great Divorce* (1946), Lewis discusses the problems that a busload of ghosts from hell might experience should they be allowed to visit heaven. Among the ghosts' complaints are that the light is too bright, the grass is too hard, and reality is too real. The ghosts do not enjoy their visit, nor do they wish to remain in heaven—they cannot "see" its majesty or beauty because of the smallness of their own interests and perceptions (1946, 26–31, 50–59).

Perhaps Lewis's clearest example of the role the mind plays in our perception of reality can be found in his Chronicles of Narnia. In the seventh book of this series, *The Last Battle* (1956), the king of Narnia and his troops are defeated in battle by the Calormenes, captured, bound, and thrown into a small stable where a monster presumably stands ready to devour them. Once inside the stable, however, they find that they are in Aslan's country (heaven). Some rebel dwarves are also captured by the Calormenes and thrown into the stable, but they are unable to see the beautiful new world into which they have fallen. Sitting in the middle of a sunlit, flower-strewn field, the dwarves huddle together, believing themselves still to be imprisoned in a dark, smelly stable. Because of their character and attitude, they can see only evil in other things and other people. Despite the best efforts of others to bring them to their senses, the dwarves continue to see reality as they want to see it:

> "Oh the poor things! This is dreadful," said Lucy. Then she had an idea. She stopped and picked some wild violets. "Listen, Dwarf," she said. "Even if your eyes are wrong, perhaps your nose is all right: can you smell *that*." She leaned across and held the fresh, damp flowers to Diggle's ugly nose. But she had to jump back quickly in order to avoid a blow from his hard little fist. "None of that!" he shouted. "How dare you! What do you mean by shoving a lot of filthy stable-litter in my face? There was a thistle in it too. It's like your sauce! And who are you anyway?" (1956, 145)

Because science cannot provide us with absolute truth, our interpretation of the limited facts we do have available is very much subject to our preexisting desires, beliefs, and attitudes. Our senses become filters that allow certain types of information to pass into our minds but selectively screen out other types of information. If a person is given to unbelief, as soon as one barrier to faith is dismantled (such as the clockwork universe), he or she will erect a new one (such as the quantum universe). If a person is given to belief, models and paradigms of the universe may change, but the handiwork of God is ever present and apparent. In this sense, we are all self-made individuals; we believe only what we want to believe. As the cartoon character Popeye might say, "I am whats I am, and I believes whats I wants to believe."

Perhaps the most blatant example of this attitude can be found in scientific discussions concerning the creation of the universe. One of the fundamental tenets of Judaism and Christianity is that God created the universe. Many scientists, however, have been unable to accept the idea that this vast cosmos, composed of billions upon billions of galaxies that stretch out to the very edge of space and time, could have been created by an intelligent, self-conscious being. Humanity has now reached the point in its scientific sophistication—or godlikeness—that we have begun to speculate about not only how the universe came into existence but also how we ourselves might create such a universe. Alan Guth, the creator of the inflationary model of the universe, suggests that our universe may be someone else's experiment:

> "You might even be able to start a new universe using energy equivalent to just a few pounds of matter," Guth suggested, in a 1987 interview. "Provided you could find some way to compress it to a density of about 10^{75} grams per cubic centimeter, and provided you could trigger the thing, inflation would do the rest." And if *we* could do it, so, perhaps, could someone else have done it long ago. "For all we know," said Guth, who had a gift for the laconic statement of radical ideas, "our own universe may have started in someone's basement." (Ferris 1988, 361–62)

It is obvious, therefore, that although many scientists cannot tolerate the idea that God created the universe, they are not so intolerant in their speculations as to how humans or other alien creatures might have created such a universe—in their basement. These scientists present a picture of blind guides who "strain out a gnat but swallow a camel" (Matt. 23:24).

So long as individuals *want* to disbelieve, they will find ample support for their unbelief. From this standpoint, there can never be enough evidence (scientific or historical) to convince nonbelievers in the authenticity of the Bible. Archaeologists could discover the remains of Noah's ark, the foundation walls of Sodom and Gomorrah, and the golden ark of the covenant, but nonbelievers would still find a means to explain away such evidence. As Abraham said to the rich man in hades who wanted to return to earth to warn his brothers, "If they do not listen to Moses and the Prophets, they will not be convinced even if someone rises from the dead" (Luke 16:31). Someone did indeed rise from the dead, but unbelief has not abated from the earth. We continue to see what we want to see and believe what we want to believe—at least for the present.

Problems with Hearing

Andrei Linde and Carl Sagan: Missing the Message

As discussed in chapter 13, Russian cosmologist Andrei Linde developed a model of creation called "chaotic inflation." His model states that new universes are constantly "budding off" from our universe in a process that he called "eternal inflation." Linde speculated that an advanced civilization might learn to control this process, thereby gaining control of creation itself. He also recognized the apparent futility of such an effort:

> Like Alan Guth and several other cosmologists, Linde liked to speculate on the feasibility of creating an inflationary universe in a laboratory. But only Linde asked: Why would one *want* to create another universe? What purpose would it serve? Once some cosmic engineer created a new universe, it would instantaneously dissociate itself from its parent at faster-than-light speeds, according to Linde's calculations. No further communication would be possible. (Horgan 1996, 101)

Why, indeed, bother creating a universe if you immediately lose the potential for future contact or control of that universe? Linde's answer to this problem was that perhaps such godlike engineers might also be able to weave into the very fabric of each new universe a message that clearly stated who had created it. Any intelligent life that might arise in this new universe would eventually discover the signature of the creator(s) clearly stamped on the laws and forces that governed the universe. In like manner, an artist signs his name at the bottom of a painting, thereby ensuring that, even if he loses contact with his creation, strangers and even future generations will always know that this work is his creation. Linde speculated about such a message having been encoded into our universe:

> In fact, Linde suggested, our own universe might have been created by beings in another universe, and physicists such as Linde, in their fumbling attempts to unravel the laws of nature, might actually be decoding a message from our cosmic parents. Linde presented these ideas warily, watching my reaction. Only at the end, perhaps taking satisfaction in my gaping mouth, did he permit himself a little smile. His smile faded, however, when I wondered what the message imbedded in our universe might be. "It seems," he said wistfully, "that we are not quite grown up enough to know." (Horgan 1996, 101)

Cornell astronomer Carl Sagan also suggested the dream of finding a message from the creator embedded in the fabric of the universe. In his science fiction novel *Contact*, Sagan's primary character is a brilliant female astronomer named Eleanor Arroway. Like Sagan himself, Arroway is an atheist, simultaneously repelled by the anti-intellectualism of many Christians but still attracted to religion through the mystery and grandeur of the universe that she is studying. While discussing religion with a popular minister named Palmer Joss, Arroway expresses her frustration with the apparent discrepancies between what we find in Scripture and what scientists find in science:

> What I'm saying is, if God wanted to send us a message, and ancient writings were the only way he could think of doing it, he could have done a better job. And he hardly had to confine himself to writings. Why isn't there a monster crucifix orbiting the Earth? Why isn't the surface of the Moon covered with the Ten

Commandments? Why should God be so clear in the Bible and so obscure in the world? (1985, 170)

In the last chapter of Sagan's *Contact,* titled "The Artist's Signature," Arroway discovers that God has indeed left a clear message embedded in the fabric of the universe. Using a supercomputer to analyze pi, she discovers that by using Base 11 arithmetic (which can be written out entirely as zeros and ones), "Hiding in the alternating patterns of digits, deep inside the transcendental number, was a perfect circle, its form traced out by unities in a field of noughts" (430). Here was clear evidence that the very geometry and mathematics that scientists use to study the universe are themselves formed by the hand of God:

> The universe was made on purpose, the circle said. In whatever galaxy you happen to find yourself, you take the circumference of a circle, divide it by its diameter, measure closely enough, and uncover a miracle—another circle, drawn kilometers downstream of the decimal point. There would be richer messages farther in. It doesn't matter what you look like, or what you're made of, or where you come from. As long as you live in this universe, and have a modest talent for mathematics, sooner or later you'll find it. It's already here. It's inside everything. You don't have to leave your planet to find it. In the fabric of space and in the nature of matter, as in a great work of art, there is, written small, the artist's signature. Standing over humans, gods, and demons, subsuming Caretakers and Tunnel builders, there is an intelligence that antedates the universe. The circle had closed. She found what she had been searching for. (430)

Carl Sagan and Paul the Apostle: Dreams versus Reality

It is unfortunate that Carl Sagan was never personally able to make the discovery that his fictional character, Eleanor Arroway, makes. For Sagan, the discovery of divine meaning in the universe remained an elusive dream. Near the end of his life, while discussing his recurring fight with cancer in a chapter titled "In the Valley of the Shadow," Sagan wrote,

"I would love to believe that when I die I will live again, that some thinking, feeling, remembering part of me will continue. But as much as I want to believe that, and despite the ancient and worldwide cultural traditions that assert an afterlife, I know of nothing to suggest that it is more than wishful thinking" (1997, 214).

The Bible states that the message about which Linde theorized and of which Sagan dreamed does indeed exist—not only in written form but also impressed upon the very structure of the physical universe—if we choose to hear the message: "For since the creation of the world God's invisible qualities—his eternal power and divine nature—have been clearly seen, being understood from what has been made, so that men are without excuse" (Rom. 1:20). In a subsequent passage, the apostle Paul writes about the judgment of God: "For God does not show favoritism. All who sin apart from the law will also perish apart from the law, and all who sin under the law will be judged by the law" (Rom. 2:11–12). God could not be a just God and be willing to punish people who did not have access to His written revelation—unless He had also provided an equally clear, nonverbal revelation of Himself that was available to all humanity. The previous passage from Romans states clearly that God has indeed written His signature upon the universe that He created. Therefore, because of the dual nature of God's revelation, *all* of humanity is "without excuse" (Rom. 1:20). Nonetheless, as Jesus said, "Though seeing, they do not see; though hearing, they do not hear or understand" (Matt. 13:13). The problem lies not with the existence or clarity of the message, but with one's willingness to hear and understand that message.

Problems with Interpreting

Hugh Ross and Robert Jastrow: Finding Evidence of Design

Many scientists who have not allowed their biases to blind and deafen them to the facts have found clear evidence of God's eternal power and divine nature embedded within the structure of the physical universe. Perhaps the most striking form this evidence takes is that of purposeful design. The idea that the universe, the galaxy, the solar system, the earth, life upon the earth, and the human mind all arose by random chance and therefore have no real meaning staggers the human imagination. Yet, this very belief has been repeated over and over again for many years in many scientific textbooks.

Many ideas are initially appealing to the human mind simply because they are so foreign to common sense. Such radical ideas present a challenge; it takes strenuous effort to believe in them. Nevertheless, many scientists have prided themselves in believing the unbelievable and condemning the rest of society for not placidly following their example. As the White Queen boasted to Alice in Lewis Carroll's *Through the Looking Glass,* "Why, sometimes I've believed as many as six impossible things before breakfast" (1946, 76).

Merely because some ideas are difficult to believe does not necessarily mean that they are false—or true. The problem with many of our theories and ideas is that we fail to carry these lines of thought to their logical conclusions. Many radical ideas can easily be shown to be untrue or nonsensical if their implications are fully considered. For instance, the statement "All things are relative" is self-negating because that statement, by its own definition, must be relative—and therefore no more worthy of belief than any other statement. Similarly, the belief that "All things arose by chance" is also self-negating and therefore illogical. If all things are due to chance, then even the formulation of thoughts in the human mind can be explained by the random movements of electrical charges back and forth between the neurons of the brain. In such a nondirected process, one randomly generated thought—such as "All things arose by chance"—can have no more claim to validity than any other randomly generated thought—such as "I am really a toast and cheese sandwich." Therefore, if one were to embrace totally the idea of random chance, all human ideas would lose their significance, and rational thought would cease to exist; the created idea would destroy its creator—the mind. In other words, some ideas seem to be mental cul-de-sacs. Perhaps God has placed a limit on how far we can follow certain lines of unproductive thought.

Christian astronomer Hugh Ross has been cataloging the various lines of evidence for purposeful design in the physical universe. In his book *The Creator and the Cosmos* (1993), Ross identifies no less than twenty-six physical parameters that must fall within extremely limited ranges in order for life to exist anywhere within the universe (118–21). He identifies another thirty-three parameters that must be precisely set for life to be possible on the earth (138–41). The viable range of variation among some of these parameters is exceedingly minute. As Ross notes, "Three different characteristics of the universe must be fine-tuned to better than one part in 10^{37} for life of any kind to exist" (118). As seen in chapter 13, one of the factors that stimulated Alan Guth to develop inflation theory was the "flatness problem." This problem centers on the fact that the critical density of the universe at the big bang could not have deviated by more than one part in 10^{59}; otherwise, the universe would have expanded too slowly or too rapidly for life to appear. Thus, science has found repeatedly that the statistical probabilities for life arising by chance in the universe are ridiculously low. These "problems," however, are only problems to those who want to believe that both life and the universe arose by chance.

Many astronomers and physicists have not missed the implications inherent in the fine-tuning of the universe. Ross has noted, "The discovery of this degree of design in the universe is having a profound theological impact on astronomers" (1993, 121). He goes on to cite examples of a number of scientists who have reached out to touch the exquisite fabric of creation and have ended up thinking in terms of a Creator. In *The Symbiotic Universe,* astronomer George Greenstein briefly ponders the signature of God in the universe:

> As we survey all the evidence, the thought insistently arises that some supernatural agency—or, rather, Agency—must be involved. Is it possible that suddenly, without intending to, we have stumbled upon scientific proof of the existence of a Supreme Being? Was it God who stepped in and so providentially crafted the cosmos for our benefit? (1988, 27)

For every scientist who has reached out to examine the apparent design in nature and ended up—like Adam in Michelangelo's painting *The Creation of Adam* in the Sistine Chapel—touching the finger of God, many more have been puzzled by what they have touched or have immediately turned away from such contact. In the previous quotation from

The Symbiotic Universe, for example, George Greenstein quickly dismisses his musings on purposeful design as "illusory."

Another instance of an astronomer (astrophysicist) who had a close encounter with God is Robert Jastrow. Jastrow was so moved by the evidence that the universe had a beginning (i.e. the big bang), he wrote a book titled *God and the Astronomers.* The evidence that inspired him to write this book, however, did not persuade him to abandon his own agnosticism (1978, 11). Instead, he suggested that the discovery of the big bang in the twentieth century was, for many astronomers, very much like a bad dream come true.

Many astronomers, like Jastrow, had rejected the biblical account that God created the universe. They went off in search of a scientific explanation for the universe—perhaps the universe was eternal, it had always been and it always would be. Therefore, it was quite a shock for many agnostic and atheistic astronomers when they found strong evidence that the universe did indeed have a beginning—just as the theologians had been saying. To make matters worse, scientists also found that, because the density, energy, and temperature of the universe reach infinity at the big bang, the laws of physics begin to break down as the moment of Creation is approached. Therefore, scientists were not only wrong about the universe not having a beginning, they could not even study that beginning with their scientific tools. As Robert Jastrow laments,

> Now we would like to pursue that inquiry farther back in time, but the barrier to further progress seems insurmountable. It is not a matter of another year, another decade of work, another measurement, or another theory; at this moment it seems as though science will never be able to raise the curtain on the mystery of creation. For the scientist who has lived by his faith in the power of reason, the story ends like a bad dream. He has scaled the mountains of ignorance; he is about to conquer the highest peak; as he pulls himself over the final rock, he is greeted by a band of theologians who have been sitting there for centuries. (115–16)

It is sad, however, that many astronomers have not rushed forward with open arms to greet their theological counterparts as the evidence for a beginning, or other evidences of purposeful design, have become clear. Instead, they have found ingenious ways to maintain their former beliefs in spite of the evidence.

Robert Dicke and Brandon Carter: Explaining Away Design

Perhaps one of the most popular theories that astronomers have devised to explain away the evidence for purposeful design in the universe is the anthropic principle. This principle simply states that if the universe had not been suitable for life, we would not be here to talk about it. Life exists in the universe because conditions were such that life was possible. Robert Dicke (1916–1997) was one of the first astronomers to apply this principle to the evidence for design in cosmology. In a paper titled "Dirac's Cosmology and Mach's Principle" (1961), Dicke "pointed out that the number of particles in the observable extent of the Universe, and the existence of Dirac's famous Large Number Coincidences '*were not random but conditioned by biological factors*'" (Barrow and Tipler 1986, 16). According to John Gribbin, however, cosmologists did not really become interested in this concept until the mid-1970s, "when the British researcher Brandon Carter drew a distinction between the 'weak anthropic principle' and the 'strong anthropic principle'" (Gribbin 1996, 24).

Precise definitions of the two basic forms of the anthropic principle are given by John Barrow and Frank Tipler in a book titled *The Anthropic Cosmological Principle* (1986):

Weak Anthropic Principle (WAP): The observed values of all physical and cosmological quantities are not equally probable but they take on values restricted by the requirement that there exist sites where carbon-based life can evolve and by the requirement that the Universe be old enough for it to have already done so. (16)

Strong Anthropic Principle (SAP): The Universe must have those properties which allow life to develop within it at some stage in its history. (21)

In other words, the Weak Anthropic Principle argues that there had to be times and places within the physical universe where the forces and laws of the universe were compatible with the appearance of life; otherwise, we would not be here.

> On this picture, an infinite universe might be separated into "domains" which have different laws of physics. These domains might be separated from one another in space, beyond the range of our telescopes, or in time—in some sense, perhaps, "before" the Big Bang. Or they might exist in some extradimensional superspace, connected by *wormholes*. Life forms like us would exist only in domains where stars lived long enough for complex creatures to evolve, and where other conditions were, like baby bear's porridge, "just right." (Gribbin 1996, 24–25)

The Strong Anthropic Principle argues that the entire universe had to be structured such that the forces and laws of the universe were compatible with the appearance of life; otherwise, we would not be here.

> The strong version of the anthropic principle suggests that the Universe had no choice about how it emerged from the Big Bang, and is in some sense "tailor made" for humankind. Some physicists, notably John Wheeler, have linked this to ideas from quantum physics, which suggest that nothing is real unless it is observed—that is, that the physical reality of our Universe depends on the presence of intelligent observers who notice its existence, and that this ensures that the fundamental interactions and the constants of nature, such as the strength of gravity, have the values we know. (Gribbin 1996, 25)

Both of these principles are based on the assumption that physical forces and laws that govern this universe (or the visible portion of this universe) *could* have been otherwise. In another universe, the strong nuclear force could have been a bit weaker, or the weak nuclear force could have been a bit stronger. Had these forces been even slightly different, life might not have been possible.

Of all of the possible universes that could exist (each having its own unique set of laws and forces), only certain types of universes would be compatible to life as we understand it. In a universe with only two spatial dimensions, for instance, a being that possessed a digestive tract would be cut in half by this structure (Hawking 1988, 164); in a universe with more than three spatial dimensions, electron and planetary orbits would be unstable, so atoms and planetary systems could not exist (Barrow 1994, 132). A universe in which the force of gravity was slightly stronger would briefly inflate out of a singularity and then collapse rapidly back upon itself—long before life had the opportunity to make its appearance. A universe in which the force of gravity was slightly weaker would inflate so rapidly that matter would be dispersed as a vapor across space; it would never condense into planets, stars, and galaxies. This phenomenon is often called the "Goldilocks Effect": one universe is too hard, another universe is too soft, and only one universe is just right—ours! (Gribbin 1996, 25).

Based on the preceding observations, astronomers with agnostic or atheistic beliefs are able to look at the evidence for purposeful design in creation and say, "But of course the laws and forces governing this universe seem to have been marvelously crafted to meet the unique needs of living creatures! Had this universe (or this part of the universe) not been structured in a manner compatible to life, humans would not be here to make these observations. In other words, the universe is as it is because we are as we are." A fundamental linkage exists between the presence of life in the universe and the physical character of that universe.

Perhaps the anthropic principle is news to twenty-first-century humanity, which has become accustomed to thinking of life as a Darwinian struggle for survival and has become used to seeing the universe as an inhospitable place that humans are able to make amenable to their needs by sheer willpower or technological sophistication. Our forefathers, on the other hand, whose lives were more closely tied to nature, might not have been as impressed by the anthropic principle. To them, this principle might have seemed little more than stating the obvious. Even John Gribbin (1996, 24) notes that this principle comes perilously close to being a tautological argument (one that is "true by virtue of its logical form alone" [*Merriam Webster's Collegiate Dictionary*, 11th ed., s.v. "tautologous"]).

Scientists have often attacked Christians as being intellectually unsophisticated in their explanations of the physical world. They argue that one of the most common Christian responses to the mysteries of nature is simply, "The universe is as it is because God created it so—case closed!" In other words, the only one who needs to know about such things is God Himself; humans should mind their own business and not go probing into the secrets of the Deity. Scientists rightly point out that such an attitude is not only stifling to the inquiring mind but also would, if widely adopted, sound the death knell for all scientific research and inquiry. Many scientists, however, fail to recognize that exactly the same criticism can be applied to the anthropic principle. The response of many scientists to evidence for purposeful design in nature is simply, "Of course the universe is marvelously adapted to life; if it weren't, we wouldn't be here!" In other words, "The universe is as it is because chance created it so—case closed!" If scientists approached all mysteries in the physical universe thus, the death knell for all scientific research and inquiry would just as surely sound. As Sir Fred Hoyle (1915–2001) notes, the anthropic principle "is a modern attempt to evade all implications of purpose in the Universe, no matter how remarkable our environment turns out to be" (1983, 217–18).

Under close scrutiny, the anthropic principle does not seem to offer much enlightenment about the nature of the universe. One might suspect, in fact, that advocates of this approach are more interested in justifying their particular belief systems than in searching for the answers to the mysteries of the universe. Through their discovery of purposeful design in the cosmos, many astronomers might have literally reached out and touched the Truth but failed to recognize it as the Truth. "The light shines in the darkness, but the darkness has not understood it" (John 1:5).

Purposeful Design in the Macrouniverse

How is it possible that humans can even begin to understand the processes of Creation and perhaps emulate some of those processes? Many of science's greatest minds have pondered this question:

"The most incomprehensible thing about the Universe is that it is comprehensible" is one of the best known of Einstein's sayings—it has become a cliché. He meant by it that the basic physical laws, which our brains are attuned to understand, have such broad scope that they offer a framework for interpreting not just the everyday world but even the behavior of the remote cosmos. (Gribbin and Rees 1989, 284)

If the universe is only a chance occurrence, "the ultimate free lunch," then it is indeed miraculous that the human mind can at least partially understand the structure of that universe. On the other hand, if a Creator purposefully designed the universe, and if we ourselves are created in the image of that Creator, then it is not too surprising that the structure of the universe is somewhat understandable to us. From this perspective, perhaps it is forgivable if, occasionally, as we discover ever more about the beautiful symmetry and logical structure of the universe, we are overwhelmed with such a strong sense of empathy with our Creator that we are inclined to say, "If I were God, I would have made the universe in exactly the same way!" We, being thinking beings, can recognize the work of another thinking being. The juxtaposition of the logical structure of our minds and the logical structure of the universe provides irrefutable evidence of purposeful design; it is the signature of the Creator written large across the face of His creation.

IGNORING THE
BIOLOGICAL EVIDENCE

THE FIELDS OF ASTRONOMY and cosmology are not the only scientific areas where new evidence of purposeful design has surfaced recently. Nothing in the physical universe is more complicated than life. Truly, we know more about the internal working of distant stars and galaxies than we know about the human mind. If the complex structure of the cosmos (which makes life possible) suggests purposeful design, it should not be surprising that the far more intricate structure of the life that inhabits this cosmos provides even clearer evidence of intelligent manufacture. Purposeful design has, in fact, long been an issue in the field of biology. Many biologists see this evidence as not just a bad dream but a bad dream that keeps recurring.

Throughout the ages, humans have looked at their own physical bodies and been amazed at the complexity residing therein. King David, for example, was moved to exclaim, "I praise you because I am fearfully and wonderfully made; your works are wonderful, I know that full well" (Ps. 139:14). Perhaps the most famous advocate of purposeful design in nature was William Paley (1743–1805). In 1802 Paley published his most famous work, *Natural Theology*, in which he pointed out various lines of evidence for purposeful design in nature. His most famous evidence for intelligent creation is the intricate design of the human eye—a clear example, he believed, of the hand of God at work: "As far as the examination of the instrument goes, there is precisely the same proof that the eye was made for vision, as there is that the telescope was made for assisting it. They are made upon the same principles; both being adjusted to the laws by which the transmission and refraction of rays of light are regulated" (1854, 13).

Since the 1859 publication of Charles Darwin's *On the Origin of Species*, evolutionists have expended a great deal of effort in attempting to show that natural selection, not a divine Creator, is responsible for the uniqueness of adaptation and the complexity of design in all living things. Nearly one hundred fifty years after Paley's book was first published, evolutionists are still trying to explain how evolution produced the human eye. Richard Dawkins, for example, one of the most popular modern exponents of evolution, discusses this problem in his books *The Blind Watchmaker: Why the Evidence of Evolution Reveals a Universe Without Design* (1987) and *River Out of Eden: A Darwinian View of Life* (1995). These explanations usually take this form: "Although natural selection cannot produce the human eye in a single large step, it can produce the human eye in a series of small steps." In other words, by merging simple, preexisting structures into more complex forms, natural selection can eventually produce organs as intricate as the human eye. As a recent textbook, *How Humans Evolved*, explains,

> An eye is only useful, it is claimed, once all parts of the complexity are assembled; until then, it is worse than no eye at all. After all, what good is 5% of an eye? Darwin's answer, based on the many adaptations for seeing or sensing light that exist in the natural world, was that 5% of an eye *is* often better than no eye at all. It is quite possible to imagine that a very large number of small changes—each favored by selection—led cumulatively to the wonderful complexity of the eye. (Boyd and Silk 2000, 17)

The authors then go on to discuss various types of "eyes" that are found in nature, from the light-sensitive cells in the eye pit of a limpet, to the lens eyes of the Atlantic dog whelk. Based on these examples, Boyd and Silk argue that there are various ways of "seeing," from very simplistic structures (such as the limpet), to extremely complex structures (such as the human eye). Therefore, nature clearly demonstrates that 5 percent of an eye (i.e., very primitive forms of vision) may indeed be better than no vision at all (Boyd and Silk 2000, 17–18).

Michael Behe: Finding Evidence of Design

Despite the ingenuity of their explanations, every time evolutionists think the issue of purposeful design in biology has finally been laid to rest, new evidence appears. In *Darwin's Black Box: The Biochemical Challenge to Evolution* (1996), Michael Behe argues that late twentieth-century biochemistry has discovered evidence for "irreducible complexity" at the molecular level of life. When Charles Darwin was formulating his theory of evolution, the discoveries of Gregor Mendel (1822–1884) in heredity were still unknown to most scientists. When the synthetic theory of evolution was developed in the 1930s, effectively merging Darwin's theory of evolution with modern genetics, the field of biochemistry had not yet been developed. Behe argues that throughout the history of biology, there have always been "black boxes" that have remained unopened, secrets of life that have remained beyond the reach of science. Although biologists could see the external manifestations of various processes, the internal workings of these processes remained a mystery. In this state of ignorance, evolutionists could always assume that complex structures, such as the human eye, could have arisen through the process of natural selection. Natural selection, by favoring the retention of more-adaptive traits over less-adaptive traits, could—over long periods of time—lead to the transformation of earlier, quite primitive structures into later, more complex forms (such as the human eye).

At the end of the twentieth century, however, Behe pointed out, biochemistry successfully opened the last black box of biology. Biologists are now able to understand the workings of life at the molecular level. Because molecules are made of atoms (the building blocks of both the organic and the inorganic worlds), no deeper level exists to which biologists can descend; they have finally reached the ultimate foundation of life. Now that they have opened this last black box and allowed the searing light of science to penetrate into its inner recesses, what have biologists found? According to Behe, they've found that the fundamental building blocks of life are molecules, and that these molecules are, themselves, highly complex machines. Because molecules are built of atoms, no structures of intermediate complexity exist from which they could have evolved. Consequently, these molecular machines display irreducible complexity. Their existence cannot be explained in terms of Darwinian natural selection. Therefore, Behe believes that these molecular machines provide irrefutable evidence of purposeful design: "The result of these cumulative efforts to investigate the cell—to investigate life at the molecular level—is a loud, clear, piercing cry of '*design!*' The result is so unambiguous and so significant that it must be ranked as one of the greatest achievements in the history of science" (1996, 232–33).

It is interesting, however, that when the evidence for intelligent design began to emerge from their studies of the cell, few biologists were ready to shout their discovery from the housetops. Indeed, as Behe points out, no celebrations accompanied this major scientific discovery:

> But no bottles have been uncorked, no hands slapped. Instead, a curious, embarrassed silence surrounds the stark complexity of the cell. When the subject comes up in public, feet start to shuffle, and breathing gets a bit labored. In private people are a bit more relaxed; many explicitly admit the obvious but then stare at the ground, shake their heads, and let it go at that. (1996, 233)

Biologists were no more elated to find evidence for intelligent design than astronomers were to find evidence that the universe had a beginning. In both cases, the religious implications were only too clear for those who had struggled to build a wall between scientific truth and religious truth.

Although Behe believes that the molecular complexity that underlies the structure of life provides clear evidence that life was created by intelligent design, he has no illusions that this discovery will have a significant impact on the religious perceptions of his biology colleagues. As he points out, "No scientific theory can compel belief in a positive religious tenet by sheer force of logic" (1996, 247). Certainly the theory posited in the early twentieth century that the universe had a definite beginning in the big bang did not lead most astronomers to a religious conversion (at least initially). Therefore, the recognition of intelligent design in biology should prove no great threat to scientists who wish to retain their agnosticism or atheism. Instead, unbelieving biologists, like their astronomy colleagues, will undoubtedly find ways to explain the evidence for intelligent design in life without having to invoke the name of God. Before examining some of these alternative explanations, however, one other line of biological evidence for purposeful design should be discussed.

Charles Lyell and Charles Darwin: The Early Appearance of Life

Biological evidence for purposeful design in nature can be found in not only the irreducible complexity of the molecular building blocks of life but also the rather abrupt appearance of life upon the earth. Most evolutionists, from Darwin's time onward, believed that life could have arisen on the earth through natural processes—given enough time. This idea is often illustrated by the argument that a room full of monkeys, banging away at random on typewriters, could, if given enough time, produce the entire works of Shakespeare—completely by chance (Dawkins 1987, 46). The key qualifier necessary for either of these highly unlikely events ever to occur is, of course, "given enough time."

Although Charles Darwin could not, in the later half of the nineteenth century, assign a specific date to the age of the earth, he was aware of the great vistas of time that geologists were beginning to discover in the geological record. One of the books that Darwin took with him on his famous voyage aboard the HMS *Beagle* was Charles Lyell's book *Principles of Geology* (1868). In that book, Lyell popularized many of the ideas of James Hutton (1726–1797), who is known as the father of modern geology. Hutton is most famous for two concepts: (1) the principle of uniformity—rocks and landforms of the earth were formed by slow, uniform processes acting over vast periods of time; and (2) the statement that, in the geologic record of the earth, "We find no vestige of a beginning, no prospect of an end" (Tarbuck and Lutgens 1994, 312). Darwin came to believe that the diversity of life on the earth could also be explained in terms of slow, uniform "biological" processes acting over vast periods of time.

Darwin's theory of evolution has at least three basic levels:

microevolution (genetic variation within a species), macroevolution (the genetic transformation of one species into another), and random genesis (the creation of life from inorganic matter). Few people, of whatever religious persuasion, disbelieve in microevolution—if they understand the definition. Humans have been manipulating genetic variation in plants and animals since the Agricultural Revolution, which began nearly ten thousand years ago. Breeding plants and animals for certain desirable traits is a fact of life—just as the building of machines has been a fact of life for the past two hundred fifty years. Macroevolution is more controversial because the evidence is much less abundant, complete, or precise. Random genesis, however, is the most speculative of the three levels of evolution and is the most subject to attack. Behe's argument for purposeful design was not aimed at microevolution or macroevolution but directly at random genesis.

Growing evidence against random genesis can be found in not only the field of biochemistry but also the field of paleontology (the study of fossilized plants and animals). Geologists who study fossils believed initially that life first arose in the Cambrian Period, approximately 570 million years ago. During this period an explosion of life occurred in the primeval oceans of the world, with a diversity of invertebrates filling the various aquatic niches. All the rocks that are older than the Cambrian Period were initially called "Precambrian" and were thought to be totally devoid of life. Yet, as scientific tools and research techniques became more sophisticated and we began to examine the Precambrian rocks in more detail, we found evidence of still earlier life forms. Paleontologists began slowly to move ever deeper into the past, first finding fossils that are six hundred million years, then seven hundred million years, and then a billion years old. Today, the oldest fossils acknowledged by most paleontologists are at least 3.5 billion years old. These fossils, called stromatolites, look like irregularly shaped cauliflowers and are composed of alternating layers of clay and silt, intermingled with layers of prokaryote cells from bacteria and blue-green algae.

Ancient stromatolite fossils are significant because they are composed of cells that are more advanced evolutionarily than some prokaryote cells still alive on the earth today. The prokaryote cells in stromatolites were able to produce their own food through photosynthesis (the transformation of light, air, and water into energy). Some of the more primitive prokaryotes that are alive on the earth today, however, produce their own food through fermentation rather than photosynthesis. Other, still more primitive living prokaryote cells cannot produce their own food; they must rely on naturally occurring compounds found in their environment. Because Darwinian evolution postulates that simple organisms evolved into more complex organisms, the 3.5-billion-year-old photosynthesizing prokaryotes of the stromatolites obviously must have evolved from still more primitive prokaryotes that either produced food through fermentation or were unable to produce food at all. Therefore, the origins of life likely go back farther than the oldest stromatolites. Currently, the oldest possible evidence for life on the earth is 3.8 billion-year-old trace fossils called carbon spheres that contain isotopic ratios of carbon that are normally produced only by organic processes. Scientists, however, have not yet found fossils of the organisms that produced these carbon spheres.

Although the date for the earliest appearance of life on the earth has continued to recede into the past, the same has not been true for the age of the earth itself. No longer can we rest in Hutton's view that geology presents us with "no vestige of a beginning, no prospect of an end" (Tarbuck and Lutgens 1994, 312). Based on radioactive elements found in moon rocks and meteorites, the age of the solar system (and the earth) has repeatedly been dated to approximately 4.6 billion years old. As long as life on earth was believed to have originated in the Cambrian Period, some 570 million years ago, evolutionists had a comfortable window of opportunity, over four billion years wide, in which anything might happen—including highly improbable events such as the appearance of life from inorganic matter. As the date for the appearance of life began to be pushed back, however, this window of opportunity began to shrink. If carbon spheres do indeed represent the presence of life on the earth at 3.8 billion years ago, then the window of opportunity for random genesis was only eight hundred million years wide. Many astronomers believe, however, that the first six hundred million years of earth's history was marked by repeated meteor strikes as the earth (like the other planets) swept up most of the stray debris within its orbit. Any primitive forms of life appearing on the earth between 4.6 billion and 4 billion years ago likely were snuffed out by these repeated impact catastrophes. Therefore, the window for random genesis to occur may have been only two hundred million years wide (rather than four billion years wide). Consequently, it is looking more and more likely that as soon as life was possible on the earth, life appeared.

To some scientists who have contemplated deeply the complexity of life, the likelihood of living cells, each composed of a vast number of complex molecular machines, being generated by chance in such a short time frame is no longer a viable option. Sir Fred Hoyle and Chandra Wickramasinghe have estimated that the likelihood of random chance producing all 2,000 enzymes that make life possible on the earth is only 1 chance in $10^{40,000}$ (1981, 24). When this figure is compared with the 1 in 10^{59} chance of the universe having just the right mass so that it didn't expand too quickly or too slowly (Krauss 1989, 137), or the 1 in 10^{37} chance that three other parameters in the physical universe were fine-tuned just enough for life to be possible (Ross 1993, 118), biologists clearly are faced with an even greater dilemma than their colleagues in astronomy. Both the physical conditions necessary for life to exist and the actual presence of life itself provide clear evidence for purposeful design in nature rather than random chance.

Although the discovery of such strong evidence for purposeful design in biology might logically seem to point directly toward a Creator, many biologists, though somewhat disquieted, remain unconvinced. Some scientists have begun to construct theories that can explain both the irreducible complexity of organic molecules and the early appearance of life on the earth without using random genesis or divine creation. Some of these recent theories are based more on science fiction than scientific fact. Indeed, many scientists seem to be willing to believe in just about anything rather than acknowledge the existence of a divine creator.

Francis Crick and Fred Hoyle: Explaining Away Design

Francis Crick (1916–2004) was a scientist who probed deeply into the mysteries of life. In 1962, Crick, James Watson, and M. H. F. Wilkins shared the Nobel Prize in Medicine for their discovery of the double helix structure of DNA—the genetic code of life. Because of his detailed knowledge of the complexity of the genetic code, Crick has not been particularly impressed by current evolutionary theories that attempt to explain how random genesis might have led to the appearance of life upon the earth. In *Life Itself: Its Origin and Nature*, Crick suggests, "An honest man, armed with all the knowledge available to us now, could only state that in some sense, the origin of life appears at the moment to be almost a miracle, so many are the conditions which would have had to have been satisfied to get it going" (88).

Although he is not opposed to the idea of random genesis, Crick argues that science presently does not have enough information to determine whether the appearance of life on the earth through natural processes is a likely or an unlikely event. He does not, however, allow these doubts to lead him into speculations about a divine creator. Most scientists, Crick believes, have gone beyond such "myths of yesterday" (1981, 164). Instead, he reasons that "if it turns out that it [life] was rather unlikely, then we are compelled to consider whether it might have arisen in other places in the universe where possibly, for one reason or another, conditions were more favorable" (88). If, though, life arose by random genesis outside the solar system rather than within it, then scientists must also explain how life subsequently reached the earth. Crick believes that the early appearance of complex cells on the earth may have been the result of some alien civilization's attempt to "seed" other solar systems with primitive forms of life. This nontheistic alternative to random genesis occurring upon the earth is called "directed panaspersia."

Directed panaspersia allows scientists such as Francis Crick to explain the growing evidence for purposeful design in biology. Instead of God, the creator becomes alien beings that lived on distant planets. Absolutely no scientific evidence for alien civilizations exists, of course, unless one believes in unidentified flying objects (UFOs). Most scientists, however, relegate accounts of UFOs and alien encounters to the realm of science fiction or pseudoscience. On the other hand, Christianity and Judaism, which Crick dismisses as "myths of yesterday," are solidly grounded in historical people and events. The Old and New Testaments, as well as church history, provide detailed historical documentation of God's dealings with real people in real time. Nevertheless, Crick apparently is more comfortable thinking in terms of an extraterrestrial creator than a supernatural creator.

Directed panaspersia does not resolve the problem of how complex organic molecules could have arisen through random genesis. It simply removes this problematic event from the earth and assumes that it occurred somewhere else in the vastness of space and time (Crick 1981, 142).

Given the great age of the universe (ten to fifteen billion years old), Crick speculates, there would have been ample time for life to arise through random genesis and then begin to spread itself across the universe:

> There is enough time for life to have evolved not just once, but *two times in succession*. In short, the time available would allow for life to have started on some distant planet formed nine billion years ago, for creatures like ourselves to have developed four to five billion years later and for them to have then sent some simple form of life to the earth, which by that time had cooled to the stage when the primitive oceans had already formed. (1981, 116)

Now, some 4.6 billion years later, the simple life forms that were introduced into earth's environment have evolved into an advanced civilization that is itself taking its first steps toward the exploration and possible colonization of other planets and solar systems.

In the latter chapters of *Life Itself*, Crick even speculates about what type of simple life forms might have been sent into space by this alien civilization (chap. 11: "What Would They Have Sent?") and what type of space ships they would have used (chap. 12: "The Design of the Rocket"). He concludes that, because of the distances and dangers involved in space travel, very primitive life forms such as bacteria would have stood the best chance of survival (1981, 124–29). The types of spacecraft used to carry these bacteria into space were probably small, unmanned craft propelled by solar sails (139–40). Once these spacecraft had carried their cargo of bacteria to a suitable planet—a planet, by the way, with the thirty-three finely tuned parameters necessary for life, which Hugh Ross identified—these primitive life forms might then have evolved into another advanced civilization, as they had previously done through random genesis on the home planet.

Although Francis Crick's model of directed panaspersia offers an alternate explanation for the evidence of purposeful design found in biology, it does not address the evidence for purposeful design found in astronomy. Sir Fred Hoyle, in collaboration with Chandra Wickramasinghe, developed an even more elaborate form of directed panaspersia that attempts to address the evidence for purposeful design in both biology and astronomy.

Sir Fred Hoyle was a cosmologist and astrophysicist at Cambridge University in England. He is most famous for his collaboration with Hermann Bondi and Thomas Gold in the development of a model of the universe called the steady state theory. That theory postulated that the universe had no beginning; it has existed throughout all of eternity. Hoyle, Gold, and Bondi explained the expansion of the universe, which Edwin Hubble had discovered, as arising from the spontaneous and continuous creation of small amounts of matter throughout empty space. Most astronomers eventually abandoned the steady state theory as the evidence for the big bang theory continued to accumulate. Hoyle is also famous for his model of the nuclear synthesis of heavier elements in stars. He developed his theory in conjunction with W. A. Fowler, Geoffrey Burbidge, and Margaret Burbidge. During the latter part of his career, Hoyle gained fame (or notoriety) for his work with Chandra Wickramasinghe on the extraterrestrial origins of life.

Hoyle and Wickramasinghe have written four books about the origin of extraterrestrial life: *Lifecloud: The Origin of Life in the Universe* (1978), *Diseases from Space* (1979), *Evolution from Space: A Theory of Cosmic Creationism* (1981), and *Our Place in the Cosmos: The Unfinished Revolution* (1993). Hoyle has also written an overview of his understanding of the existence of life in the universe, *The Intelligent Universe* (1983). As was noted at the beginning of this section, Hoyle thinks that the chances of life appearing on the earth through random genesis are just about nil—1 chance in $10^{40,000}$ (Hoyle and Wickramasinghe 1981, 24). Like Behe, Hoyle arrived at this conclusion by examining the complexity of life at the molecular level:

All of life (and death) could be seen, it was claimed, to spring from natural causes. With the development of microbiology in the second half of the twentieth century it became overwhelmingly clear that the truth is quite otherwise. Biochemical systems are exceedingly complex, so much so that the chance of their being formed through random shuffling of simple organic molecules is exceedingly minute, to a point indeed where it is insensibly different from zero. (Hoyle and Wickramasinghe 1981, 2–3)

In *The Intelligent Universe*, Hoyle is even more explicit about the failure of random genesis to explain the appearance of life on the earth: "As biochemists discover more and more about the awesome complexity of life, it is apparent that the chances of it originating by accident are so minute that they can be completely ruled out. Life cannot have arisen by chance" (1983, 11–12). Hoyle is so impressed by the evidence for purposeful design in biology that he completely rejects the Darwinian idea that life could have arisen on the earth by chance. Unlike most scientists, Hoyle is quite explicit about his opposition to Darwinian evolution: "If on occasions in this book my opposition to the Darwinian theory has seemed fierce, it is because of my feelings that a society oriented by that theory is very likely set upon a self-destruct course" (245).

Hoyle, however, like Crick, does not allow the evidence of purposeful design in biology to lead him to a recognition of God—or at least the God of the Bible. He notes in the last chapter of *The Intelligent Universe*, "I am not a Christian, nor am I likely to become one as far as I can tell" (1983, 251). Instead, Hoyle also invokes the theory of directed panaspersia to explain the evidence for design that science has inadvertently uncovered.

Hoyle's theory of directed panaspersia goes well beyond Crick's idea of advanced alien civilizations seeding distant solar systems with simplistic forms of life. Instead of a single superior civilization, Hoyle hypothesizes that the universe may contain a large number of superior intelligences. All of these beings (including humans) are linked in a "connecting chain of intelligence" (1983, 244–46). These beings not only live in the universe, but are directly involved in both its maintenance and its very existence:

Instead of an introverted picture with man crowded in on this particular planet, a prisoner confined to a tiny corner of the solar system, itself but a speck in our galaxy and our galaxy but a speck in the Universe, we have an open picture with life spread throughout the heavens, and quite possibly with life controlling much of what happens everywhere throughout the Universe. (250)

Hoyle believes that evidence for purposeful design found in biology can be directly attributed to a more advanced but "intermediate" intelligence. These beings might have come to recognize the inevitability of their own demise in the cosmos but, determined to perpetuate their own existence through a "deliberate act of creation" (1983, 226), they encoded their knowledge and very being into a new form of life that was carbon based. These purposefully designed molecules of carbon had the potential, given the right conditions, to someday evolve into self-aware, intelligent beings (such as ourselves). As Hoyle notes, "We are the intelligence that preceded us in its new material representation—or rather, we are the re-emergence of that intelligence, the latest embodiment of its struggle for survival" (239).

Hoyle goes on to suggest the existence of still higher forms of intelligence than the intermediate beings that were responsible for the creation of carbon-based life. These higher-level intelligences are probably responsible for the other lines of evidence for purposeful design that astronomers and physicists are discovering within the physical laws that govern the universe. These laws regulate everything from atoms to the expansion of the universe and must be fine-tuned to one part in 10^{37} or one part in 10^{59} if life is to be possible on earth or anywhere else in the universe.

At the very top of Hoyle's hierarchy of intelligence is a being that approaches "the Judaeo-Christian idea of a deity outside the Universe" (1983, 249). Hoyle describes this being as "The overriding intelligence in the infinite future, which masterminds the development of intelligence in our present time" (248). Unlike the God of the Bible, however, Hoyle's deity is constrained by its own creation. This being is so closely tied to its creation that it "must exercise its controlling influence simply in order to exist" (248). Should this god cease to govern and intervene in the universe, it would itself cease to exist; "God is the universe" (Hoyle and Wickramasinghe 1981, 143). In the end, Hoyle's pantheistic god is quite unlike the God of the Bible, who stands apart from the space-time universe that He created; the Judaeo-Christian God is a God who governs His creation, but is in no way constrained by it.

Purposeful Design in the Microuniverse

The theories of directed panaspersia that Crick and Hoyle have developed are good examples of how far scientists will go to avoid acknowledging the God of Abraham, Isaac, and Jacob. The message from God that Sagan longed for, and about which Linde theorized, is indeed written across the face of creation in the clear, bold letters of purposeful design! It is a tragic failing that many scientists fail to see or hear this message. Other scientists who are more sensitive perceive the message, but then they immediately attempt to explain it away by creating "cleverly invented stories" (2 Peter 1:16) such as the anthropic principle or directed panaspersia. That such eminent scientists as Crick and Hoyle could endorse these ideas shows clearly how strong is the scientific bias against the very idea of God.

To those scientists whose senses have not been impaired by an overriding belief in random chance, the evidence for purposeful design is quite abundant. As scientists grow ever more sophisticated in understanding the physical universe, the logical structure of the universe becomes ever more apparent. As scientists continue to unlock nature's secrets, they are beginning to catch glimpses of how and why God created the universe as He did. Some scientists are beginning to recognize that the machines that humans can build are far inferior to the machines that are found in nature. Compare, for example, computers to DNA. Now that binary codes have been developed for the storage of massive amounts of information in our computers, we can more fully appreciate the far superior information storage capability of the DNA code that contains the blueprints for all life forms upon the earth. As Ehud Shapiro, a professor at the Weizmann Institute of Science in Israel, has noted, "The living cell contains incredible molecular machines that manipulate information-encoding molecules like DNA and RNA in ways that are fundamentally very similar to computation." The information storage capacity of DNA, however, is far superior to any computer that humans have ever built: "It [DNA] can hold more information in a fifth of a teaspoon than a trillion CDs" (Reuters 2001).

By the late 1990s, a few scientists were suggesting that we might be able to build truly "super" computers if we used DNA code rather than the binary code (Adleman 1998). By late 2001, scientists announced that they had made the first tentative steps toward achieving that goal (Benenson et al. 2001). Nevertheless, one of the scientists involved in this project, Ehud Shapiro, had to admit, "Since we don't know how to effectively modify these machines or create new ones just yet, the trick is to find naturally existing machines that, when combined, can be steered to actually compute" (Reuters 2001).

One of William Paley's most famous arguments for design in his book on *Natural Theology* (1854) was an analogy between a watch and a living organism. Palely argued that, if a man found a watch lying in a field, opened the back, and saw the complex mechanisms within, he would not think that the watch had arisen by chance. So too, when we look at the internal complexity of living organisms, it is obvious that the organism did not arise by chance.

David Hume, however, attacked Paley's argument on the basis that it was not a strict analogy—a living organism is not a machine. Hume's claim is no longer valid. Today, microbiology has shown that the cells of living organisms are actually composed of numerous tiny machines. Indeed, human technology has now advanced to the point at which attempts are being made to build similar microscopic machines—but with only limited success. As Ehud Shapiro noted above, in order to build DNA computers, we are borrowing the miniature machines of life (that God designed), because they are far superior to the miniature machines that humans can design. Hume could hardly have asked for a stricter analogy than this: the tiny organelles within the cell are not *like* machines, they *are* machines.

It has been more than two hundred and fifty years since the Industrial Revolution began. Since that time, humans have made all kinds of machines in various shapes and sizes and for various purposes. It is probably safe to say, then, that most humans in industrialized countries know a machine when they see one. Therefore, the continued refrain of many scientists that complex biological structures, such as molecular machines and the DNA code, arose purely by chance is becoming a bit tiresome. Scientists who are dedicated to seeking the truth should be willing to follow truth wherever it leads, and then readjust their theories to fit the new truths they discover.

CHAPTER 16

THE WAGES OF WILLFUL IGNORANCE

SCIENTISTS ARE FINDING THAT the distortion of their perceptions and their fabrications to replace truth exact a price. As noted in chapter 5, since the time of Francis Bacon, science has been an experiential rather than a philosophical discipline. Scientists have taken pride in their empiricism, relying entirely on their senses to study the physical universe. As David Hume once boldly stated, anything that cannot be apprehended by the five senses is "nothing but sophistry and illusion" (Hume 1975, 165). What happens, though, when perceptions become insensitive? What happens when the secular public continually witnesses scientists using the same sensory data to arrive at totally different conclusions?

What happens is that the secular public and scientists themselves, without science to provide absolute truth, without a Higher Power as a source of absolute truth, begin to question the existence of truth itself. They begin to ask, as Pontius Pilate asked Jesus prior to sentencing him to be crucified, "What is truth?" (John 18:38). This collective loss of faith in the existence of absolute truth has led modern culture to turn to another, new philosophy of life—a philosophy positing that *all* cultural practices have equal value and are equally acceptable. This new philosophy, which is growing in popularity, is cultural relativism.

Franz Boas and Melville Herskovits: Cultural Relativism

The modern concept of cultural relativism first arose in anthropology, the scientific discipline that focuses on human beings. Within anthropology are three major subfields:

Anthropology

1. *Cultural anthropology:* the study of the beliefs, practices, and material culture of living peoples;
2. *Archaeology:* the study of the beliefs, practices, and material culture of peoples no longer living;
3. *Physical anthropology:* the study of the human body (its phenotype, genotype, and evolutionary history).

The father of American anthropology was Franz Boas (1858–1942). Born in Germany, Boas immigrated to the United States in 1888. He eventually settled in New York and held dual appointments, teaching anthropology at Columbia University and working for the American Museum of Natural History. Many of his students at Columbia subsequently became famous anthropologists, including Margaret Mead, Ruth Benedict, Melville Herskovits, and Alfred Kroeber. Among his many accomplishments, Boas is often credited with developing the concept of cultural relativity.

Boas was particularly interested in studying the native cultures of North America. During the course of his research, Boas found that many of the beliefs and practices of Native Americans were radically different from those of Europeans. From the perspective of Western civilization, many of the manners and customs of native peoples seemed to be silly or were morally repugnant. Because native cultures were rapidly disappearing under the onslaught of Western civilization, however, Boas taught his students that they could not afford the luxury of making judgments about the cultures they were studying. Anthropologists needed to collect as much information about these disappearing cultures as possible and not waste time prejudging which elements of these cultures were good or bad, valuable or useless. Boas believed that anthropologists must learn to temporarily suspend their own personal values and beliefs while doing fieldwork. They must attempt to understand each culture in terms of its own ideas and standards. This fieldwork technique became known as cultural relativism.

An idea that might be good and profitable in one setting might, however, cause great harm when misapplied to other situations. This happened with cultural relativism. Many anthropologists were so proud of the open-minded attitude they had developed for doing fieldwork that they wanted to share the merits of this approach with the broader public. Terms such as *ethnocentric, cultural bondage,* and *xenophobic* were applied not only to other anthropologists who failed to adhere to a relativistic stance during their fieldwork but also to anyone who failed to adopt this approach when dealing with people in other cultures. Consequently, cultural relativism eventually spread from anthropology into society and was thereby transformed from a field technique into a general philosophy of life. Herskovits focuses on the tolerance inherent in cultural relativism:

> For cultural relativism is a philosophy which, in recognizing the values set up by every society to guide its own life, lays stress on the dignity inherent in every body of custom, and on the need for tolerance of conventions though they may differ from one's own. Instead of underscoring differences from absolute norms that, however objectively arrived at, are nonetheless the product of a given time or place, the relativistic point of view brings into relief the validity of every set of norms for the people whose lives are guided by them, and the values these represent. (1948, 76)

To many cultural relativists, anyone—scientist or citizen—who takes exception to the beliefs or practices of another culture, or suggests that some cultural practices or beliefs are superior or inferior to others, is obviously a narrow-minded bigot or racist. Such individuals are doubtless deficient in their mental and moral development and are, therefore, held up to public censure or scorn. Much of the political correctness movement in the 1990s grew out of this philosophy of cultural relativism.

Although cultural relativism had great value as a technique of anthropological fieldwork, its adoption by the masses has had disastrous consequences for the secular public as well as for scientists. If all values, beliefs, practices, and customs are totally relative to the culture in which they occur, then the whole concept of absolute truth is a delusion. Science, recall, claimed to have the lock on absolute truth. But under cultural relativism, one idea or theory is just as true as any other—it all depends on your cultural frame of reference. The only absolute left standing is the statement "All things are relative."

To the perceptive person, this statement is, of course, self-negating. If all things are relative, then so is the statement "All things are relative." No more reason exists to believe or disbelieve the statement—"All things are relative"—than exists to believe or disbelieve the statement "All things are absolute." Cultural relativists are forever trapped in this fundamental inconsistency.

Consequently, it is not difficult to understand why the thinking of cultural relativists is often fuzzy. They will attempt to obliterate every trace of Christianity from American society, while at the same time adamantly defending the rights of atheists, anarchists, and Neo-Nazis to express their views publicly. They will castigate all history, literature, and science as being poisoned by male, patriarchal bias while at the same time they themselves are exhibiting the most blatantly sexist attitudes (i.e., men are chauvinist pigs). For practicing cultural relativists, truth has meaning only within the context of the personal beliefs and ideas they want to advance. Anything that runs counter to their personal opinions is obviously racially or sexually biased. It is nearly impossible to reason or debate with those who have taken such a stance; they are totally oblivious to the inconsistency of their position.

Henry Bagish and Allan Bloom: Abandonment of Absolutes

Even some anthropologists have begun to recognize the deleterious effects of cultural relativism on society. In "Confessions of a Former Cultural Relativist" (1990), Henry H. Bagish bemoans the fact that college students are losing the ability to make value judgments: "I find students generally very reluctant to judge anyone's behavior, to evaluate it in any way. Most of them resist saying that anyone else's ideas or behavior are *wrong,* or *bad.* One student said recently in class that he doesn't even use the words 'good' or 'bad'—it's all relative" (31). Allan Bloom, in his controversial book *The Closing of the American Mind: How Higher Education Has Failed Democracy and Impoverished the Souls of Today's Students* (1987), makes a similar observation:

> There is one thing a professor can be absolutely certain of: almost every student entering the university believes, or says he believes, that truth is relative. If this belief is put to the test, one can count on the students' reaction: they will be uncomprehending. That anyone should regard the proposition as not self-evident astonishes them, as though he were calling into question $2 + 2 = 4$. (25)

Bagish believes that this situation has resulted largely from two erroneous conclusions that have been drawn from cultural relativism: (1) the belief that "all cultural practices are equally *valid*"; and (2) the belief that "all cultural practices are equally *worthy of tolerance and respect*" (1990, 34). As to the first erroneous conclusion, Bagish argues that most anthropologists, faced with a life-threatening infection, would not argue that a witch doctor would be just as effective as antibiotics. Therefore, he counters the idea that *all cultural practices are equally valid* with what he calls his "pragmatic principle": "That which *works* is 'better' than that which *doesn't* work. Or more accurately, when people are given a choice, that which *works better,* to *achieve certain valued ends,* is what most people end up choosing, most of the time" (34).

Regarding the belief that *all cultural practices are equally worthy of tolerance and respect,* Bagish points out that, again, few anthropologists would be willing to sanction such activities as wife-burning, headhunting, or genocide as being morally relative to the culture in which they occur. To remedy this situation, Bagish suggests a "hierarchy of values" in which tolerance is not necessarily the supreme value—as most avid cultural relativists seem to believe. In the case of human slavery or torture, for instance, "compassion for my fellow humans" might outweigh my "tolerance and respect" for other cultural practices (1990, 36). For a former cultural relativist, these ideas are not a bad beginning, but are still a long way off from affirming that there are absolute truths that must govern our beliefs and behaviors. To pre-twentieth-century peoples, untainted by modern cultural relativism, Bagish's pragmatic principle (that which works is better than that which doesn't) and his hierarchy of values (some values are more important than others) would have seemed glaringly obvious to both the educated and the uneducated masses—but not today.

Max Horkheimer and Theodor Adorno: Critical Theory

The extreme impact that cultural relativism can have—on both scientific and historical truth is perhaps best exemplified in the work of the Frankfurt School of critical theory. Founded in 1924 in Frankfurt, Germany, the Institute for Social Research was set up for the express purpose of studying the history of socialism and the labor movement, as well as the propagation of Marxist philosophy. After Max Horkheimer became the director of the institute in 1931, the school began to exert a wider influence on society. Like Comte and the logical positivists, Horkheimer was interested in merging various scientific disciplines into a unified whole. In particular, he advocated the integration of philosophy (particularly Marxist philosophy) and social science. He believed that all human societies could best be understood in terms of Marxist explanations.

Despite the Marxist orientation of the Frankfurt Institute, Horkheimer was not willing to adopt every aspect of orthodox Marxist philosophy. Instead, he and his followers were selective as to which aspects of Marxism they used in their study of society. This hybrid form of Marxism came to be known as critical theory. In part, this term was used to camouflage or disguise the Marxist underpinnings of the school, but it was also meant to distinguish the Marxism of the Frankfurt School from the orthodox Marxism of that time (Wiggershaus 1994, 5). Members of the Frankfurt School believed that, although the main ideas of Marxism were basically true, there was nonetheless room for improvement. Critical theory would correct and perfect historical Marxism, thereby expediting the spread and adoption of this philosophy by societies around the world.

The early Marxist idealism of the Frankfurt School was badly damaged by World War II. Because many members of the school were Jewish, they had to flee Germany to survive the Holocaust. After the war ended, the Iron Curtain descended around Russia and Eastern Europe, and the Cold War between communism and capitalism began. The communist reign in the Soviet Union became more and more repressive, deviating sharply from the socialism envisioned by the Frankfurt School. On the other hand, capitalism in the West seemed more firmly entrenched than ever. The school's bright hope that socialism would march triumphantly from one culture to another began to fade. This growing disillusionment among members of the Frankfurt School marks the second phase in the development of critical theory: "This skepticism regarding the emancipatory potential of science as a whole during this period led them [the Frankfurt School] to abandon the former goal of an empirical, scientific interdisciplinary research program and to focus their theoretical attention increasingly on cultural and aesthetic criticism" (Hunter 1993, ix).

The growing skepticism of the Frankfurt School during the period from 1940–1950 is clearly seen in the *Dialectic of Enlightenment* (1972), which was published by Horkheimer and his colleague, Theodor W. Adorno. In this book, they attempt to show how, by a "dialectical twist," the Enlightenment, which had attempted to use rational thought as a vehicle for freeing humanity from the bondage of religious and political domination, was itself transformed (by capitalism) into a means for further subjugating nature and humanity. Therefore, although the leaders of the Frankfurt School no longer believed they could significantly alter the continued disintegration of Western civilization under capitalism, they could at least document and criticize the processes by which this domination was occurring.

Based on its Marxist orientation, critical theory attempts to examine the mechanisms of control by which capitalism has come to dominate nature and humanity in Western civilization. It attempts to "explain how a person, group, or society has come to be engaged regularly in practices that, in fact, are not in his, her, or its interest, as a result of some feature of that society" (Braaten 1991, 10–11). Karl Marx argued that religion is "the opium of the people" (1977, 64). He suggested that religious beliefs that promise heavenly rewards for submission to earthly rulers are like powerful drugs that can be used to keep the proletariat—workers/employees—docile in the face of oppression by the bourgeoisie—owners/employers. The Frankfurt School argued that it is not just religion but all aspects of Western society—including science—that act to keep the oppressive system of capitalism in power. Poster sets forth the premise of Frankfurt School texts:

> Workers, now considered "the masses," were viewed as manipulated, depoliticized, and reconciled to capitalist values by all aspects of popular culture. Jazz, astrology columns, sports, television, consumer goods generally—the entire panorama of leisure and daily life since World War II—narcotized and numbed the working class. The Frankfurt School presented a monochromatic picture of mass culture in which a dubious functionalist analysis operated. A unified and mystifying intention to disrupt the class struggle stood behind every manifestation of the culture industry. The discourse of the Frankfurt School staged contemporary life as a parody of crude capitalist greed and stupid working-class gullibility. (Poster 1989, 2)

Therefore, according to critical theory, everything about society—including science, art, and religion—has an ideological role that legitimizes the position of those in power. Following this line of reasoning, they argue that (1) ancient cultures had different absolute truths than modern cultures, (2) industrialized cultures have different absolute truths than agrarian cultures, and (3) Eastern cultures (India, China, etc.) and Native American cultures have different absolute truths than Western cultures (Europe, America, etc.). Absolute truth is always relative to the culture in which it occurs. Change the power structure of a society, and you will inevitably change the truths that the masses believe in.

Marxism has always had a strong element of cultural relativism running through it. Marx was a materialist; he believed the material world was the driving force behind all human beliefs and behaviors. He and his followers argued that the framework of human culture (social organization, trade, law, etc.) is built on the foundation of economic production—how material goods are produced for human consumption.

Covering the framework of culture is a roof of philosophy and religion that helps to maintain the integrity of the structure. The roof, however, is always relative to the framework, and the framework is always relative to the foundation—that is, you can't build a house by starting with the roof. According to Marx, religion and philosophy are always relative to the society in which they occur and can subsequently be swept aside as irrelevant. The critical theorists expanded the cultural relativism of Marx to include all aspects of culture—including science.

P. K. McCary and Karen Armstrong: The Rise of Subjectivism

The little spark of cultural relativism that Marx ignited and the Frankfurt School fanned into critical theory has become a wildfire that threatens to engulf all cultures and societies, whether they are capitalistic, socialistic, or of some other political persuasion. Individuals in non-Western societies are now arguing that Western philosophies and beliefs—including Marxism—are themselves products of subjectivism, biased by the cultures out of which they grew. Larry J. Zimmerman explains that some Native Americans now dismiss archaeological reconstructions of the prehistory period as the biased imaginings of the White Man:

> University of Arizona anthropologist J. Jefferson Reid believes that Native Americans see archaeological accounts of their past as a threat to traditional, Indian accounts of that same past. They fear that the archaeological version eventually will replace the traditionally constructed past and their culture, once again, will be eroded. Indians told Reid, during a recent archaeological conference, that the archaeology of the Southwest had no relevance for southwestern Indians; in their view "... archaeology was only relevant to other archaeologists." (Zimmerman 1994, 65, 67)

Feminists are conducting a similar critical analysis of world literature, history, science, and religion. They have identified numerous examples of what they consider to be patriarchal, subjective bias and male chauvinism. The Bible has been a major target for such sexist attacks. During a ten-part PBS series titled *Genesis: A Living Conversation,* hosted by Bill Moyers, "P. K. McCary, the author of an Old Testament storybook aimed at black youth, dismisses the whole biblical episode [Abraham's willingness to sacrifice his son Isaac] as an exercise in patriarchal machismo. 'I don't think God would have asked the same of [Abraham's wife] Sarah,' she says, 'knowing what her answer would be'" (Woodward 1996, 78). During the same series, another so-called religious scholar attempted to implicate God for displaying what Stephen Jay Gould might call "species bias":

> In a discussion of Noah and the Flood, what seems like straightforward punishment for a world turned radically evil becomes an occasion for rejecting a God who would resort to such an extreme measure. Karen Armstrong, the British author of one new interpretation of Genesis, blames God for "behaving in an evil way." He destroys not only sinners but also "animals who haven't done anything wrong at all." (Woodward 1996, 78–79)

These examples illustrate that, with critical theory, all things are subject to attack and revision. The world of knowledge becomes a wasteland of shifting sand with no fixed landmarks. The interpreter alone plays the role of god, free to create his or her own subjective reality from a constantly changing kaleidoscope of unconnected facts.

Critical theorists believe that all knowledge is culturally biased. They point out that the rich and powerful in a society (the bourgeoisie) exert a strong influence over the businesses and industries, schools and churches, and media and entertainment of that society. Critical theorists argue that the bourgeoisie use this influence to interpret and manipulate facts to their own personal advantage, thereby helping them maintain their positions of power and privilege. Taken in its extreme form, critical theory says that culture is nothing more than stories and lies that the elite feed to the masses, the better to control them. Whereas Marx taught that religion is the opiate of the masses, critical theorists believe that the entire culture acts as a drug. They hold that "all knowledge is historical, distorted communication, and that any claims to seek 'objective' knowledge are illusory" (Renfrew and Bahn 1996, 464). Therefore, one might argue that critical theory is the ultimate conspiracy theory—*everyone* in a position of power is out to get you.

One of the logical flaws in critical theory is that if *all* knowledge is subjective and culturally biased, then the knowledge that critical theory attempts to convey must *also* be subjective and culturally biased. Special interest groups using critical theory seem to believe that they should be permitted to critique all of the beliefs and practices of others without themselves being critiqued. They can fault other groups and cultures for their failings while many of their own pronouncements are blatantly biased (e.g., all whites are evil, all Christians are hypocrites).

In the final analysis, critical theory is a vicious, cyclical game that has no end. If all knowledge is subjective and culturally biased, then critical theorists and other special interest groups have no more solid ground upon which to stand than the worst bigot; they are simply promoting their own biases. Concepts such as scientific and nonscientific, truth and falsehood, objective and subjective, sacred and profane are all equally meaningless. All of these so-called philosophical debates about cultural, historical, and literary bias degenerate into nothing more than a naked struggle for power with no moral high ground whatsoever. In such circumstances, the strongest and most aggressive are usually the victors. Darwinian "survival of the fittest" becomes social reality.

The growing popularity of cultural relativism and critical theory provides strong evidence that our senses have indeed become dulled. Critical theory/cultural relativism/subjectivism is an intellectual cancer that threatens to destroy the very fabric of logical thought. Yet many scientists have failed to recognize the symptoms of this potentially fatal disease. Rather, some scientists have worried publicly that religion may be dragging science into a new dark age (Asimov 1983, 5–15). In reality, scientists have far less to worry about from the religious right than from the nonreligious left.

If science, religion, and philosophy are the primary avenues by which humans have sought truth down through the ages, what happens to these disciplines if critical theory and cultural relativism continue to spread and humanity completely abandons its belief in absolute truth? It is an old maxim that a person who disbelieves everything will eventually fall for anything. The philosopher Paul Feyerabend certainly demonstrated this principle of relativism as he rejected the traditional teachings of science, philosophy, and religion, while championing the cause of alternate forms of understanding, such as magic, mysticism, and the occult (1978, 295, 298–299). "Falling for anything" may ultimately be the price that all humanity will have to pay if we continue to reject absolute truth and embrace philosophies such as cultural relativism and critical theory.

Part 4 of this book discussed the problems related to the cultural limitations of scientific truth, the problems of science as history, science as literature, science as propaganda. Critical theory has used many of these same problems to argue that there is no absolute truth. There is great danger in this argument, and Christians must take great care that in their zeal to discover the limitations of scientific truth they do not follow the critical theorists into the black hole of relativism. It is one thing to recognize one's limitations in apprehending absolute truth; it is quite another thing to argue that there is no absolute truth.

One must tread carefully, then, that narrow path that lies between the abyss of relativism (there is no absolute truth) on the left and the chasm of scientism (scientific truth is absolute truth) on the right. It is far easier to fall into one of these two extremes than it is to balance on the narrow divide that lies between them. Christ expects us to follow that narrow path by keeping our eyes firmly fixed on Him, who is Truth: "Enter through the narrow gate. For wide is the gate and broad is the road that leads to destruction, and many enter through it. But small is the gate and narrow the road that leads to life, and only a few find it" (Matt. 7:13–14).

Scientific Subjectivity

The willful dulling of perceptions, which part 6 has documented, provides one last example of the limitations of scientific knowledge. Modern science seeks truth by means of the scientific method, which relies on observation and experimentation to test hypotheses and to formulate laws. The senses are the windows through which scientists acquire facts about the physical universe, but if their senses are dulled, how can scientists see clearly? Our senses are governed by our minds, and too often we see what we want to see, hear what we want to hear. Once again, *facts do not speak for themselves; they must be interpreted!* Despite their desire for objectivity, scientists, like all mortals, are prone to subjectivity in their interpretation of empirical observations. This is not to say that scientists can't rise above subjectivity, but it is an ever-present liability.

The reality, of course, is that some scientists have indeed interpreted facts in a subjective manner, especially with regard to issues relating to religion or a belief in the supernatural. Some scientists have ignored or perverted the empirical evidence of purposeful design that God has written across the face of His creation. The resulting variability in the interpretation of empirical data among scientists has made a significant contribution to the growing popularity of cultural relativism and critical theory, both inside and outside academic circles.

If science is determined to apprehend absolute truth, then scientists should expect to find some surprises along the way. If the God of the Bible is indeed the Creator of the universe, then science will find, if it ever approaches absolute truth, that its truths converge with the truths of Christianity. The God who revealed Himself through Christ and the Scriptures is also the God who reveals Himself through purposeful design in the physical universe. C. S. Lewis, speaking from his own experience as a former atheist, noted in his book *Surprised by Joy*, "A young man who wishes to remain a sound Atheist cannot be too careful of his reading. There are traps everywhere—'Bibles laid open, millions of surprises,' as Herbert says, 'fine nets and stratagems.' God is, if I may say it, very unscrupulous" (1955, 191).

A scientist attempting to understand the structure of the physical universe may be in no less danger of conversion than if he or she were sitting down to read the Bible for the first time. Many scientists—such as Dicke, Greenstein, Jastrow, Crick, and Hoyle—have been able to avoid the fate of C. S. Lewis only by ignoring their senses or by creating anthropic principles and elaborate tales of alien civilizations or extraterrestrial intelligences to explain away the clear evidence of purposeful design in the physical universe. Such "close encounters" with the Almighty must surely be unnerving experiences for confirmed agnostics and atheists. Perhaps a similar experience led Francis Thompson to write "The Hound of Heaven":

> I fled Him, down the nights and down the days;
> I fled Him, down the arches of the years;

I fled Him, down the labyrinthine ways
Of my own mind; and in the mist of tears
I hid from Him, and under running laughter.
Up vistaed hopes I sped;
And shot, precipitated,
Adown titanic glooms of chasmed fears,
From those strong Feet that followed, followed after.
But with unhurrying chase,
And unperturbèd pace,
Deliberate speed, majestic instancy,
They beat—and a Voice beat
More instant than the Feet—
"All things betray thee, who betrayest Me."

([c. 1888] 1946, 101)

PART 7

THE HUMAN QUEST:
FINDING TRUTH

Jesus answered, "I am the way and the truth
and the life. No one comes to the Father
except through me."
—John 14:6

CHAPTER 17

AN ALTERNATE MODEL

OF SCIENCE

HUMANS HAVE THREE BASIC avenues for finding truth: science, philosophy, and religion. In the past, religion or philosophy was thought to provide the superior pathway to truth. Today, many people believe that scientific truth is not only superior to religious or philosophical truth but also is the *only* truth. This book has shown the inaccuracy of this belief, documenting some of the major limitations of science in arriving at absolute truth. Those areas include temporal, logical, cultural, spatial, and empirical limitations.

Absolute truth, however, is not a mirage; it is the ultimate goal toward which science, philosophy, and religion are oriented. Merely because science and philosophy have not yet arrived at absolute truth has no bearing on whether such truth actually exists. Indeed, the very existence of these disciplines and their striving after truth is strong evidence that absolute truth does exist. Fred Hoyle has argued that one of the most important evidences for the purposeful design of life is the instinct, or hard wiring of the human brain, that causes us to search continually for truth. The codeveloper of the theory of evolution, Alfred Russell Wallace, described the instinct as "a mysterious sanctity whereby truth is invested as the highest of virtues" (Hoyle 1983, 250–51).

Indeed, many scientists have a vision of absolute truth—pure and perfect, shining in the darkness just beyond their reach. Many Christians, however, have a similar vision of God, the perfect embodiment of absolute truth. Thus, while scientists understand absolute truth as a goal, Christians understand absolute truth as a Person—the ultimate meaning of the universe can be found only in the Creator of the universe.

Science, then, is but one manifestation of humanity's quest for absolute truth—not the ultimate acquisition of absolute truth. Because scientific truth is constantly changing, it cannot be absolute truth. Because modern science is not absolute truth, it must contain a mixture of truths and nontruths. This situation arises, in part, because of the limitations that have already been discussed. Whether science can someday overcome these limitations and arrive at absolute truth is certainly open to debate. What cannot be debated is the current incomplete (nonabsolute) state of modern scientific knowledge.

People often ask scientists who are Christians, "How can you be a scientist and a Christian when many scientific theories contradict the Bible?" A Christian can be scientist if he or she understands the limitations of scientific knowledge and the current transitory nature of scientific truth. From that perspective, it is natural to expect numerous discrepancies between the perfect truth of God's revelation and the imperfect truths of current scientific understanding.

What, then, should be the Christian's attitude toward science—since scientific truth is not absolute truth, since scientific knowledge is a mixture of truths and falsehoods? Should Christians simply reject all scientific understanding as irrelevant? To take this approach is akin to throwing the baby out with the bath water. Many of the facts that science has uncovered *are* truths. How we interpret these facts may change, but the facts themselves do not change—from day to day, year to year, or century to century. Such truths are a part of the absolute truth—but not its total embodiment.

A Christian who truly loves truth must accept truth wherever it is found. Nuggets of gold in the gravel of a stream are not the mother lode, but they are pieces of the mother lode. Similarly, scientific facts are not the absolute truth about the universe, but they are pieces of that truth. Therefore, to reject science is to reject not only its falsehoods but also its truths.

Science as a Tool

One way to look at science is simply as a tool. Like all tools, science can be used for great good or great evil. As a hammer can be used to build a house or to crack a skull, science can be used to make medicines or poisons, to create alloys for construction or bombs for destruction. Most of the time, however, science is neither good nor bad—it is neutral, just another tool that humans use for various purposes.

Because of its limitations, science is an imperfect tool but still a very powerful tool. The cars we drive are often far from perfect. Sometimes they are noisy, provide an uncomfortable ride over long distances, and sometimes won't start. Most of the time, however, our cars get us where we want to go. We are not about to start walking everywhere because our cars are imperfect. Similarly, science might have its limitations, but it is a vast improvement over ignorance. Although science might never be able to explain the universe completely, we still know a great deal more about the universe today than we did a thousand years ago, or one hundred years ago, or even ten years ago. We might never be able to acquire absolute truth through science, but we can certainly decrease our level of ignorance about the physical universe in which we live—as well as develop a deeper appreciation of what God has made.

It is unfortunate, though, that many Christians are only too happy to abandon science. They are like school children wanting the schoolhouse to burn down so they can have a permanent vacation from learning. The Christian's attempt to demonize science is just as foolish as a scientist's attempt to deify it.

Because we are not omniscient, humans must make decisions "to the best of our knowledge." In this context, science has a very important role to play. Scientific knowledge is neither absolute truth nor utter nonsense. While its pronouncements should not be allowed to replace the Word of God, the knowledge that it provides is nonetheless valuable. Christians are not commanded to live in ignorance. God has made us in His image. He has given us minds capable of understanding His creation. He has given us souls with an unquenchable thirst for truth. Science can provide us with innumerable opportunities to understand the world around us better. What use we make of this tool is entirely in our hands.

The Christian who by default rejects scientific knowledge embraces scientific ignorance. Other than giving a brief outline of how God created the heavens and the earth, the Bible does not give us much information about the nature of the physical universe. Therefore, when we attempt to explain anything about the universe that is not clearly spelled out in the Bible, we are dependent on a human explanation. Do you reject Einstein's model of the universe? If so, what do you substitute for Einstein's explanation—the Newtonian universe? Do you reject Newton's model of the universe in favor of Ptolemy, or do you reject Ptolemy's model in favor of the pre-Aristotelian Greeks who thought the stars and planets were gods? Whichever choice you make, you are still dependent upon humanly derived knowledge. None of these models is divinely sanctioned, nor have any of them achieved the status of absolute truth. Although Einstein's model of the universe will someday be proven to be neither complete nor perfect, it is a drastic improvement over earlier models. Therefore, lacking God's specific revelation on the subject, we are dependent on the most informed, up-to-date models that are available to us. To do otherwise is to live in willful ignorance. A little light is better than no light; limited truth is better than no truth.

Therefore, science is neither bad nor good; it is just a tool that humans use in their search for truth. In this sense, the scientific pursuit of truth seems divinely justified on two grounds: (1) God has given us minds that hunger for truth; and (2) God has structured the universe such that it is comprehensible to us. As Einstein said, "The most incomprehensible thing about the Universe is that it is comprehensible") (Gribbin and Rees 1989, 284). God also holds us accountable, however, for the use we make of this tool that He has given us. As with any tool, it is helpful to know the strengths and weaknesses that the instrument possesses. If we use a wrench for a hammer, it might break; if we use a screwdriver as a pry bar, it might bend. Science is a powerful tool, but it also has its limitations—the temporal truths of science are not superior to the absolute truth of divine revelation.

Science as a Servant

Another approach to science that attempts to factor in both its strengths and weaknesses was developed by Harry Collins and Trevor Pinch. They visualize science not as a tool, but as a servant. A tool has no volition or will of its own; if you don't pick up the tool, it just lies there and does nothing. A servant, on the other hand, is a separate being who can function and act with or without external intervention. Thus, a servant is more than a tool and has greater potentials and greater liabilities. With proper instruction, a servant can continue to work in our absence. Without good direction, however, a servant may act against our desires or best interests. Science has the same potentials and liabilities as a servant.

In *The Golem: What Everyone Should Know About Science* (1993), Collins and Pinch argue that science is like a golem:

> A golem is a creature of Jewish mythology. It is a humanoid made by man from clay and water, with incantations and spells. It is powerful. It grows a little more powerful every day. It will follow orders, do your work, and protect you from the ever threatening enemy. But it is clumsy and dangerous. Without control, a golem may destroy its masters with its flailing vigor. (1)

This image of science as a Frankensteinlike creature with great strength but small intelligence is in stark contrast to the godlike image of science that is commonly presented for popular consumption. How, then, did these two scientists arrive at this conclusion?

Following in the footsteps of Thomas Kuhn and Imre Lakatos, Collins and Pinch were primarily concerned with discovering how science actually works rather than with how it is supposed to work. To see science more clearly as it really is, they focused on periods of "controversial science," those episodes in which current scientific orthodoxy is challenged by new theories or experiments. Such periods are often marked by controversy between scientists before a consensus is finally reached. These controversies may be over individual theories (such as cold fusion versus hot fusion) or over an entire scientific paradigm (such as Newtonian physics versus Einstein's theory of relativity). According to Collins and Pinch, the manner in which these controversies are resolved gives us the clearest picture of how science actually works in the real world (1993, xiii–xiv, 114–16).

Drawing material from seven major scientific controversies (including chemical memory, cold fusion, gravity waves, and solar neutrinos), Collins and Pinch came to three interesting conclusions: (1) scientific experiments are often inconclusive; (2) scientific controversies are frequently settled by social rather than scientific factors; consequently, (3) science is more like a golem than a god (1993, xiv).

Inconclusive Scientific Experiments

The scientific experiment has been the litmus test of scientific truth since the days of Francis Bacon. Once a hypothesis has been formulated through inductive observations, it must be tested experimentally. Only thus can it be learned whether a hypothesis is true or false. A key element in the experimental method is replication: Can the results of a scientific experiment performed by one scientist be reproduced (replicated) by other scientists? If a scientific experiment actually has the power to reveal the truth or falsehood of a hypothesis, other scientists should be able to perform the same experiment and reach the same conclusion. Collins and Pinch found, however, that "Experiments in real science hardly ever produce a clear-cut conclusion" (1993, 149). This situation arises out of the natural complexity of the universe. Any scientific experiment may have a number of variables such as temperature, pressure, chemical composition, light intensity, age of specimen, length of test, sensitivity of measuring instruments, and so forth. All of these variables may influence the outcome of a scientific experiment. In addition, during periods of scientific controversy, "previously ignored minutiae become highly relevant and hotly debated" (117). As scientists continue to factor in more and more variables, the experiments become even more complex, and comparisons between experiments become even more uncertain (11–12). As a result, it is often very difficult to determine whether two experiments are identical. Have both experiments given the same weight to all the same variables?

Controversies and Social Factors

To make matters worse, during periods of scientific controversy, when alternative theories are in competition, scientists are often uncertain about what the results of an experiment actually mean. Do the results of an experiment indicate that a particular hypothesis is true or false, or do they simply indicate that the experiment itself was flawed? Collins and Pinch refer to this dilemma as the "experimenter's regress" (1993, 98). Experimenter's regress can be compared to one of Douglas Hofstadter's "strange loops" (1979, 10) in that it keeps bringing the scientist back repeatedly to the same point of indecision. In other words, if your experiment confirms your hypothesis, is it because your hypothesis is true, or is it because your experiment was flawed and failed to test your hypothesis adequately? Conversely, "Negative results could be explained away by believers [scientists who believe the hypothesis to be true] as being due to differences in the replicating experiment. To those who failed to find anything [scientists who did not believe the hypothesis to be true], however, this was simply confirmation that there was nothing to be found" (Collins and Pinch 1993, 69). Therefore, the strange loop that Collins and Pinch call "experimenter's regress" always brings the scientist back to the same position of indecision in which he or she was before the experiment was performed: Is the hypothesis true or false? The way that scientists break out of the experimenter's regress brings us to Collins and Pinch's second point, the social (subjective) component of experimental science (101).

Scientists may disagree about not only the adequacy of an experiment but also the competency of the individuals performing the experiment. Did the scientist fail to consider certain critical variables? Did the scientist neglect to perform this or that standard procedure? An attack on the competency of an experiment can easily degenerate into an attack on the competency of the experimenter because the two are closely bound (Collins and Pinch 1993, 74). Although scientists normally display to the general public a veneer of professionalism and mutual respect for each other, during periods of scientific controversy, they often drop such pretenses, put on their gloves, and give us a clearer view of how scientific decisions are often made (114–15).

One of the examples of controversial science that Collins and Pinch cite was the debate over the discovery of "gravity waves." In the early 1970s, Professor Joseph Weber built an elaborate device for detecting the gravity waves that Einstein had predicted in his general theory of relativity.

Although Weber believed his device had detected such gravity waves, other scientists had trouble replicating his results. Soon, a controversy arose between those who believed that gravity waves could be detected and those who believed that they couldn't be detected. Most of the subsequent experiments were rendered inconclusive because of the unfortunate problem of experimenter's regress. Therefore, scientists eventually made their decisions about the validity of Weber's gravity wave detector based on a variety of social rather than scientific considerations. Among the reasons that scientists cited for accepting or rejecting Weber's results were the following (Collins and Pinch 1993, 101):

1. "Faith in a scientist's experimental capabilities and honesty, based on a previous working partnership";
2. "The personality and intelligence of experimenters";
3. "A scientist's reputation gained in running a huge lab";
4. "Whether or not the scientist worked in industry or academia";
5. "A scientist's previous history of failures";
6. "'Inside information'";
7. "Scientists' style and presentation of results";
8. "Scientists' 'psychological approach' to experimentation";
9. "The size and prestige of the scientist's university of origin";
10. "The scientist's degree of integration into various scientific networks";
11. "The scientist's nationality."

In other words, scientists ultimately judged the results of Weber's experiments on not only the basis of the adequacy of the experiments themselves but also their perceptions of Weber's character and abilities. Although the experimental evidence was never conclusive one way or the other, the tide of scientific opinion was eventually turned against Weber, and the majority of scientists rejected his discovery of gravity waves.

Repeatedly in their book, Collins and Pinch demonstrate that scientific controversies are settled not on the basis of decisive experiments but on the basis of much more subjective factors (including one's nationality): "The struggle between proponents and critics in a scientific controversy is always a struggle for credibility" (1993, 74). Collins and Pinch argue, therefore, that scientists are no different from businessmen or politicians in how they reach a consensus: "The meaning of an experimental result does not, then, depend only upon the care with which it is designed and carried out, it depends upon what people are ready to believe" (42).

Therefore, in controversial situations, we often see scientists resolving their problems in much the same way as the average person—people believe what they want to believe. In the face of contrary evidence, they will find justification for ignoring the evidence. Conversely, the lack of evidence is not always perceived as a reason for abandoning a favorite belief. As Collins and Pinch point out, "No experiment is alone definitive, and loop-holes [sic] can always be found by a determined critic" (1993, 135).

Science as Golem

Collins and Pinch show that the scientific method includes a strong sociological element in its decision-making process. Scientific experiments are evaluated by other members of the scientific community who eventually reach a consensus as to whether the evidence is admissible. "In history, as in science, facts do not speak for themselves" (Collins and Pinch 1993, 54)—the scientist must interpret what the facts actually mean. Thus, the scientific method includes a strong subjective element. Collins and Pinch, however, do not believe this is a fault of science. Science is simply made up of individual human beings behaving like human beings, using both their knowledge and their biases to interpret information and arrive at conclusions (2). Consequently, "It is our image of science which needs changing, not the way science is conducted" (78). To Collins and Pinch, the correct image of science should be that of a golem rather than a god: "There is an unfortunate tendency these days for scientists writing for a popular audience to compare themselves and their subject with God. The final lesson is that science is less of a God and more of a golem" (xiv).

Science in Perspective

Science is exciting, exhilarating, and intellectually gratifying to those who practice and understand it. It does not, however, provide its followers with absolute truth. Many of the "scientific truths" that scientists believe today will be the "scientific mistakes" of tomorrow. Maintaining perspective is critical for a scientist to survive in this rapidly changing world of knowledge. Many scientists, however, become embittered as they see their life's work swept away by new theories and discoveries. If, though, scientists can maintain perspective (and humility) and view their work as only part of an unfinished dance—but not the dance itself—as the assembling together of fragments of truth—rather than the absolute truth—then they can take satisfaction in their work, even though its results may be transitory. Stephen Jay Gould advocates such an approach to science in his introduction to *The Mismeasure of Man:*

> I criticize the myth that science itself is an objective enterprise, done properly only when scientists can shuck the constraints of their culture and view the world as it really is. . . . Rather, I believe that science must be understood as a social phenomenon, a gutsy, human enterprise, not the work of robots programmed to collect pure information. I also present this view as an upbeat for science, not as a gloomy epitaph for a noble hope sacrificed on the altar of human limitations. (1981, 21)

Science is a powerful tool, a strong and compliant servant, but it has its limitations. Actor Clint Eastwood is known for the catch phrase "A man's just got to know his limitations." The same is true of the scientist: a scientist has "just got to know his limitations"—and the limitations of the scientific method. Otherwise, many scientists will spend their lives seeking that which the scientific method cannot deliver—absolute truth. They will build their houses on a foundation of sand—knowledge that is constantly shifting—and will end up mistaking golem for God, worshiping the creation rather than the Creator.

CHAPTER 18

AN ALTERNATE ATTITUDE
TOWARD SCIENCE

BECAUSE MANY CHRISTIANS DO not fully understand how science works, they feel threatened by it. Their knowledge of science is based on the popular model of science which states that: (1) scientists are completely objective; (2) the scientific method is completely rational; (3) scientific truth is superior to biblical truth; and (4) scientific truth has disproved the existence of God. In this book it has been shown that all four of these premises are false. Scientists are not—and cannot be—completely objective. They are cultural beings and are subject to the same cultural biases that bedevil all humans (chaps. 8–10). Moreover, even empirical observations are biased by personal beliefs and experiences (chaps. 14–16). The scientific method is not totally rational because it is built upon a foundation of induction. Hume has shown that this foundation is logically flawed because it is impossible to ever "prove" a universal statement that had been derived from induction (chap. 5–7). If scientific statements can't be proven, then what makes them superior to other forms of truth? Conversely, if scientists are unable to prove any universal statements, how could they possibly prove that God doesn't exist? Christians, as well as scientists, need to reject the popular model of science because it is simply untrue.

As discussed in chapter 17, many Christians, like many scientists, need to develop a new model of science—a model that takes into account both the strengths and the weaknesses of scientists and the scientific method.

Models that depict science as a tool or a servant are quite helpful in this regard. Such alternative models have the potential to free Christians from their fear of and animosity toward science. These alternative, more realistic models of science also have some important implications for the Christian.

Science Does Not Provide Absolute Truth

Christians should not get too excited about scientific claims of having found—or of eventually finding—absolute truth. While some individuals want to believe that scientific truth is absolute truth, the reality is far different. Nowhere is this more clearly revealed than by the constant flux in scientific knowledge and scientific truth. As the pace of scientific discovery continues to accelerate, the only assurance we have concerning scientific truth is that what we think we know today will likely be proven wrong tomorrow (see chapters 3 and 4).

Another impediment to science's achieving absolute truth are the boundaries that exist in the microuniverse (such as the Planck boundary) and the macrouniverse (such as Hubble's radius) (chaps. 11 and 12). The gates to the undiscovered countries on the other side of these boundaries appear to be permanently locked. Consequently, the realm of the very small and the realm of the very large hold secrets about the universe that science may never be able to apprehend.

The goal of absolute truth continues, like a rainbow, to retreat into the distance whenever scientists attempt to approach that fabled land. The deeper that science probes into the secrets of the universe, the deeper the mystery becomes. Many scientists have argued that the supernatural must be excluded from science because it can't be empirically studied. Because of quantum uncertainty, however (chap. 11), and the possible existence of hidden dimensions or multiple universes (chap. 13), significant parts of the physical universe may exist that can't be empirically studied. Should these parts also be excluded from science? Instead of a well-defined clockwork universe, a vast undiscovered cosmos stretches off into the darkness. The prospects for science obtaining absolute truth about such a universe are not bright.

Under such conditions, surely wisdom dictates that Christians—as well as non-Christians—should not invest too much faith in a discipline (science) that cannot, by its own admission, hope to resolve many of the mysteries of the physical universe. To do otherwise would be like "a foolish man who built his house on sand. The rain came down, the streams rose, and the winds blew and beat against that house, and it fell with a great crash" (Matt. 7:26–27).

Scientific Truth Is Not Superior Truth

Although scientific truth cannot be equated with absolute truth, many scientists would nevertheless argue that scientific truth is superior to biblical truth because scientists (1) focus on the (knowable) physical world, (2) rely on empirical observations, (3) generate scientific facts, (4) create hypotheses, and (5) verify their hypotheses through experimentation and further observation. This claim of scientific superiority leads some of the more vocal representatives of the scientific community to champion ideas that are clearly in opposition to what the Bible teaches. Many scientists teach, for instance, that the universe arose by chance, but the Bible states that God created the heavens and the earth. Many scientists argue that human beings are merely the result of random evolutionary processes, but the Bible reveals that humans were made in the image of God. Many scientists state that there is neither a God nor an afterlife, but the Bible promises that God will judge the nations at the end of time. Given these major differences between what many scientists teach and what the Bible teaches, it is not surprising that many Christians wonder whether scientific truth is indeed superior to biblical truth.

The popular model of science states that scientific truth is the superior form of truth. This belief has been widely disseminated among the general public. Teachers are encouraged to teach science in their classrooms, but religion is forbidden. Science textbooks, as well as secular movies, often portray religion as the great persecutor of science and free thought. But is scientific truth really superior to biblical truth? Repeatedly in the Old Testament, when the people of Israel or Judah placed their trust in false gods, they suffered for their idolatry. Perhaps the modern world's deification of scientific truth will have similar dire consequences, which is the message of the angel in the following poem:

He turned blue at the wingtips and disappeared as another
    angel approached me.
This one was quietly but appropriately dressed in cellophane,
    synthetic rubber and stainless steel,
But his mask was the blind mask of Ares,
    snouted for gas-masks.
He was neither soldier, sailor, farmer, dictator
    nor munitions-manufacturer.
Nor did he have much conversation,
    except to say,
"You will not be saved by General Motors
    or the pre-fabricated house.
You will not be saved by dialectic materialism
    or the Lambeth Conference.
You will not be saved by Vitamin D
    or the expanding universe.
In fact,
    you will not be saved."
                  —Stephen Vincent Benét (1936, 75)
                     "Nightmare, with Angels"

On the other hand, if scientific truth is *not* superior to biblical truth, then the recognition of this fact should have a liberating effect on the lives of many believers. Many Christians would no longer need to live in doubt, perhaps secretly wondering if scientists do indeed have an inside track on the truth. They would no longer have room in their hearts for the constant fear that someday science might make a discovery that would absolutely and irrevocably prove there is no God.

The good news is that scientific truth is not superior to biblical truth. Not only are scientific truths incomplete and subject to constant revision, but each element in the scientific process has been found to have significant problems. Although science only studies the physical universe, scientists no longer believe that all aspects of that universe are knowable (chaps. 11–13). Empirical observations are not always objective, they are often interpreted according to subjective beliefs and experiences (chaps. 14–16). Throughout this book it has been repeatedly pointed out that scientific "facts" cannot stand alone—they must be interpreted before they have any meaning. Numerous examples were presented to show that scientific interpretations of facts are frequently colored by the historical, literary, or racial biases of the culture in which the scientist is working (chaps. 8–10). Because of the problem of induction, science cannot even generate a provable universal statement (chaps. 5–7). As Stephen Jay Gould has pointed out,

> Science, since people must do it, is a socially embedded activity. It progresses by hunch, vision, and intuition. Much of its change through time does not record a closer approach to absolute truth, but the alteration of cultural contexts that influence it so strongly. Facts are not pure and unsullied bits of information; culture also influences what we see and how we see it. Theories, moreover, are not inexorable inductions from facts. The most creative theories are often imaginative visions imposed upon facts; the source of imagination is also strongly cultural. (1981, 21–22).

Moreover, during periods of scientific controversy, the experimental method itself proves to be ineffective as it degenerates into the closed loop of "experimenter's regress" (chap. 17). If, therefore, the truths of science are transitory and incomplete, if the study area of science is restricted by spatial boundaries, if the methodology of science is logically flawed, and if the techniques of science are subject to personal and cultural biases—exactly what is it that makes scientific truth superior to biblical truth? The answer is, of course, nothing!

Science Should Not Be Feared

The Christian, then, does not need to fear the pronouncements of science that contradict (or appear to contradict) the Bible. Scientific truth is neither absolute truth, nor a superior form of truth. Science is a powerful tool for collecting data, creating hypotheses, testing hypotheses, and generating provisional truths. Science has not, however, proven itself capable of arriving at absolute truth. Moreover, scientists themselves have feet of clay; they are subject to the same motivations, biases, and limitations that bedevil all of humanity. Therefore, the scientific truths that scientists apprehend are not absolute truth; instead, they are a mixture of fact and fiction.

All scientific theories, then—not just those that seem to run counter to the Scriptures—should be questioned. They are based on scientific truths that are themselves provisional. Why, therefore, should Christians fear the truths of science if those truths are here today and gone tomorrow? To paraphrase Franklin Delano Roosevelt, *We have nothing to fear from science except our fear of science.*

Science Should Not Dictate Doctrine

Because of the transitory nature of scientific truth, a Christian would be foolish to link his or her faith too closely with any particular scientific truth. Yet many ministers, theologians, churches, and seminaries have altered their religious beliefs to be more in line with scientific truths. Whenever Christians link biblical truths with scientific truths, however, they will eventually find themselves in conflict with science. This is because the adopted scientific truths become intertwined with theology and church doctrine. When, as invariably happens, an older scientific truth is replaced with a newer scientific truth, the newer scientific truth will naturally appear to be in conflict with the theology and church doctrine that is attached to the old scientific truth. This is exactly what happened when the early church merged its theology of creation with Ptolemy's earth-centered model of the heavens. When Copernicus first presented his sun-centered model of the heavens, many Christians believed that this new theory contradicted the Bible—but they were, of course, wrong.

Viewed from a Christian perspective, the conflict between the church and astronomers such as Copernicus or Galileo would never have happened if Christian doctrine had not been merged with scientific theories. Once this merger had been effected, conflict between science and the church was inevitable because the gospel is eternal while scientific theories are temporal.

The same thing will happen in the future if, for example, we attempt to harmonize Einstein's theory of relativity with the Bible. To the Christian, the Bible is the eternal, inerrant word of God. This belief does not arise from some abstract philosophical or scientific reasoning but is plainly stated in the Scriptures:

> I tell you the truth, until heaven and earth disappear, not the smallest letter, not the least stroke of a pen, will by any means disappear from the Law until everything is accomplished. (Matthew 5:18)

> All Scripture is God-breathed and is useful for teaching, rebuking, correcting and training in righteousness, so that the man of God may be thoroughly equipped for every good work. (2 Timothy 3:16–17)

> But even if we or an angel from heaven should preach a gospel other than the one we preached to you, let him be eternally condemned! (Galatians 1:8)

> Heaven and earth will pass away, but my words will never pass away. (Matthew 24:35)

These Scriptures are based on the divine revelation of an eternal, unchanging God. How, then, can we link the truths of the "eternal gospel" (Rev. 14:6) with scientific truths that are constantly changing? Any bridges we attempt to build between these two types of truth will eventually collapse.

Thus, to link the current scientific thought with Christian belief is to embrace chaos. The Christian who would link religious beliefs to the latest scientific theory must be willing to constantly readjust his or her faith to fit each new scientific discovery, theory, or paradigm. Christians who adopt this approach soon find themselves adrift on a sea of subjectivism with no solid ground on which to stand. In such a situation, they easily fall prey to every passing fad or fancy of modern culture and thereby lose their ability to witness to a fallen world. To whom can the scientist turn for solid answers to life's ultimate questions if Christian beliefs are themselves constantly being adjusted to conform to the current teachings of science? Jesus said, "You are the salt of the earth. But if the salt loses its saltiness, how can it be made salty again?" (Matt. 5:13).

Science Is Useful

Science is a stumbling block for many Christians in the modern world. For some, science is a source of lies and falsehoods. These individuals feel that they must constantly be on guard against the teachings of science that threaten to undercut their beliefs and destroy their faith. For others, science has become a light in the darkness, a standard of truth against which even scripture must be measured. In the middle are many more Christians who maintain an uneasy truce between the two extremes.

A more accurate model of science makes it possible for Christians to benefit from, or even participate in, science's quest for truth, without becoming blinded to its weaknesses. The Christian does not need to fear science—nor completely embrace it. Science should not be demonized or deified. Science is a tool that can be used; it is a servant that can be supervised. It has both strengths and weaknesses. The more we know about science and its limitations, the better we can use it to achieve our goals, as well as understand the nature of the truths that it gives us.

CHAPTER 19

WHEN THE FINITE MEETS
THE INFINITE

CHRISTIANS HAVE NOTHING TO fear from science. After learning about the limitations of scientific truth, however, Christians face another danger— that of coming to believe that their own grasp of truth is far superior to that of the scientist. The debate between modern science and Christianity has been going on for several hundred years. The various arguments of scientists seem perfectly logical to the scientists making them. The various arguments of Christians seem perfectly logical to the Christians making them. No clear victor, therefore, has emerged.

If the arguments of one side were clearly true and the arguments of the other side clearly false, such a debate would have little longevity. Perhaps the debate between Christianity and science has continued for so many centuries because the arguments of both sides contain a mixture of truth and falsehood.

Theological Limitations

While it is true that scientists have limitations in attaining absolute truth, it is also true that Christians are subject to similar limitations. We are finite beings trying to understand an infinite God, but we are not in a position to dictate the terms of that relationship. We cannot know God unless He reveals Himself to us. God has promised that if we seek Him with all of our hearts and souls, we will surely find Him (Deut. 4:29). He has never promised, however, that we will be omniscient. Although we are "fearfully and wonderfully made" (Ps. 139:14), we are not God; neither is our knowledge infinite nor our understanding perfect. We must ever keep these limitations before us as we seek absolute truth.

Christians believe that God is omniscient, knowing all things. Christians believe that God's revelation of Himself is a perfect revelation, capable of accomplishing all that He desires it to accomplish. We should worry, however, about how much of God's perfect revelation we fully understand. The very fact that Christianity has fragmented into a multiplicity of creeds, doctrines, denominations, and sects is clear evidence that we do not fully understand either God's revelation or His will. Divisions among Christians have proliferated, even though Christ prayed that His followers "may be one" (John 17:21). Can this be because we have failed to completely understand and/or obey His revelation?

Over the centuries, God revealed Himself and His divine purposes to humanity. The breadth and depth of this revelation was preserved through the written Word. In that Word we read, for instance, of His covenant with Abraham, that Abraham's offspring would become as numerous as the stars but also that, through his offspring, all of the nations of the earth would be blessed. God Himself wrote the Ten Commandments on tablets of stone during the Exodus. Through divine inspiration, God directed Moses to write the Pentateuch (Genesis–Deuteronomy), which records His dealings with humanity since the Creation. The later historical books (Joshua–Job) record God's dealings with the nation of Israel in the Promised Land.

In the poetic books, prophecies concerning the coming of the Messiah begin to emerge, and this revelation becomes more complete in the Major and Minor Prophets. In the New Testament, the Gospels record the fulfillment of the Old Testament prophecies concerning the Messiah. The Word of God becomes incarnate—as the gospel of John records: "The Word became flesh and made his dwelling among us" (John 1:14). In the book of Acts and the Epistles, we read of the establishment of the church and the beginning of its spread across the world. And finally, in the book of Revelation, God reveals to John future events and the ultimate return of Christ to judge the living and the dead.

Christians believe that the Old and New Testaments represent God's full and perfect revelation of Himself and His will for humanity; the Scriptures are literally "God-breathed" (2 Tim. 3:16). Given the scope and range of God's revelation, however, it is not surprising that our finite minds often have a difficult time taking it all in. Some areas of God's revelation are not completely clear to us for a variety of reasons including (1) the difference in scale between the finite mind of man and the infinite mind of God and (2) the chasm between the sinful state of man and the holy character of God.

Moreover, there are topics about which we would like to know more but about which God has chosen to reveal little or nothing. God desires, we know, that we obey Him out of love rather than compulsion, as children for a father rather than as slaves for a master. Consequently, He has purposefully not spelled out all of the dos and don'ts of behavior. Instead, He has given us guiding principles. When one of the scribes asked Jesus, for example, "What is the greatest commandment?" the Lord responded,

> "The most important one," answered Jesus, "is this: 'Hear, O Israel, the Lord our God, the Lord is one. Love the Lord your God with all your heart and with all your soul and with all your mind and with all your strength.' The second is this: 'Love your neighbor as yourself.' There is no commandment greater than these." (Mark 12:29–31)

Based on these two commands, it is obvious that the rightness or wrongness of each thought we think, each word we speak, and each deed we do during the course of a day is ultimately dependent on the quality of love that each action expresses toward God or our fellow humans. Christian ethics, as revealed in the New Testament, goes much deeper than a simple laundry list of right and wrong behaviors. God wants and expects us to go far beyond mere rule keeping. He has given us a revelation that forces us to ponder deeply how each of His commands is to be obeyed.

Because of the difficulties that God's perfect revelation presents to humanity's imperfect mind and soul, Christians have created the discipline of theology—the study of God. By examining the full revelation of

God in both the Old Testament and the New Testament, theologians hope to find information that will help them clarify some of the more complex passages of Scripture. They also hope to find guidance or insights that will help answer questions that the Scriptures have not addressed fully. As with all intellectual disciplines, however, theology must use human understanding and human interpretations in its efforts to explain various aspects of God's revelation. It is unfortunate that with human understanding and interpretation of Scripture come all of the perils of human ignorance, willful blindness, and cultural bias that we have already documented regarding scientific understanding and interpretation of facts in the physical world. Thus, theological truth, like scientific truth, also has its limitations.

A knowledge of the dispute between science and Christianity, which arose around the work of Copernicus and Galileo, should make Christians much more careful in their handling of biblical truth. The past is littered not only with failed scientific theories but also with failed theological interpretations. God's Word is perfect and complete—but we are not. Many of the things we think are obvious in the Scriptures might not be so. We might be blind to the truth; we might be biased in our own feelings, cultural backgrounds, emotions, and sins; we might choose not to hear the message that God wants us to hear; we might not understand the Bible as well as we think we do. Therefore, Christians should exercise humility in their handling of the Word of God. Just because scientists are sometimes wrong does not mean that Christians are always right.

Beyond Truth

Perhaps the most difficult concept for the finite mind of man or woman to comprehend is the idea of the infinite—that which has no bounds and no end. One of the ways humans attempt to make the unknowable knowable is through hypothetical questions and answers such as the following:

Question: In eternity, how much time will be left after a billion years have passed?

Answer: In eternity, as much time will be left after a billion years has passed as when eternity first began.

Similarly, we might address the problem of knowing the mind of God:

Question: After thousands of years of study, how close are humans to understanding the infinite mind of God?

Answer: After thousands of years of study, humans are no closer to understanding the infinite mind of God than when they first began.

Because our minds are finite, we can never hope to comprehend the infinite. This is the ultimate limitation in humanity's quest for truth, the absolute boundary beyond which we cannot go. In our attempt to know the mind of God, perhaps we should adopt the same attitude that has been advocated for philosophers in their search for truth: "We should combine unashamed pride in the loftiness of our goal with undiluted modesty about the poverty of our achievement" (Kenny 1994, 369).

Because we cannot know the mind of God, our theologies are but imperfect reflections of the truth. Because of these imperfections, some theologies have often done more harm than good. As one of my seminary professors was fond of saying, "We will be saved in spite of our theologies, not because of them." Straining at a gnat and swallowing a camel, we debate the inconsequential and ignore the essential. The items over which we argue are legion: premillennialism, postmillennialism, amillennialism, dispensationalism, short chronologies, long chronologies, consubstantiation, transubstantiation, how many angels can dance on the head of a pin. Like doomed prisoners, we whittle away the hours in the cells of our minds, awaiting judgment and execution—anything to avoid true repentance and obedience. God is much more pleased with the lone man or woman who is obedient to His commands that are clear and specific, than with the multitude who debate endlessly over issues that God has not thought important enough to reveal clearly in His Word.

The reality of the human situation is that we all have feet of clay, whether we are believers or nonbelievers, whether we are scientists or theologians. Before the infinite mind of the omniscient God, we all stand

shamefaced and abashed as our theories and theologies become super-
fluous in the searing light of His presence: "For the wisdom of this world
is foolishness in God's sight. As it is written: 'He catches the wise in their
craftiness'; and again, 'The Lord knows that the thoughts of the wise are
futile'" (1 Cor. 3:19–20). Therefore, knowing the limitations of scientific
truth, we should not allow scientific pronouncements to cast shadows of
doubt upon our faith. On the other hand, neither should we be overly
confident in our own understanding of God's written revelation or His
created universe. To think that we know more than we really know is a
dangerous position for both the Christian and the scientist.

> He has showed you, O man, what is good.
> And what does the LORD require of you?
> To act justly and to love mercy
> and to walk humbly with your God.
> —Micah 6:8

Because of the limitations of both scientific truth and theological truth,
there seems little hope of reaching a rapport between science and
Christianity any time in the near future. Both sides are arguing from the
vantage point of limited knowledge. Both sides have beliefs that are a
mixture of truth and falsehood. Scientists are seeking absolute truth but
have not yet found it; Christians, through God's revelation, have received
absolute truth but do not yet fully understand it. God has revealed
Himself to humanity through both verbal and nonverbal means, through
both Scripture and evidence for purposeful design in the physical
universe. It is a tragedy that both Christians and scientists often ignore
or misinterpret this revelation.

To scientists wishing to remain nonbelievers, scientific facts that provide evidence for a divine creator can always be reinterpreted. To Christians wishing to ignore God's specific commands, the Scripture can always
be reinterpreted. The ultimate question, therefore, becomes, *How will
you interpret this evidence?* Will you cast your lot with the age-old rebel-
lion of mankind against God, or will you submit to His authority and
mercy? This is the most important question each of us will ever answer.
This is the ultimate question of all ultimate questions.

To pursue truth for the sake of truth is a worthy goal, but it should not be an end in itself. Like other desires, our longing for truth can be perverted to bad ends. God has a reason for placing an unquenchable thirst for truth in the human mind. Even as water seeks to return to the sea from whence it came, so truth flows back toward its Creator. The ultimate purpose of our quest for truth is not to satisfy our intellectual curiosity—it is to lead us back to our Creator, who is the source of truth.

The Christian in search of truth should have but one guiding principle in all studies and endeavors: all truth, no matter where it is found, will ultimately lead to Christ because Christ is Truth (John 14:6). The absolute meaning and truth of any created object—be it a house, a painting, a poem, or a universe—must ultimately lie with its creator. The creator alone can explain the purpose for which something has been created. Christ is not only the Savior of the world but also its Creator:

> In the beginning was the Word, and the Word was with God, and the Word was God. He was with God in the beginning. Through him all things were made; without him nothing was made that has been made. In him was life, and that life was the light of men. The light shines in the darkness, but the darkness has not understood it. (John 1:1–5)

Once we understand the limitations of human knowledge—whether it be science, philosophy, or theology—once we have identified man's endeavors for exactly what they are—the searching after truth, not its apprehension—then we are freed to move beyond the mere pursuit of truth and focus our attention on developing a personal relationship with the One who is Truth. In Him alone will we find true rest and peace. The truth, indeed, shall set us free.

As the apostle Paul preached to the Athenians on the Areopagus nearly two thousand years ago,

> The God who made the world and everything in it is the Lord of heaven and earth and does not live in temples built by hands. And he is not served by human hands, as if he needed anything, because he himself gives all men life and breath and everything

else. From one man he made every nation of men, that they should inhabit the whole earth; and he determined the times set for them and the exact places where they should live. God did this so that men would seek him and perhaps reach out for him and find him, though he is not far from each one of us. "For in him we live and move and have our being." As some of your own poets have said, "We are his offspring." (Acts 17:24–28)

EPILOGUE

IN THIS BOOK, I HAVE attempted to address one of the great fears that has assailed many Christians, including me—the fear of science. Has science disproved the Bible? Will science someday discover absolute and undeniable evidence that there is no God? Will my faith in Christ one day wither upon the flame of scientific truth? I have had this fear hanging over me since I was a child.

It has been said that a person's fears often drive that person to do the very thing they fear most. Some people who fear heights climb mountains; some people who fear water become scuba divers; some people who fear darkness or enclosed spaces explore caves. Such people, by defying their fears, are able to overcome them. I suppose that a similar motive led me into science. Certainly, my own experience has been that the more deeply I became involved in science, the less fearful I became of its pronouncements.

We cannot become an intimate acquaintance of another person without learning that person's hidden weaknesses as well as his or her visible strengths. The same holds true in regard to any area of study. Thus, the more deeply I have become involved in science, the less confidence I had in the absoluteness of its pronouncements. Somewhere during this process, my fear of science ceased to be a threat to my faith, but I cannot pinpoint the exact moment when that happened. Instead, the process was like having a cut that heals slowly. My fear of science gradually diminished as the limitations of scientific truth became more and more apparent. I eventually realized that the wound no longer hurt—all that was left was a scar.

People often ask me, "How can you be a scientist and a Christian?" As I noted in the introduction to this book, I have not had an easy time answering that question. There are many reasons, but none of them can be explained easily during a brief conversation. Consequently, in this book I have provided some of the major reasons that I no longer find my faith threatened by science.

Any one of these reasons in itself might prove adequate to justify my rejection of scientific truth as absolute or superior truth, but most convincing is the sheer weight of the evidence. I hope that other Christians will find these reasons as liberating as I have.

REFERENCES

Adleman, Leonard M. 1998. Computing with DNA. *Scientific American* 279 (2): 54–61.

Aristotle. 1955. *The Organon.* Translated and edited by Harold P. Cooke and Hugh Tredennick. Cambridge, Mass.: Harvard University Press.

Asimov, Isaac. 1972. *Isaac Asimov's Biographical Encyclopedia of Science and Technology: The Lives and Achievements of 1195 Great Scientists from Ancient Times to the Present Chronologically Arranged.* New York: Avon Books.

———. 1976. *Asimov on Physics.* New York: Avon Books.

———. 1983. The Army of the Night. In *The Roving Mind,* 5–15. Buffalo, N.Y.: Prometheus Books.

Ayer, A. J. 1936. *Language, Truth and Logic.* Oxford: Oxford University Press.

———, ed. 1959. Editor's introduction to *Logical Positivism.* Edited by A. J. Ayer, 3–28. Glencoe, Ill.: Free Press.

———. 1978. Logical Positivism and Its Legacy: Dialogue with A. J. Ayer. In *Men of Ideas,* by Bryan Magee, 116–33. New York: Viking Press.

Bacon, Lord. 1901. *Novum Organum.* New York: P. F. Collier and Son.

Bagish, Henry H. 1990. Confessions of a Former Cultural Relativist. In *Anthropology 90/91,* edited by Elvio Angeloni, 30–37. Guilford, Conn.: Dushkin.

Barrow, John D. 1994. *The Origin of the Universe.* New York: Basic Books.

Barrow, John D., and Frank J. Tipler. 1986. *The Anthropic Cosmological Principle.* Oxford: Clarendon Press.

Bartusiak, Marcia. 1993. *Through a Universe Darkly.* New York: Avon Books.

Behe, Michael J. 1996. *Darwin's Black Box: The Biochemical Challenge to Evolution.* New York: Free Press.

Benenson, Yaakov, Tamar Paz-Elizur, Rivka Adar, Ehud Keinan, Zvi Livneh, and Ehud Shapiro. 2001. Programmable and Autonomous Computing Machine Made of Biomolecules. *Nature* 414:430–34.

Benét, Stephen Vincent. 1936. Nightmare, with Angels. In *Burning City: New Poems*, by Stephen Vincent Benét, 73–75. Murray Hill, N.Y.: Farrar and Rinehart.

Bintliff, John L. 1984. Structuralism and Myth in Minoan Studies. *Antiquity* 58:33–38.

Bloom, Allan. 1987. *The Closing of the American Mind: How Higher Education Has Failed Democracy and Impoverished the Souls of Today's Students.* New York: Simon and Schuster.

Bohr, Niels. 1958. Discussion with Einstein on Epistemological Problems in Atomic Physics. In *Atomic Physics and Human Knowledge*, by Niels Bohr, 32–66. New York: John Wiley and Sons.

Boorstin, Daniel J. 1983. *The Discoverers.* New York: Vintage Books.

Boslough, John. 1981. The Unfettered Mind: Stephen Hawking Encounters the Dark Edges of the Universe. *Science 81*, 2 (9): 66–73.

———. 1992. *Masters of Time: Cosmology at the End of Innocence.* New York: Addison-Wesley.

Boyd, Robert, and Joan B. Silk. 2000. *How Humans Evolved.* New York: W. W. Norton.

Braaten, Jane. 1991. *Habermas's Critical Theory of Society.* Albany: State University of New York Press.

Bradley, John P., Leo F. Daniels, and Thomas C. Jones. 1969. *The International Dictionary of Thoughts.* Chicago: J. G. Ferguson.

Brigham, Carl C. 1922. *A Study of American Intelligence.* Princeton: Princeton University Press.

Brinton, Daniel G. 1890. *Races and Peoples: Lectures on the Science of Ethnography.* New York: N. D. C. Hodges.

Burke, James. 1985. *The Day the Universe Changed.* Boston: Little, Brown.

Calder, Nigel. 1979. *Einstein's Universe.* New York: Penguin Books.

Carroll, Lewis. 1946. *Through the Looking Glass: And What Alice Found There.* New York: Random House.

Cassidy, David C. 1992. Heisenberg, Uncertainty and the Quantum Revolution. *Scientific America* 266 (5): 106–12.

Casti, John L. 1989. *Paradigms Lost: Images of Man in the Mirror of Science.* New York: William Morrow and Company.

———. 1994. *Complexification: Explaining a Paradoxical World Through the Science of Surprise.* New York: HarperCollins.

———. 1996. *Five Golden Rules: Great Theories of Twentieth-Century Mathematics—and Why They Matter.* New York: John Wiley and Sons.

Chase, Allan. 1976. *The Legacy of Malthus: The Social Costs of the New Scientific Racism.* New York: Alfred A. Knopf.

Clifton, James A. 1968. *Introduction to Cultural Anthropology: Essays in the Scope and Methods of the Science of Man.* New York: Houghton Mifflin.

Collins, Harry, and Trevor Pinch. 1993. *The Golem: What Everyone Should Know About Science*. Cambridge, England: Cambridge University Press.

Comte, Auguste. 1853. *The Positive Philosophy of Auguste Comte*. Vol. 1. Translated by Harriet Martineau. New York: D. Appleton.

Copleston, Frederick. 1946. *A History of Philosophy*. Vol. 1, Greece and Rome. London: Search Press.

Crick, Francis. 1981. *Life Itself: Its Origin and Nature*. New York: Simon and Schuster.

Daintith, John, et al., eds. 1989. *The Macmillan Dictionary of Quotations*. New York: Macmillan.

Dames, Michael. 1992. *Mythic Ireland*. London: Thames and Hudson.

Davies, Paul. 1983. *God and the New Physics*. New York: Simon and Schuster.

———. 1984. *Superforce: The Search for a Grand Unified Theory of Nature*. New York: Simon and Schuster.

Davies, Paul, and John Gribbin. 1992. *The Matter Myth: Dramatic Discoveries That Challenge Our Understanding of Physical Reality*. New York: Simon and Schuster.

Dawkins, Richard. 1987. *The Blind Watchmaker: Why the Evidence of Evolution Reveals a Universe Without Design*. New York: W. W. Norton.

Dawson, John W. Jr. 1988. Kurt Gödel in Sharper Focus. In *Gödel's Theorem in Focus*, edited by S. G. Shanker, 1–16. New York: Croom Helm.

D'Este, Carlo. 1995. *Patton: A Genius for War*. New York: HarperCollins.

Durant, Will. 1953. *The Story of Philosophy: The Lives and Opinions of the Greater Philosophers*. New York: Simon and Schuster.

Eiseley, Loren. 1960. How the World Became Natural. In *The Firmament of Time*, 1–30. New York: Atheneum.

Feferman, Solomon. 1986. Gödel's Life and Work. In *Kurt Gödel Collected Works*. Vol. 1, Publications 1929–1936, edited by Solomon Feferman et. al., 1–36. Oxford: Clarendon Press.

Ferris, Timothy. 1983. *The Red Limit: The Search for the Edge of the Universe*. New York: Quill.

———. 1988. *Coming of Age in the Milky Way*. New York: William Morrow.

———. 1992. *The Mind's Sky: Human Intelligence in a Cosmic Context*. New York: Bantam Books.

———. 1997. *The Whole Shebang: A State-of-the-Universe(s) Report*. New York: Simon and Schuster.

Feyerabend, Paul. 1978. *Against Method: Outline of an Anarchistic Theory of Knowledge*. London: Verso.

———. 1995. *Killing Time: The Autobiography of Paul Feyerabend*. Chicago: University of Chicago Press.

Gardner, Martin. 1962. *Relativity for the Millions*. New York: Macmillan.

Gödel, Kurt. 1986. On Formally Undecidable Propositions of *Principia*

Mathematica and Related Systems I. In *Kurt Gödel Collected Works*. Vol. 1, Publications 1929–1936, edited by Solomon Feferman et. al., 144–95. Oxford: Clarendon Press.

Gould, Stephen Jay. 1977a. Racism and Recapitulation. In *Ever Since Darwin: Reflections in Natural History*, 214–21. New York: W. W. Norton.

————. 1977b. Racist Arguments and IQ. In *Ever Since Darwin: Reflections in Natural History*, 243–47. New York: W. W. Norton.

————. 1980. Dr. Down's Syndrome. In *The Panda's Thumb: More Reflections in Natural History*, 160–68. New York: W. W. Norton.

————. 1981. *The Mismeasure of Man*. New York: W. W. Norton.

————. 1983. Science and Jewish Immigration. In *Hen's Teeth and Horse's Toes*, 291–302. New York: W. W. Norton.

————. 1989. *Wonderful Life: The Burgess Shale and the Nature of History*. New York: W. W. Norton.

————. 1991. Literary Bias on the Slippery Slope. In *Bully for Brontosaurus: Reflections in Natural History*, 241–52. New York: W. W. Norton.

Greene, Brian. 1999. *The Elegant Universe: Superstrings, Hidden Dimensions, and the Quest for the Ultimate Theory*. New York: W. W. Norton.

Greenstein, George. 1988. *The Symbiotic Universe: Life and Mind in the Cosmos*. New York: William Morrow.

Grenz, Stanley. 1992. *The Millennial Maze: Sorting Out Evangelical Options*. Downers Grove, Ill.: InterVarsity.

Gribbin, John. 1996. *Companion to the Cosmos*. Boston: Little, Brown.

Gribbin, John, and Martin Rees. 1989. *Cosmic Coincidences: Dark Matter, Mankind, and Anthropic Cosmology*. New York: Bantam Books.

Guth, Alan H. 1997. *The Inflationary Universe: The Quest for a New Theory of Cosmic Origins*. New York: Addison-Wesley.

Hanfling, Oswald. 1981. *Logical Positivism*. New York: Columbia University Press.

Haviland, William A. 1999. *Cultural Anthropology*. New York: Harcourt Brace College Publishers.

Hawking, Stephen W. 1988. *A Brief History of Time: From the Big Bang to Black Holes*. New York: Bantam Books.

————. 1993. *Black Holes and Baby Universes and Other Essays*. New York: Bantam Books.

Herrnstein, Richard J. and Charles Murray. 1994. *The Bell Curve: Intelligence and Class Structure in American Life*. New York: Free Press.

Herskovits, Melville J. 1948. *Man and His Works: The Science of Cultural Anthropology*. New York: Alfred A. Knopf.

Hodder, Ian. 1984. Archaeology in 1984. *Antiquity* 58:25–32.

Hoffmann, Banesh. 1959. *The Strange Story of the Quantum*. New York: Dover.

Hofstadter, Douglas R. 1979. *Gödel, Escher, Bach: An Eternal Golden Braid*. New York: Vintage Books.

Horgan, John. 1993. The Worst Enemy of Science. *Scientific American* 268 (5): 36–37.

———. 1996. *The End of Science: Facing the Limits of Knowledge in the Twilight of the Scientific Age.* New York: Broadway Books.

Hoyle, Fred. 1983. *The Intelligent Universe.* New York: Holt, Rinehart and Winston.

Hoyle, Fred, and Chandra Wickramasinghe. 1981. *Evolution from Space: A Theory of Cosmic Creationism.* New York: Simon and Schuster.

Hume, David. 1845. *An Essay on Miracles.* New York: G. Vale.

———. 1975. *Enquiries Concerning Human Understanding and Concerning the Principles of Morals,* ed. L. A. Selby-Bigge. Oxford: Clarendon Press.

———. 1978. *A Treatise of Human Nature,* ed. L. A. Selby-Bigge. 2nd ed. Oxford: Clarendon Press.

Hunter, G. Frederick. 1993. Introduction to *Between Philosophy and Social Science: Selected Early Writings,* by Max Horkheimer, vii–x. Cambridge, Mass.: MIT Press.

Jastrow, Robert. 1978. *God and the Astronomers.* New York: W. W. Norton.

Johnson, George. 1995. *Fire in the Mind: Science, Faith, and the Search for Order.* New York: Alfred A. Knopf.

Kenny, Anthony. 1994. *The Oxford History of Western Philosophy.* Oxford: Oxford University Press.

Kramer, Samuel Noah. 1963. *The Sumerians: Their History, Culture, and Character.* Chicago: University of Chicago Press.

Krauss, Lawrence M. 1989. *The Fifth Essence: The Search for Dark Matter in the Universe.* New York: Basic Books.

Kuhn, Thomas S. 1970. *The Structure of Scientific Revolutions.* Chicago: The University of Chicago Press.

Lakatos, Imre. 1976. *Proofs and Refutations: The Logic of Mathematical Discovery.* Cambridge, England: Cambridge University Press.

———. 1978. *The Methodology of Scientific Research Programmes.* Philosophical Papers. Vol. 1, edited by John Worrall and Gregory Currie. Cambridge, England: Cambridge University Press.

Lang, Andrew, ed. 1967. *The Crimson Fairy Book.* New York: Dover.

———. 1969. *The Blue Fairy Book.* New York: Airmont.

Lederman, Leon M., and David N. Schramm. 1995. *From Quarks to the Cosmos: Tools of Discovery.* New York: Scientific American Library.

Lerner, Eric J. 1991. *The Big Bang Never Happened.* New York: Times Books.

Lewin, Roger. 1987. *Bones of Contention: Controversies in the Search for Human Origins.* New York: Simon and Schuster.

Lewis, C. S. 1943. *The Pilgrim's Regress: An Allegorical Apology for Christianity, Reason and Romanticism.* Grand Rapids: Eerdmans.

———. 1946. *The Great Divorce.* New York: Macmillan.

———. 1954. *The Horse and His Boy*. Chronicles of Narnia. New York: Collier Books.

———. 1955. *Surprised by Joy: The Shape of My Early Life*. New York: Harcourt Brace Jovanovich.

———. 1956. *The Last Battle*. Chronicles of Narnia. New York: Collier Books.

Lindley, David. 1993. *The End of Physics: The Myth of a Unified Theory*. New York: Basic Books.

Locke, John. 1961. *An Essay Concerning Human Understanding*. Edited by John W. Yolton. New York: Dutton.

MacDonald, George. 1964. *The Princess and the Goblin*. Baltimore, Md.: Penguin Books.

Magee, Bryan. 1975. *Popper*. Glasgow: William Collins Sons.

———.1985. *Philosophy and the Real World: An Introduction to Karl Popper*. La Salle, Ill.: Open Court.

Marshack, Alexander. 1972. *The Roots of Civilization: The Cognitive Beginnings of Man's First Art, Symbol and Notation*. New York: McGraw-Hill.

Marx, Karl. 1977. Towards a Critique of Hegel's *Philosophy of Right*: Introduction. In *Karl Marx: Selected Writings*, edited by David McLellan, 63–74. Oxford: Oxford University Press.

Morris, Richard. 1993. *Cosmic Questions: Galactic Halos, Cold Dark Matter and the End of Time*. New York: John Wiley and Sons.

Nelson, Harry, and Robert Jurmain. 1991 *Introduction to Physical Anthropology*. New York: West Publishing Company.

Orwell, George. 1977. *1984*. New York: New American Library.

Overbye, Dennis. 1991. *Lonely Hearts of the Cosmos: The Scientific Quest for the Secret of the Universe*. New York: HarperPerennial.

Paley, William. 1854. *Natural Theology: Evidences of the Existence and Attributes of the Deity, Collected from the Appearances of Nature*. 1802. Reprint, Boston: Gould and Lincoln.

Pears, David. 1971. *Wittgenstein*. Glasgow: William Collins Sons.

Popkin, Richard H. 1999. Introduction (to Origins of Western Philosophic Thinking). In *The Columbia History of Western Philosophy*, edited by Richard H. Popkin, 1–6. New York: Columbia University Press.

Popper, Karl R. 1965. *Conjectures and Refutations: The Growth of Scientific Knowledge*. New York: Harper and Row.

———. 1966. *The Open Society and Its Enemies*. Vol. 1, The Spell of Plato. Princeton: Princeton University Press.

———. 1968. *The Logic of Scientific Discovery*. New York: Harper and Row.

———. 1976. *Unended Quest: An Intellectual Autobiography*. La Salle, Ill.: Open Court.

Poster, Mark. 1989. *Critical Theory and Poststructuralism: In Search of a Context*. Ithaca: Cornell University Press.

Rees, Martin. 1997. *Before the Beginning: Our Universe and Others*. New York: Simon and Schuster.

Renfrew, Colin, and Paul Bahn. 1996. *Archaeology: Theories, Methods and Practice*. London: Thames and Hudson.

Reuters. 2001. Scientists Build Tiny Computer Using DNA Molecules. In *The New York Times*, 27 November 2001.

Ross, Hugh. 1991. *The Fingerprint of God*. Orange, Calif.: Promise Publishing Company.

———. 1993. *The Creator and the Cosmos: How the Greatest Scientific Discoveries of the Century Reveal God*. Colorado Springs: NavPress.

———. 1994. *Creation and Time: A Biblical and Scientific Perspective on the Creation-Date Controversy*. Colorado Springs: NavPress.

Rouse, W. H. D. 1957. *Gods, Heroes and Men of Ancient Greece*. New York: New American Library.

Rubenstein, James M. 1994. *An Introduction to Human Geography*. New York: Macmillan.

Russell, Bertrand. 1945. *A History of Western Philosophy: And Its Connection with Political and Social Circumstances from the Earliest Times to the Present Day*. New York: Simon and Schuster.

Russell, Colin A. 1985. *Cross-Currents: Interactions Between Science and Faith*. Grand Rapids: Eerdmans.

Sagan, Carl. 1979. *Broca's Brain: Reflections on the Romance of Science*. New York: Ballantine Books.

———. 1980. *Cosmos*. New York: Random House.

———. 1985. *Contact: A Novel*. New York: Simon and Schuster.

———. 1996. *The Demon-Haunted World: Science as a Candle in the Dark*. New York: Random House.

———. 1997. *Billions and Billions: Thoughts on Life and Death at the Brink of the Millennium*. New York: Random House.

Sarich, Vincent M., and Allan C. Wilson. 1967. Immunological Time Scale for Hominid Evolution. *Science* 158:1200–3.

Schaeffer, Francis A. 1972. *Genesis in Space and Time: The Flow of Biblical History*. Downers Grove, Ill.: InterVarsity.

Seeds, Michael A. 1993. *Horizons: Exploring the Universe*. Belmont, Calif.: Wadsworth.

Smoot, George, and Keay Davidson. 1993. *Wrinkles in Time*. New York: Avon Books.

Stumpf, Samuel Enoch. 1971. *Philosophy: History and Problems*. New York: McGraw-Hill.

Tarbuck, Edward J., and Frederick K. Lutgens. 1994. *Earth Science*. New York: Macmillan.

Theocharis, T., and M. Psimopoulos. 1987. Where Science Has Gone Wrong. *Nature* 329:595–98.

Thompson, Francis. 1946. "The Hound of Heaven." In *The Poems of Francis Thompson,* 99–106. London: Hollis and Carter.

Tolkien, J. R. R. 1966, *The Hobbit: Or There and Back Again.* Boston: Houghton Mifflin.

Turner, Mark. 1996. *The Literary Mind.* Oxford: Oxford University Press.

Weinberg, Steven. 1993. *Dreams of a Final Theory.* New York: Vintage Books.

Weyl, Hermann. 1949. *Philosophy of Mathematics and Natural Science.* Princeton: Princeton University Press.

Wheeler, John Archibald with Kenneth Ford. 1998. *Geons, Black Holes, and Quantum Foam: A Life in Physics.* New York: W. W. Norton and Company.

Whitehead, Alfred North, and Bertrand Russell. 1910. *Principia Mathematica.* Vol. 1. Cambridge, England: Cambridge University Press.

———. 1912. *Principia Mathematica.* Vol. 2. Cambridge, England: Cambridge University Press.

———. 1927. *Principia Mathematica.* Vol. 3. Cambridge, England: Cambridge University Press.

Wiggershaus, Rolf. 1994. *The Frankfurt School: Its History, Theories, and Political Significance.* Cambridge, Mass.: MIT Press.

Wittgenstein, Ludwig. 1922. *Tractatus Logico-Philosophicus.* London: Routledge and Kegan Paul.

———. 1953. *Philosophical Investigations.* Translated by G. E. M. Anscombe. Oxford: Basil Blackwell.

Wolf, Fred Alan. 1981. *Taking the Quantum Leap: The New Physics for Nonscientists.* San Francisco: Harper and Row.

Woodward, Kenneth L. 1996. In the Beginning. *Newsweek,* 21 October, 74–79.

Wunderlich, Hans Georg. 1974. *The Secret of Crete.* Glasgow: William Collins Sons.

Zimmerman, Larry J. 1994. Sharing Control of the Past. *Archaeology* 47 (6): 64–68.

Hofstadter, Douglas R., 68–69
Hooker telescope, 166
Horgan, John, 184
Horkheimer, Max, 242–45
"Hound of Heaven, The"
    (Thompson), 249–50
How Humans Evolved (Boyd and
    Silk), 222–23
Hoyle, Fred, 218, 228, 231–34, 253
Hubble, Edwin Powell, 35, 165–
    72, 181–82, 191, 231
Hubble radius, 171–72, 180, 264
Hubble's Law, 169–72, 180
Hume, David, criticism of
    science, 18, 56–60; empiricism
    of, 62, 64, 67, 82, 86, 91, 235,
    263; skepticism of, 85, 88, 142,
    151, 197, 205, 237. *See also*
    Hume's Problem.
Hume's Problem, 58–60, 65,
    73–74, 82, 87
Hutton, James, 225, 227
hypotheses, 51, 76–77; hard-core,
    80–81; inductive method and,
    52–56, 74; nature of, 17;
    testing, 258

I

Immigration Restriction Act
    (1924), 130–31
"Immunological Time Scale for
    Hominid Evolution" (Sarich
    and Wilson), 110–11
implicate universe, 151
inductive method, 17, 51–60, 145;
    Hume and, 56–60, 61; logical

positivism and, 65, 67, 71;
    Popper and 73–77
infinite, 271–78
inflationary theory, 190–97
"Inflationary Universe" (Guth),
    190
intelligence tests, 128–33
Intelligent Universe, The (Hoyle
    and Wickramasinghe), 231,
    232
"Is the Universe a Vacuum
    Fluctuation?" (Tryon), 194

J

Jastrow, Robert, 214
Johnson, George, 194

K

Kaluza, Theodor, 188
Kant, Immanuel, 166
Kepler, Johannes, 31
Knossos, 97–100
knowledge, change in, 27–35
Krauss, Lawrence, 8
Kroeber, Alfred, 238
Kuhn, Thomas, 18, 37–47, 51, 77,
    85, 86, 91

L

Lakatos, Imre, 18, 79–82, 84, 86,
    87, 91
Landau, Misia, 106–7, 112
Language, Truth and Logic (Ayer),
    66
Laplace, Pierre-Simon de, 146,
    152, 157, 163

LaVergne, TN USA
20 December 2010
209532LV00002B/1/P